Overdoing It

OVERDOING IT

How To Slow Down
And Take Care
Of Yourself

Bryan E. Robinson, Ph.D.

Foreword by Gloria Steinem

Health Communications, Inc.
Deerfield Beach, Florida

Library of Congress Cataloging-in-Publication Data

Robinson, Bryan E.
   Overdoing it: how to slow down and take care of yourself / by Bryan
E. Robinson; with foreword by Gloria Steinem.
     p.   cm.
   Includes bibliographical references.
   ISBN 1-55874-237-9
   1. Overachievement. 2. Overachievement — Case studies. 3. Stress
management. 4. Conduct of life. I. Title.
BF637.094R63   1992   92-19228
158'.1—dc20   CIP

©1992 Bryan E. Robinson
ISBN 1-55874-237-9

Publisher: Health Communications, Inc.
                3201 S.W. 15th Street
                Deerfield Beach, Florida 33442-8190

Cover design by Andrea Perrine

Dedication

To Jamey McCullers,
for 22 years of love and concern
and guidance on how to slow
down and take care
of myself

Acknowledgments

I want to thank the many wonderful people in my life who helped make this book a reality. My special thanks to Bertie Billups for such a beautiful job of typing the manuscript. Thanks to Marie Stilkind for her steady and calm source of moral support throughout this project and all others, and to Diane Zarowin for her excellent job of editing the manuscript. Dr. Nancy Chase has given me valuable support, feedback and enduring love. And my publicists, Diane Glynn and Arlene Nepomucenco, have given me steadfast support and assistance in making my work more visible. Randy McKenzie, Barbara Nichols, Peter Vegso and all others at Health Communications have my personal and heartfelt thanks.

My special appreciation goes to Gloria Steinem for reading my previous book, *Work Addiction*, and agreeing to write the foreword to *Overdoing It*. The following people generously gave of their time to be interviewed or write their own experiences of how overdoing had ·impacted their personal lives:

Debbie Becker
Rob Becker
Audrey Belk
Sylvia Bracket
Nancy Chase
Bettie Dibrell
Elaine Farthing
Brian Federal
Stephanie Felder
Robin Hanes

Bob Kennedy
Joan Kofodimos
Cheryl Libby
Sue Patterson
Jan Phillips
Marilyn "Sam" Price
Lyn Rhoden
Beverly Rodgers
Stephen Smith
Dennis Stabler

Lauren Stayer   Lib Willis
Patty Stayer   Carla Wills-Brandon

Finally I give special thanks to my anonymous clients who gave me permission to use some of their personal accounts and to all the people not mentioned by name for their love, support and sharing of themselves in the preparation of this book.

I would like to extend my appreciation to the following for permission to use their material:

Workaholics Anonymous World Service Organization, for material excerpted from "Workaholics Anonymous: A Brief Guide," including the preamble, the 20 signs of *How Do I Know I'm A Workaholic?*, The WA Tools of Recovery, How WA got Started and the 12 Steps.

Quotations in Chapter 8 by Joan Kofodimos and The Values-Behavior Discrepancy Activity from: Joan Kofodimos (1993). *Executives Out of Balance: Integrating Successful Careers and Fulfilling Personal Lives.* San Francisco: Jossey-Bass.

Section in Chapter 6 titled "Caretaking Versus Caregiving" was written by Marilyn "Sam" Price and excerpted from *To Life Newsletter,* copyright 1991. Used with permission of the author.

Tim Funk for Hillary Clinton quote in Chapter 2. Quotation excerpted from "Meet Hillary Clinton" by Tim Funk, copyright 1992, *The Charlotte Observer.*

Section titled "Overworked Pastors Need A Break; Give It To Them" was used with permission of Ken Garfield, copyright 1992, *The Charlotte Observer.*

Contents

Foreword

Gloria Steinem

A few years ago I picked up a pioneering book called *Work Addiction* and read the story of its author, Bryan Robinson, a therapist and university professor, who had been wise enough to include his own personal journey (read about his story in Chapter 10), along with those of the many people he had helped. As the child of a well-meaning and accomplished but often terrorizing and alcoholic father, he had grown up feeling "different" and fearful of the uncontrollable chaos he might find at home. He believed his family's problems were unique and shameful, as children do when their suffering is denied or concealed, and he strove to gain control and approval by excelling in school and the world outside his home.

Thus, from his earliest boyhood, he had cultivated the seeds of overdoing it, or workaholism — the use of work to conceal emotion and a true self instead of expressing them — that was to flower in his professional life. Only going back to uncover and uproot those deep and early causes had freed him from numbness and compulsion; a process made all the more difficult by society's approval of work as a drug of choice.

On the surface, there seemed to be no similarities between Bryan's childhood and my own. Unlike his father, mine had been a kind-hearted and gentle man who took care of me more than my mother did. Because her spirit seemed to have been broken before I was born, she was often a figure lying on the couch, talking to unseen voices, and only able to make clear that she loved me and my sister. There was no violence in my house, and I grew up with the sureness that my parents were treating us as well as they treated themselves. That not only satisfied my need to feel loved and therefore lovable, but also the sense of fairness that seems innate in children.

Nevertheless, as I read about Bryan's feelings, I felt deep parallels. He had felt ashamed of his home and parents — and so had I. A house filled with dirty dishes, stacks of unwashed clothes, and a "crazy" mother had made me fantasize about a normal home where I could invite my friends. He had adopted cheerfulness and competence in school as a way of concealing the shame of sad feelings and "differentness" — and so had I.

Only many years later when I wrote an essay about my mother after her death did the outpouring of response from readers make me realize how many women's spirits have been broken in patriarchies that cannot allow females to be full, unique human beings, and thus how many of us have grown up with "crazy" mothers. I realized that Bryan had turned to the more rational and controllable world of first school and then work as a way of escaping emotions he did not want to feel — and so had I. I had even denied my need for vacations and periods of introspection, just as he had done. Though I had been lucky enough to find feminist work that was a direct way of helping myself and other women — and an indirect way of helping my mother — I had sometimes carried on these efforts at the expense of my own writing, and as an anesthetic to buried childhood emotions.

Like so many people, and women especially, I badly needed to reverse the Golden Rule, and treat myself as well as I treated others; yet even the life-saving luck of living in a time of growing feminism was often changed by me into a time of helping others *instead* of myself, not *along with* myself. It was the old "feminine" pattern of subordinating oneself to a husband and children, but transposed into a modern movement style.

Only when I, like Bryan Robinson, was forced by one too many episodes of burnout to uncover those childhood sadnesses did I begin to see work as an irreplaceable part of my life, but not the *whole* of my life. And only then did I begin to focus on what I could uniquely do instead of trying to do *everything* — thus beginning to be far more effective as a worker.

The value of personal stories like that of the author and many other people included in these pages — people whose diverse experiences he has assembled to expose the full range of problems, from work addiction to just "doing too much" — is that they allow us to see ourselves, to know we are not alone, and so to find the heart and hope to change.

Burnout, the need to be needed, an inability to say no: all these are masks of overdoing it that are especially evident in women. Burnout, the need to be in control, an inability to let go: all of these are symptoms of overdoing it that are especially evident in men. But whatever its gender mask, the emotional burnout that comes from obsessive doing and denial of authentic feeling is serious self-abuse that is as epidemic to workaholics as cirrhosis of the liver and other more recognized damages are to alcoholics.

In addition to looking at causes of overdoing it in our personal pasts, we need to look at the politics that create and reward work addiction in society. If "masculinity" in a male-dominant culture did not require impossible control over others, accomplishment and denial of "feminine" emotion, men like Bryan Robinson's father might be less subject to alcoholism and violence as a way of creating delusions of power and control. If "femininity" in the same culture did not mean living through others, an impossible sacrifice of self, and denial of masculine intellect or ambition, women like my mother might be less subject to depression and literal delusions as a way of escaping powerlessness and lack of control over their own lives. Futhermore, a "masculine" paradigm often becomes even more punishing when race, class or sexuality stands in the way of realizing the impossible ideal of power that is not only male, but white, heterosexual and successful. And a "feminine" paradigm is often re-doubled for women of color, poor women, lesbians and others who cannot "find" themselves through subordination to the proper kind of husband or family, and so are made to feel lacking.

Because women are rebelling at these kinds of deep gender roles, there is a backlash that several women in this book describe: the notion that women must be Superwomen who are able to add work outside the home to all the traditional work *in* the home;

that we must "do it all." Because the goal of any backlash against equality is to convince the public that equality is actually bad for those who are demanding it — whether that means saying civil rights and affirmative action are bad for African-American men and women, or feminism is bad for women of every race — the message has been that Superwoman is a damaging creation of the women's movement. Nothing could be further from the truth.

An anti-equality culture first said that women could not do the work of lawyers, television repair people, physicians, tennis players — whatever the job that females had been forbidden by tradition. When women showed they *could* do that work, a second message was necessary to protect male dominant systems against change: "Yes, you can do that work, but only if you continue doing all the work you did before. Only if you keep raising children — essentially alone — caring for the house, cooking meals and being a husband's supporter and servant."

Of course, it's impossible to do two full-time jobs. Only when we as women realize that overdoing it actually protects an unjust system — one that robs children of nurturing fathers as well as robbing women of a sense of self — will we rebel against it. If the message of the first stage of the women's movement 20 years ago was "Women can do what men can do", we are now ready for the message of the second stage: "Men can do what women can do." Only when men are equal *inside* the home can women be equal *outside* the home. Women's overdoing it — and the male-dominant culture that compels it — allows this country to be the only industrialized democracy in the world without a national system of child care, the rudiments of flexible work schedules, parental leave for fathers as well as mothers, shortened workdays or work weeks for *both* parents of young children — and so much more.

As always, compulsive overdoing it creates not only incomplete individuals, but a world around us that is out of balance.

I'm grateful to Bryan Robinson for telling his own story and for emphasizing personal and diverse journeys in this book. But, as you read it, remember, the life you save must be your own.

Gloria Steinem

Introduction

The way to do is to be.
– Lao-tzu

The airplane, engines whining, sounded as if it were slicing chunks out of the atmosphere as it cut its way through icy clouds. Eyes closed, I was experiencing the stillness of my life on this blustery winter day, relishing this rare moment that might not come again for a long time. I paid attention to the sounds around me, sounds I usually shut out as I speed to get somewhere. This was a silent time for me to collect my thoughts and to slow down and center myself.

When my friends and colleagues heard that I was writing a book called *Overdoing It*, they laughed. Generally, I am perceived as a hopeless compulsive overworker who doesn't practice what he preaches. Okay, I admit it. It was very difficult for me not to overdo it while writing this book. I had a tight deadline on getting the manuscript to the publisher.

So I reserved a beachfront room in South Carolina. I planned to pile my car with computer, boxes of books, attache case, pencils, pens, reams of computer paper and notepads and head out for the four-hour drive. Once there, I was going to lock myself in the room from Thursday to Sunday and complete at least one chapter. It occurred to me that this was classic "overdoing it" behavior. There was no difference between my working around the clock in a beachfront motel room and Jack Lemmon and Lee Remick, playing two alcoholics in the movie *The Days of Wine and Roses*, closing themselves off to binge in a sleazy motel room.

This analogy helped me see my behavior more clearly. I knew I was no longer the insufferable work addict of ten years ago. I really had changed from the chain-smoking, caffeine-drinking madman who worked every night, weekend and holiday. Back then I was obsessed with my career. I lived to work. Work had become my bottle. Even when vacationing, my thoughts centered around my next project.

Despite how it might look to my concerned friends and skeptical colleagues, I am different on the inside. I have made significant changes, although I still lead a very productive and busy life. I have learned how to set boundaries around my overworking. I no longer smoke. I exercise regularly and meditate as often as possible. But I still have a lot to change. My desire to overdo it continues to plague me . . . in exercise, meditation and even over-caring for friends and clients.

They say that we teach (or in this case write about) what we need to learn ourselves, and that's certainly true in this case. I am well-qualified to write this book. I am constantly walking that blurry line between taking care of myself and working and living in today's world, and I probably always will. The line between office and home seems to get more blurry for many of us as we approach the next century. Overdoing it is a habit that we get into without thinking.

Modern technology has given us more time on our hands than ever before, and the average worker is spending more of it on the job. More women are blending careers with managing a home and rearing children. More people are going back to school for a "better life" and exercising to live a "longer life." In an attempt to squeeze in personal errands more people are getting shoe shines, haircuts and manicures at the office and using their lunch hours to shop, exercise, study for an exam or dash to their therapist for a session.

My dental technician told me that she often goes home on her lunch hour to have sex with her husband because otherwise they are both too busy. She works full time, has been a part-time student for the past eight years, teaches aerobics every morning at 6:15 and fills the rest of her hours studying, sleeping and managing a house.

The stress of trying to do everything has become overwhelming, and almost everyone suffers some effects of overdoing it. But slowing down is not easy. There never seems to be enough time to do what needs accomplishing.

In fact, how we fill our time has become the measure by which we judge our lives.

With these thoughts in mind, I resisted the temptation to go to the beach motel to binge on work because today I understand those strong urges. More and more when I want to overdo it I know my inner self is asking for care — the need to do something for myself, such as meditate, exercise, have fun with friends or just sit and relax. I'm learning that the antidote to overdoing it is self-nurturance.

I think of the words of the philosopher Lao-tzu: "To do is to be" or of Aesop: "Plodding wins the race." I learned this lesson perhaps a thousand times this last year in the course of writing this book. Next year maybe I'll have to learn it only one hundred times. Who knows? Maybe one day I'll learn the lesson for good, maybe not. The point is I haven't arrived anywhere and never expect to. I try to practice what I preach, but I'm not perfect; my goal is progress, not perfection.

This book shows you how to accept and participate in our fast-paced society without letting it erode your spirits. It reminds you that you can always find time for yourself, once you stop denying you are worth it. This book helps you find that place within yourself where you can always go to keep yourself balanced and content. By the time you finish reading, you will know more about special times to pamper yourself and idle moments with nothing to accomplish. You might not be ready to pack your bags and head for the woods, but your refrain on time will sound more like that of Henry David Thoreau, who said, "Time is but the stream I go a-fishing in."

1
Are You Overdoing It?

*Americans generally spend
so much time on things that are
urgent that we have none left to spend
on those that are important.*

— Henry Ward Beecher

Stephanie Felder is a 45-year-old mother of three. She teaches full time and manages a household. This is her story of overdoing it:

I guess some people would say I'm overdoing it. But I don't think I am because I'm really hard on myself. I expect perfection from myself and expect myself to do everything well. Partially because of the women's movement and partially because of my parental expectations.

I feel like I have this thing to prove: I'm a woman, but I'm not going to use that as an excuse. I want to show people that women can do as much as men. And yet I really feel like there's not enough time in the day for me to do a good job at any of this stuff. I always feel that I'm behind the eight ball. I'm never caught up, never. Constant guilt. The guilt is related to my kids.

Every year before school, I'm up all night long, tossing and turning and agonizing. I always feel that I'm cheating or short-changing them by not staying home with them like my mother did. But I judged her harshly for that for some reason, I don't know why. I didn't have any models for women who combined career and home. And I judge other women harshly also.

I'm really hard on one friend of mine. I feel like telling her, "You are a total failure, you don't do anything right. You don't work. You don't keep your house clean. You don't cook. I pride myself on my cooking, on my clean house. I pride myself on my job at school. How can you show your face on the street? What do you do?"

I feel like people judge me on what I do. On what I accomplish, achieve and on what products I produce and what effect I have in the world. And if I'm not doing the best job I know how, I feel like a failure. And because I can't possibly be doing the best job at everything, I feel like a failure most of the time. I get depressed.

I guess I could scale back but I don't know what I'd cut out. I feel like every part of the job I do is important. At school I tried scaling back. I used to be on a million committees and take on a lot of extra stuff. And now I haven't picked up any new ones. Still, I never get anything done at school because there are always kids coming by, but that's my reason for being there, to relate to the kids and deal with them. If I'm going to hide during my free periods, then what's the point?

I judge myself by how much I accomplish. That's why I like to cook so much. That's concrete evidence. Here it is. I made this and isn't it good? People can share it, or I can enjoy it myself and say, "Yeah, I've achieved something." I'm incredibly achievement-oriented, although it's hard to measure your achievements as a teacher. I always wish I could let something go. I say the first thing I'm going to let go is housework. But I never can because I look around my house and think, "This is disgusting." I can't stand to live in squalor.

My therapist tells me I should delegate more responsibilities to my children for their own good. When my husband was out of town for a week, the kids picked up the slack and helped out a lot more. But once he came back, they slid back into their old ways.

I'm very hard on myself. I had parents who were very judgmental and never satisfied. And I have that parenting model in my head of judging myself harshly. I'm working with my therapist to accept myself more just for who I am and not just for what I do. But that's hard to do after all this time. If I make a mistake or don't do something well enough in my own view, I punish myself, I fall on myself hard.

I feel like I'm a good mother. That's what I do best if I had to choose one. I understand my kids. I don't have unrealistic expectations of them, and I accept them for who they are. I'm not always making suggestions on ways they can improve themselves, like my mother and father did. I always tell them how adorable and smart they are. I feel like they can tell me anything and come to me with anything. And that's good, that's the kind of relationship I wanted with my parents and didn't have.

I don't ever take care of myself. I drive myself. I feel like anytime I take care of myself, I'm decadent. Some days my toenails get so long when I don't take time to clip them that my shoes hurt. I don't have time for that; I've got places to go and people to see. One thing I would like to do is find the time to go exercise at the Y. But anytime I've done that I've felt narcissistic and undeserving. My mind says, "Taking all that time? You should be at home baking bread, making cookies, doing schoolwork or being with your kids." And I don't ever take that time. I have to be occupied with other people.

I don't know why I don't like to be alone. I guess I haven't had any practice at it. I can't remember the last time I was alone. I went from being somebody's daughter, to somebody's wife, to somebody's mother.

There are some women who can do it all, I guess. I have to think that since I'm trying to do it. That's my model: You can do it all, you can do it well, you can have it all, you can be all and don't offer any excuses for why you can't. But the price I pay is feeling like a failure most of the time because I have such high standards for myself that I never can reach them. I also think my standards are just. As I approach a standard, I think it's like the Groucho Marx joke, "Anybody who would have me as a member, I wouldn't want to belong to that club." So anytime I set a goal for myself that I can actually achieve, I think, "That wasn't worth it; that was nothing." So I create a higher goal which I can't possibly reach.

The Epidemic Of Overdoing It

I squeezed myself into the tiny sports car of a psychologist friend who whisked me onto the beltway around St. Louis. As we zipped down the interstate, the conversation was interspersed with business calls on his cellular phone. He retrieved messages from his office voice mail, returned a few calls to patients and then dialed the car phone of a mutual friend in Houston whose line was also busy.

I had given a lecture earlier in the day at a St. Louis hospital and was spending the evening with Rob and his wife, Debbie. Rob called Debbie, who was on her way to rendezvous with us at one of their favorite eating spots, on her car phone. They chatted for a while and synchronized watches and locations so that we could arrive at approximately the same time. We were approaching a huge shopping mall from different directions. There was a swirl of activity in this, the largest shopping mall in the world, and after a wonderful dinner we browsed. After 15 minutes of strolling by a string of seemingly endless stores I heard a telephone ringing. The sound was coming from right beside me.

"Hold it!" Debbie urged. "I have a call." She stopped in the middle of the mall, shoppers swarming around us, unzipped her purse and pulled out a cellular phone. It was the babysitter, who wanted to know why she was already 30 minutes late. We continued our stroll while Debbie got a report on the four kids and pleaded for another 30 minutes.

I was astounded! A high-tech family in direct and constant contact with one another, run just like a business. They were coordinating, synchronizing, planning and checking 24 hours a day. I felt such deep admiration and respect for them. I couldn't help but feel a tinge of sadness too.

Is this what we have evolved into? When do they get a break from all the hustle and bustle? When do they turn it off? I knew my reaction had to be significant because I was a recovering work addict. If I saw this as excessive, then surely it must be. Although my friends are nowhere close to being addicted to work, they live on the fast track nonetheless. They have developed their own brand of overdoing it that has become so common for most of us as we near the end of the twentieth century.

If you're awash in a sea of errands, appointments and job commitments — whose schedule includes a nonstop whirlwind of meetings, chores and list-making — take a deep breath and ask yourself the following questions:

- Do you rush around moaning about the shortage of time?
- Do you wail at the clock and shake your fist because there's not enough time to do everything?
- Is your life fast-paced and high-pressured without time for self-renewal, joy and serenity?
- Do you have a pervading sense of guilt because you cannot get everything done?

If you answer yes, you could be overdoing it, trying to cram 48 hours into 24.

Many of us are caught up in the frantic pace of today's world, trying to do too much in too little time. Whether you are a bus driver, factory worker, grocery-store clerk or president of your own company, you may be speed-reading, quick-fixing, rush-houring, fast-tracking and hustling and bustling yourself to death. On the job or in the home overdoing it has no boundaries — whether it's painting the house, shuffling the kids to and from school, preparing dinner or bringing work home from the office. Our relationships are becoming brittle from neglect.

Overdoing it has become an epidemic in our nation. It is estimated that millions of people in this country — from supermoms to high-powered executives to school-age overachievers to the clergy — overdo it in one form or another with sports, grades, work, being overly responsible for others or compulsive busyness around the house. It is known by many names: overdoing, careaholism, work addiction, fast-track living, busyholism, superwoman or superman syndrome. Whatever we choose to call it, we have become a nation that is unbalanced and out of control. Unless we learn how to slow down and take care of ourselves, we will self-destruct as a society.

Ironically modern technology, which promised more leisure time, has whipped us into deeper overdoing. We're bringing home to work and work to home. Fax machines, lap-top computers, cellular phones, enable us to do something literally every minute of the day, at home or at play. The Broadway playbill for "Phantom of the Opera" contained a statement asking audiences to please turn off their cellular phones because of distracting calls during performances. We have come to value life in the fast lane and to see it as inescapable. We even hold up the fast-paced lifestyle as a standard for modern family life.

One good example is the hit movie, *Home Alone,* in which the typical American family is so busy doing so many things that in their rush to get to an overseas vacation they left one of their children home alone. Although this is somewhat extreme, part of the movie's appeal was the moviegoer's identification with the lifestyle.

Our society is producing a legion of human doers rather than human beings. This book is an outgrowth of many observations and discussions and takes a broad look at how we overdo it and the many forms it takes. Gathering information for this book, I spoke with many clients in my private practice and interviewed hundreds more from around the United States. I spoke with housewives burned out trying to be all things to all people; college students depressed because of cramming for tests and working their way through school; clergy fatigued from attending to the never-ending needs of their flocks; corporate executives crashing from an inability to cut it off — all of whose lives were shattered with broken relationships, physical illnesses and personal misery. I spoke with family after family on the verge of destruction because a loved one was working out of control and some who still grieved a loved one who died from overdoing it.

Staying busy by maximizing time and getting things accomplished is the only way overdoers know how to make their lives matter. And the compulsion is aggravated by religious and cultural support with such maxims as "Idle hands are the devil's workshop." The Puritan work ethic, still alive and well, values hard work and productivity and extols it as the antidote to sin and evil. "Stay busy and you won't get into trouble." Overdoing it is so highly valued our society applauds people when they overdo, even when it is life-threatening. If marriages crumble and kids get into trouble, overdoers are exonerated and other family members swiftly accused: "They work so hard for their families, and that's the thanks they get."

Overinvestment In Work

Work addiction is only one variation on the theme of overdoing it. Millions of Americans satisfy their "do-aholism" by overinvesting in their jobs. A survey of 500 hotel executives by Hyatt Hotels and Resorts reported that one half took work with them on vacation because they wanted to feel their time off was productive.

For many Americans overdoing it leads to broken marriages and friendships, serious health problems and even death. Overdoing it on the job is so common in Japan, where 10,000 workers a year drop dead from putting in 60- to 70-hour workweeks, that the Japanese coined the term *karoshi*, which means death from overwork. Otherwise healthy, they keel over at their desks after a long stretch of overtime or a high-pressured deal, usually from stroke or heart attack. According to *The World Press Review*, more than half a million Canadians moonlight and for many free time is just a good excuse to find another job.

Since writing *Work Addiction* several years ago, I have lectured on this deadly condition in the United States and throughout the world. I co-produced and narrated a documentary for a PBS affiliate that traced the lives of seven men and women suffering from work addiction. (See appendix for more information.)

Everywhere I go compulsive overworkers and their families are desperate for help in understanding the problem and regaining balance and serenity in their lives. The staggering realization is that it's not the *work* that's addictive, it's the *doing*. Overly-responsible, overcaring and overscheduled, even off the job, they overdo it with hobbies, exercise, vacations, working around the house, volunteering or carpooling.

The Supermom Syndrome

Our society depicts the ideal woman of today as the one on the fast track who can get everything done. The best mom is the supermom who can accomplish everything. Asked who would make the best woman candidate for president, children in a 1992 national survey listed Mom as second only to Barbara Bush. Asked why, they said, "Because she can do everything." When women compare themselves with this mystical standard, they feel like failures. Not only must they be full-time moms, they must have full-time careers and manage homes and relationships, a social life and, if there's time left over, leisure for themselves.

Because they cannot deliver, supermoms feel guilty about everything: for staying home, for not having a career, for having a career, for putting kids in day care, for taking off early, for not making enough money, for not disciplining children more, for not making it to PTA meetings. The list goes on and on; women can cite endless reasons for not being good enough.

The ideal dad is the fast-track father who is a superachiever, makes lots of money and provides all the material comforts but cannot express feelings and intimacy.

What lies behind the supermom syndrome? Stephanie Felder attributes her overdoing it to the message women get from society that, "You can do it all":

> On a typical day I get up at 5:00 A.M., get out of bed, get ready and wash for school. This takes 20 minutes max. Then I go into the kitchen and make a hot breakfast for the family because I think it's important that they have a healthy start in the morning. Then I pack the kids' lunches and my lunch. Then I have to get the kids up and out of bed and into the shower. That's not easy because they don't like to wake up. Then I have to run back downstairs and make sure nothing's burning. So there's a lot of running up and down stairs in the morning trying to get ready. We're all out of the house by 7:15. I get to school and school starts.
>
> I live on coffee as a crutch to keep going. Caffeine helps me be "on" and "up." I do my best work when I'm sizzling, so I drink two cups of strong coffee in the morning to get going because I have to be up for my first class. I'm on the go every single period of the day, and at the end of the day I have a ton of work to bring home with me.
>
> I come home from school and there's kid stuff to do. There's taking kids up and down to practices and to children's theater, athletic events, being with the kids, making sure they do their homework. There's going to the grocery store, and then I make a big meal for my husband and the children every night. By that time we're up to dinner, plus I have a therapy group and other activities in the late afternoon.
>
> I also try to get to laundry, housework, picking up things. I can't stand a messy house. I don't want to have a cleaning woman; I want to do it all myself there too. If there's gardening to be done, I try to do it then also.

Then it's dinnertime. After dinner I have a lot of schoolwork to do, grading papers and planning. Plus a lot of nights I go out with my husband and do things. Most nights I don't get to bed until 1:00 A.M. So I get four and one half hours of sleep every night, maybe.

I'm wondering what's going to happen with the women's movement. There are enough of us in my generation now who've come through women's lib from the beginning and who have received that message, "Yes, you can do it all." And I don't know how the next generation is going to view this and what kind of backlash there's going to be. Are these younger women going to come in and manage to do it all? Are they going to juggle being president of IBM, a mother and Martha Stewart — and be an accomplished gardener, cook and author on every subject in the world, and then have a private physical fitness instructor to stay beautiful? Or are they going to look at people like me and say, "What a fool you were. You burned yourself out. I'm going to have a career and not have a family or go back to like it was in my mother's generation and stay home with the kids." So I'm curious to see what the next stage is.

Overinvestment In Schoolwork

It was a humdrum, business-as-usual day at the University of North Carolina at Charlotte where I teach. After my morning lecture, a student approached me, tears in her eyes, and said in a tone of desperation, "Dr. Robinson, may I please talk with you in your office. I have to talk to somebody." At first I was surprised that this student — who stood out from the others because of her sharp mind, cheery personality, beautiful face and swept-back wispy hair — could be worried about her grade or anything else for that matter.

Turned out she wasn't. She was depressed and didn't know why. She sobbed about how low she felt but couldn't put her finger on it. Her parents weren't pressuring her to excel, there was no boyfriend problem, her grades were above average. She had lots of friends. What then? I was baffled. Normally when I see clients in private practice, feelings of discontent or depression emerge fairly early in the session but not in this case. There was no obvious family dysfunction, no drugs or alcohol and no other compulsive behaviors. After 30 minutes of probing, I was suddenly slapped in the face with the source of her problem when she said she couldn't seem to fit everything in.

"Such as?" I asked.

"Such as holding down my part-time job, keeping good grades, spending time with my family and having a decent social life. I had to stop going to aerobics because I just don't have time anymore, and I feel real bad about that."

This student was suffering from overdoing it and was depressed because she felt defective when she couldn't get everything done. Many of us think there's something wrong with us if we cannot give 100 percent to every area of our lives. What was missing in the student's life was time for herself. She was so defined by what she did, she didn't know who she was. She went through the motions of overdoing it on the outside while falling apart on the inside. Studies have shown that college students are 50 percent more likely to entertain suicidal thoughts than their nonacademic peers, presumably because of the depression and stress associated with doing too much.

Students often define themselves by their grades, and when grades become all of who they are, problems erupt. For some students A minus is a failure. One college student, upset with a final grade of A minus, asked the professor if she could take the final exam over. She was given permission and got a final grade of A plus. Although she felt enormously better about herself, this pattern of pushing herself eventually led to burnout.

Lyn Rhoden, a 39-year-old doctoral student, described her drive to excel:

> I had to take three statistics courses for my Ph.D. and I made A pluses on the first two. I made an A minus on the third course. In the final outcome the A minus doesn't get figured in any less than an A plus. I had a 4.0 grade point average regardless. But it bothered me because I felt I had made better than an A minus on that exam. I felt proud of the A pluses in statistics because I didn't have a strong background in math. I wanted to make all A's, but I wasn't expecting to make A pluses. So when I started to make them, that set a new standard for myself. I thought, "Wow! I can make as many A pluses as possible instead of just making all A's." I guess those are high standards, but it's difficult to see them as high when you're surrounded by a large number of other people who are driven to excel too or they wouldn't be working for a doctoral degree.

Overdoing It With Exercise

The music blared as 50 or so sweaty bench-steppers struggled with all their might to lift heavy thighs and meaty arms toward the heavens. Gasping between breaths, Diana honked to her friend Jack, "I'm impressed!" All the other exercisers had two steps under each side of their benches. Jack, the only one with three steps on each side, smiled proudly at Diana's praise. Jack said he always puts more steps under his bench than those around him because if not, he didn't feel okay. It wasn't good enough to do the average difficulty level. It had to be higher and better than the norm.

Nowhere is the phrase "more is better" more pervasive than in exercise and sports, whether you're running more miles, doing more sit-ups, pressing more weight, winning more games or swimming more laps. The more we do, the better we are.

In my interviews for this book I heard the same stories time and again from sports enthusiasts. Doctoral student Lyn Rhoden also drives herself in her workouts:

> I was in bench class yesterday and my knees were really bothering me. I knew I could get just as good a workout if I used a lower bench. I told myself, "Just go and do that. It will be fine." I got there and I couldn't do it because it wasn't good enough. I was looking around the exercise room to see how many people had lower ones and all the people I wanted to be like had the higher benches.

More Is Better

We are judged every minute by what and how much we do. As Stephanie Felder confessed, we feel we must be doing something to have value, to feel okay. So we "do" in order to earn the right to "be" or as atonement for past shame and guilt. The more we do, the better we feel about ourselves. We carry this mind-set into work, managing a house, taking care of others, exercise, school, hobbies and even vacations. The more we can squeeze into 24 hours, the better human beings we are.

Psychotherapist Martin Helldorfer calls this attitude among the clergy perpetuating addictive caring: "Many professional church workers have a spoken and, more frequently unspoken, philosophy that to be busy is to be good, to be idle is to be bad.

Phrased another way, people who do more are better than people who do less. To the extent that church professionals accept this philosophy, they legitimize addictive behavior."

The idea that more is better causes us to overdo, overcompensate, overindulge and eventually burn out. When we try to do too much, we set ourselves up for failure because we cannot get it all done. Once we fail we kick ourselves and repeat the cycle.

"Better than average" is the yardstick Lyn Rhoden uses to measure her worth in every area of her life:

> I have a drive to not be like regular people. I have to do more, to be better or I might waste my life. That has nothing to do with being judgmental of those other people; it just has to do with me. It's always been important for me not to be average. I would like to believe in reincarnation so that I would know that I would have other chances to do other lives, but I can't count on that. So I think that when I'm near death and I look back on my life, I don't want to have any regrets about taking the easy way out or not trying real hard. That's why I don't just want to be average.

Overdoers talk about what they do, instead of how they are. I spoke with Nancy Chase in Atlanta who is disturbed by how our society defines people by what they do and how dehumanizing that can be because it encourages us to externalize the internal self through productivity. Nancy said that when her mother tells her about new acquaintances, she sounds as if she's reading their job resume: "You know she's a graduate of Smith College. She married a lieutenant colonel who just retired and their son goes to Yale," Nancy said. "She doesn't look at people for who they are, but for what they have accomplished. Even when she tells her friends about me, she describes me in terms of what I've done, that I'm an associate professor at Georgia State University, have traveled here or there, and have done this or that."

The more we define ourselves by what we do, the more we lose contact with who we are on the inside.

Myths Of Overdoing It

There are at least 10 myths that make it difficult to recognize that overdoing it is epidemic in our society:

1. Doing brings more self-worth than being.

2. You cannot be overdoing it unless you are gainfully employed in the workplace.

3. Overdoing it is a positive way of life.

4. Overdoing it is not physically or psychologically addictive.

5. Overdoing it is not harmful to emotional and physical health.

6. Overdoing it is caused by the high-pressure jobs or overdemanding family life of the 1990s.

7. Overdoing it is the only way to be effective and productive in our professional and personal lives.

8. Cutting back on the hours we work or eliminating something from our list will control our tendency to do too much.

9. Geographic escape is the solution to overdoing it.

10. Overdoing it is motivated by job loyalty or by our desire to provide a decent living for our families or to contribute to society.

The Addictive Cycle

A pattern accompanies compulsive overdoing. Some people get an adrenaline high from juggling four or five commitments, taking care of others, holding down a job while carpooling and managing a household. They get hangovers as they come off the high. The downward swing is often characterized by mood swings, crankiness, anxiety and depression. Alcoholics have blackouts. Overdoers have *brownouts*, or episodes of forgetfulness and inattention, where their awareness is impaired by stress and fatigue. Stephanie found herself browning out periodically:

> Somebody once told me about meditation: If you don't meditate, you'll find yourself zoning out during the day because your body will make you meditate, and that's what I do. Somebody will be talking to me and I realize I haven't heard what they said. I never meditate because when am I going to do that? Between one and five in the morning?

When we're living on the fast track, trying unsuccessfully to squeeze everything in, we blame it on today's lifestyles and pressures. But blaming society and modern technology lets us off the hook and we avoid taking responsibility for our actions. We do have the ability to choose the way we live and the fact is many of us choose the fast-paced lifestyle and say we have no choice. But we are only veiling our compulsive busyness.

What's behind overdoing it? Is it our fast-paced culture or the way we were brought up? Is it in our genes? What feelings rage? What memories lurk? What motivates people to push themselves and their loved ones beyond human limits? What drives us to stay on this self-destructive path, and how can we break the cycle, slow down and find balance in our lives?

The source of the problem is within us. Overdoing it results from unfulfilled needs. Blaming the job, the recession, or the need for two paychecks is like blaming a spouse for our alcoholism. These contexts contribute to and reward self-destructive behaviors but the cause is within us. Once we take responsibility for overdoing it and look at what's driving us, we empower ourselves to change.

The following chapters reveal the truth about overdoing it. They show how overachieving, overworking, overcompensating and overcaring masquerade the pain of millions of Americans.

If you are stressed out from overdoing it, if you are living your life for everyone but yourself, if you want to slow down but don't know how, this book will show you how to take care of yourself and live the full and satisfying life that you deserve.

Are You Overdoing It?

Here is a self-test to help you see if you are overdoing it. I originally developed this test, called the Work Addiction Risk Test (WART),* to evaluate overdoing it at work. But it can be applied to any area of your life. When you have responded to all 25 statements, add up the numbers in the blanks for your total score.

25 to 49 = You are not overdoing it.
50 to 69 = You are mildly overdoing it.
70 to 100 = You are highly overdoing it.

Read each of the 25 statements as follows and decide how much each one pertains to you. Use the following rating scale.

---

*NOTE: The WART has been scientifically tested and has a .83 test-retest reliability score and a .85 correlation on the individual test items. It is clinically precise and used widely in therapeutic settings as well as in research investigations.

1 = Never true
2 = Sometimes true
3 = Often true
4 = Always true

Put the number that best fits you in the blank beside each statement.

_____ 1. I prefer to do most things myself rather than ask for help.

_____ 2. I get very impatient when I have to wait for someone else or when something takes too long, such as long slow-moving lines.

_____ 3. I seem to be in a hurry and racing against the clock.

_____ 4. I get irritated when I am interrupted while I am in the middle of something.

_____ 5. I stay busy and keep many "irons in the fire."

_____ 6. I find myself doing two or three things at one time, such as eating lunch and writing a memo, while talking on the telephone.

_____ 7. I overcommit myself by biting off more than I can chew.

_____ 8. I feel guilty when I am not working on something.

_____ 9. It is important that I see the concrete results of what I do.

_____ 10. I am more interested in the final results of my work than in the process.

_____ 11. Things just never seem to move fast enough or get done fast enough for me.

_____ 12. I lose my temper when things don't go my way or work out to suit me.

_____ 13. I ask the same question, without realizing it, after I've already been given the answer.

_____ 14. I spend a lot of time mentally planning and thinking about future events, while tuning out the here and now.

_____ 15. I find myself continuing to work after my co-workers have called it quits.

_____ 16. I get angry when people don't meet my standards of perfection.

_____ 17. I get upset when I am in situations where I cannot be in control.

_____ 18. I tend to put myself under pressure with self-imposed deadlines.

_____ 19. It is hard for me to relax when I'm not working.

_____ 20. I spend more time working than socializing with friends, on hobbies or on leisure activities.

_____ 21. I dive into projects to get a head start before all the phases have been finalized.

_____ 22. I get upset with myself for making even the smallest mistake.

_____ 23. I put more thought, time and energy into my work than I do into my relationships with friends and loved ones.

_____ 24. I forget, ignore or minimize important family celebrations such as birthdays, reunions, anniversaries or holidays.

_____ 25. I make important decisions before I have all the facts and have a chance to think them through thoroughly.

2

What Drives You To Overdo It?

*Most people don't care
where they're going as long as
they're in something that gets
them there in a hurry.*

— Andy Rooney

Lyn Rhoden, 39 years old, married and a full-time doctoral student, shares more of her story:

In graduate school I carry a full course load and work 20 hours a week as a research assistant. I live in another city, two hours away from where I attend the university from Monday through Thursday. My husband, Mark, usually has dinner ready when I get home at 8:30 on Thursday evening. We spend some time together then, and on Friday while he's working, I unpack and get started on my schoolwork.

I study most of the weekends; Mark and I just have the evenings together. Saturday and Sunday mornings are the hardest because in the past they were always our time together. Sometimes I wonder how much I can ask him to give up. Every weekend it's like making that decision again. When I make the decision to spend the time with him, I try not to be thinking of other things I need to be doing . . . which is hard for me. But the quality of the time we spend together means so much that with effort I can usually be in the present and value it while we're together.

This morning we got up and had coffee, and I thought it's time for me to get organized and get started. As I was doing that, I wasn't really aware of where he was, and then I realized he was back in bed. That was an invitation. So I had to think in my mind what's the best thing to do. Ten years from now being with him will be more important than having read a certain chapter. I have to spend a few minutes getting my mind in that mode so I can experience it because I don't want to waste that time. I don't want to be with him and be thinking of school.

It gives me a sense of satisfaction to do things perfectly. It was real hard for me to acknowledge that I was tired and burned out. I had quit my teaching job to go to school full time. I thought this is a luxury to live this type of life: My work is research, reading and learning. At the end of my first semester in my doctoral program I felt guilty when I started to feel tired and down because I thought I had no right to feel this way. It took hearing a lot of different people I respect at the university say that what I was doing was hard. It was difficult for me to acknowledge that it was difficult, and I felt bad for feeling tired. I gave myself talks about not feeling sorry for myself and not feeling tired, that this was a good life, that not many people get to do this and that I had no right to feel tired.

I try very hard all the time, so I'm in high gear emotionally and stay pretty wound up. The last couple of times I had to get up to speak in class I was so charged up that I had physiological symptoms of shallow breathing and shaking but I still made it through the presentations. Knowing it was obvious to people watching that I was nervous was hard for me to deal with. I think it started out from the sheer excitement of trying too hard and preparing right up to the second that I had to get up to speak. I felt that I had failed somewhat because, although I had given the presentation well and made an A on it, I had not been perfectly relaxed and I had not done a perfect job in presenting the material, and that felt like a failure to me. I think that's a self-perpetuating thing. It sets you up next time to be scared that it will happen again. It's not something I want to continue to do, so I immediately went to find what I could do about it. I'm going to a biofeedback therapist now to learn calming and relaxation techniques. I'm hoping that will help me when I get up to speak.

Sometimes when I cannot strike the right balance at home, I feel like I should be able to fit everything in, and I beat myself up if I can't. I want everything while I'm at school to be just right, and I want everything here at home to be just right too. I like it when everything is perfect. So if Mark is in a bad mood, I try real hard to put him in a good mood again, even when it's not about me. He may be upset about something at work, for example. And if he's not ready to be in a good mood, I feel like I can't find the right thing to do, the right thing to say. I beat myself up because I can't make him better.

Sometimes I get a bad headache, which leads to a crying spell because I can't get rid of the headache. I feel guilty about having a headache because I'm not sure that other people really know how bad it is, and they might think I'm over-reacting. I get frustrated with not being able to function because of the pain, when actually the pain is just my body saying I have to stop. The frustrating times when I cannot make everything okay at home make me cry. Then the crying makes me feel out of control and more guilty and self-defeated.

I've always wanted to do things right the first time. I didn't learn to ride a bike for a long time because I couldn't accept the fact that I had to fall down all those times to learn. I just knew there had to be some way I could get on that bike and ride off into the sunset the first time. I didn't want to go through those hurtful steps on the way. I've done that about a lot of things. I've only done the things that I felt I could just step in and do well right away.

I can't swim. The reason is that as an adult it's embarrassing to go and learn how to swim. That just kills me. But the only way I could do it is if they would clear the pool so nobody would see — so nobody could witness my being inept as an adult in something that almost everybody else knows how to do.

At the conclusion of the interview, I told Lyn she definitely qualified as an overdoer. "You make an A," I told her.

"Not an A plus?" she asked.

The Driving Force

Many of us spend a great deal of time being angry at store clerks, angry because their lines move too slowly, they don't look at us or they are cold and indifferent. Actually I have come to realize that clerks are great dumping grounds for the public to deposit their frustrations. Many times we are poised for them to say one cross word or to arch one eyebrow and then we pounce!

I include myself here. On regular visits to my local pharmacy, I deal with a clerk who has an unfriendly business-as-usual air about her. She never looks at me. When I smile and ask, "How are you today?" she doesn't respond. She literally snatches the prescription out of my hand and walks away. My past reactions have been to lash out at her, which only makes her angry at me and me angrier at her. Some days I alter my approach to "get her." When she'd try to snatch the prescription, I'd clench it tightly for her to take. That would get her attention and she would look at me. It still annoyed her and that irritated me more. We were both caught in a negative cycle that threw us out of control.

Some of us move through life reacting to life's random events like rats in a maze. We respond in predictable ways without thinking about our choices. Our partner or roommate curses us and we curse back. A co-worker makes a disparaging remark, we return the insult. A neighbor calls us an ugly name, so we return the childish comment.

We can take charge of our lives by *acting* with the gift of human reasoning, not *reacting* like rats in a maze. We react when we respond in predictable ways, without conscious choice. Through reacting we are controlled by people and events. When we think and then act, we make conscious choices that put us in charge of our lives. A kind word diffuses a sour attitude. Calm in the face of hysteria has a soothing effect. Compliments reverse aspersions. In each case our behavior can turn the tone of a situation around.

Once I realized that I had some control over my actions, I began to make more conscious choices about how I wanted to think, feel and behave in all situations. One day when the pharmacy clerk persisted in her usual obstinate behavior, I smiled and asked, "How are you today?" She kept her eyes focused on the cash register and said nothing. I smiled and repeated, "How are you today?" She gruffly commented, "I'm fine," still not making eye contact and dumping the change into my hand. I continued to smile and walked away.

Changing the clerk's behavior was no longer my goal. Her rudeness had nothing to do with me. It originated from her own deep-seated unhappiness. I focused on changing *my* behavior by untangling myself from the negative interaction and choosing my actions — regardless of what she did. Whether I felt good or bad did not depend on the sales clerk being nice to me. If I wanted to enjoy my day, it was up to me. Rather than getting caught in her swirl of negativity, I stood back and let her be. I learned that I have the power to act consistently with my own beliefs, no matter how the situation bends and sways.

We can apply this same practice when we become emotionally paralyzed and helpless to do anything about our hurried and harried lifestyles. Often when we don't know what to do, we mope around, moaning about how terrible things are and hoping they will improve. But situations do not get better on their own. They improve when we change on the *inside* instead of trying to change the *outside* situation itself.

Low Self-Esteem And The Big Fix

You are not helpless; you always have choices. You are in charge of your life. But you have to claim that power.

Before you can take charge of your life, you must believe you are worth it. Not feeling worthy is the barrier that drives over-doers beyond human limits and prevents them from taking care of themselves. We overdo to fill a void. Motivated by low self-esteem, we believe nothing we do will ever be good enough. So we keep trying to do the task better, hoping that eventually we will do it perfectly and feel good about ourselves.

Characteristics Of Chronic Overdoers

Following are ten characteristics of chronic overdoers.
They tend to . . .

☐ Focus on the external world of doing, instead of the
  internal world of being.

☐ Quantify what they do (must see it and measure it) in
  order to feel good about themselves.

☐ Put their self-care needs last after everything else is
  done.

☐ Have difficulty being in the present.

☐ Focus on the final product instead of the process.

☐ Be overscheduled, inflexible and lack spontaneity.

☐ Define themselves and others by what they do, not by
  who they are.

☐ Feel incomplete and unfinished without something to
  do.

☐ Engage in critical thinking or think of themselves in
  distorted ways.

☐ Be deadly serious about most things rather than happy-
  go-lucky.

The attorney tells herself that winning just one more case will put her on top. The writer believes she will be revered in others' eyes after just one more book. The construction worker will have all the money he needs after building just one more house. The avid plant collector needs just one more rare orchid to make him happy for a lifetime. The stay-at-home mother needs to bake the perfect loaf of bread, get the bathroom painted and make it to all her children's afternoon activities as her crowning achievement. The actor needs just one more big role to make him famous.

Overdoers are the envy of their peers: accomplished, responsible and in charge of any situation. At least that's how they look to the outside world. Underneath the glitz and glitter of success, however, swirls an obsessive need to excel, a compulsive need for approval, a deep-seated unhappiness and low self-esteem.

"I didn't get anything done today," frowns Jamey McCullers, a part-time landscaper who measures his productivity in order to gauge his self-worth at the end of a long day. On days when he feels low it is often because he feels he has nothing to show for his time. Feeling incomplete and unfinished, people measure their worth by what they can produce. They must quantify their success through observable outcomes of "how much" and "how many." Outward manifestations of their importance include how much money they make, how many sales accounts they land, how many pieces of real estate they sell, how many projects they complete around the house, how quickly they can get food on the table.

Overdoers quantify all the things they do as a measurement of their personal worth. Lyn Rhoden uses this method to reassure and feel okay about herself:

> The A pluses I get in graduate school are a measure of how good I am. Sometimes I sit and count off to myself all the things I can do so that I reassure myself I'm doing okay and am accomplishing enough. I speak three languages, I can cook really well, I've been to this many countries, I work out four or five times a week, I'm getting my Ph.D., I have a 4.0 average. You're okay, Lyn. That part of me has a high self-esteem, but I have to tell myself those things and be aware of them and then there's another part of me that doesn't feel okay.

Overdoing it conveys a common message: "Look at me; I am worthy; I have value." Producing and achieving temporarily fill the inner emptiness and give a fleeting and false sense of self-fulfillment, at least until the next day.

Overdoers fear that if people really knew them, they'd be discovered for the fakes they truly are. The fear of failure drives them to produce harder and harder. They take on mountains of doing even when their professional and personal lives are already overloaded. They set themselves up for failure because their standards are so high no one could ever meet them. On the inside they feel like a small child who never does anything right, while harshly judging themselves for the most minute flaws.

Why are they so hard on themselves? Because they feel bad inside, they try to "fix" themselves, to feel better — more finished, more complete. They refuse to allow themselves to make mistakes, and when they eventually do, they judge themselves harshly. The cycle is self-perpetuating because they delve further into doing and producing as consecration for their unforgivable sins.

Stephanie soberly describes this process: "I make a vow to myself every morning when I wake up that today is going to be the day when I'm going to balance it all. I'm going to get it all right. But I never do."

The Faulty Thinking That Drives You

Those of us who chronically overdo it have a faulty belief system that sets us apart from people who can just be. These thought patterns keep us stuck in a never-ending cycle of busyness, hurrying and achieving. It's not only what we do that is important; it's what we think about what we do.

The cycle of overdoing it is self-perpetuating and very difficult to break. The cycle begins with *self-flawed thinking* and feelings of low self-esteem. You feel inadequate and unfulfilled, so you reach outside yourself to reduce the pain. Overdoing it provides you with this temporary relief. You take on too much and try to do each task perfectly — perfectionism is the killer word here — and you are bound to fail. Life becomes a juggling act and eventually one of the balls will drop.

Lib Willis, a school administrator, discovered in her bout with work addiction that self-flawed thinking was driving her:

> I thought if I did four or five projects at one time, I was smarter and that I was really up there. What I really felt was that I was less than you, so I overcompensated to make myself feel better. I kept juggling all the different things around to keep them in the air and then lost control of them. But underneath this stuff I had the feeling that I wasn't good enough the way I was, and I've had that feeling since I was a little girl — not feeling good enough.

Does Faulty Thinking Drive You To Overdo?

☐ *Self-Flawed Thinking.* Nothing I do is good enough. Something is wrong with me; I am inadequate, unworthy and unlovable.

☐ *Perfectionist Thinking.* Things have to be perfect for me to be happy, and nothing I ever do is good enough.

☐ *All-Or-Nothing Thinking.* If I cannot be all things to all people, then I'm nothing. I can either spend time with my family or financially support them — not both. I'm either the best or the worst; there is no in between.

☐ *Telescopic Thinking.* I always feel like a failure because I focus on and magnify my shortcomings and ignore my successes.

☐ *Blurred Boundary Thinking.* It's hard for me to know when to stop, where to draw the line and when to say no to others.

☐ *People-Pleasing Thinking.* If I can get others to like me, I'll feel better about myself.

☐ *Pessimistic Thinking.* My life is chaotic and stressful and full of misery and despair; that's just the way life is.

☐ *Catastrophic Thinking.* My life feels out of control and something terrible might happen, so I can't relax. I must be prepared by always expecting the worst.

☐ *Helpless Thinking.* I am helpless to change my lifestyle. There is nothing I can do to change my schedule and slow down.

☐ *Self-Victimizing Thinking.* Other people and other situations are to blame for my overdoing, my stress and my burnout.

☐ *Resentful Thinking.* I am full of bitterness and resentment, and I will never forgive others for what they did to me. I am a victim of a demanding job, a needy family or a society that says, "You can do it all."

☐ *Resistance Thinking.* Life is an uphill battle, and I must fight to enforce my way, resist what I don't want and cling to things to keep them as they are.

☐ *Wishful Thinking.* I wish I could have the things I cannot have because the things I have are of no value. If only my situation would change, I could slow down and take better care of myself.

☐ *Serious Thinking.* Playing and having fun are a waste of time because there's too much work that needs to be done.

☐ *Externalized Thinking.* Happiness can be found in the external world. If the outer circumstances of my life would change, it would fix how I feel inside.

Many overdoers feel nothing they ever did as children was good enough, and self-flawed thinking becomes their legacy in adulthood. Nothing they ever do is good enough. So they're still trying to do it right. No one can do everything perfectly all the time. Even if you don't fail, you perceive yourself as not doing well enough. You don't feel you're a good mom, you never seem to have time for the kids, the house is a mess, you're mediocre in your job. The guilt of not being there for your kids or not doing a good enough job adds to your feelings of inadequacy. So you dig your heels in deeper and determine to be the best mom in the world.

Your *perfectionist thinking* tells you to bite off more than you can chew — which leads you back to feelings of self-defeat and failure, right where you started from: self-flawed thinking. You are caught in a never-ending cycle that will never let you feel okay.

Many of us think there's something wrong with us if we cannot give 100 percent to every area of our lives, motivated by such cultural maxims as "I must be all things to all people or I'm a failure," "If you cannot do a job right, don't do it at all" or "If I cannot do it all, I might as well do none of it."

I caught myself in this type of *all-or-nothing thinking* during my 60-minute aerobics class. Thirty minutes through the class, feeling tired after a long day's work, I wanted to stop and go home and rest. My critical self-talk told me that unless I finished the full hour, I was a total failure, that I was a loser and that I wouldn't get any benefit from the exercise. It finally occurred to me that I was mentally abusing myself, holding myself hostage to my thoughts because it is clear that 45 minutes is plenty of exercise.

Overdoing it is a way to address the inner voice that says you are flawed if you cannot be all things to all people.

Even when we succeed, our critical inner voice tells us we failed. We call this *telescopic thinking* because our minds act like a telescope and zoom in on and magnify our weaknesses. This faulty thinking pattern often starts with critical parents, as Stephanie described:

> I had parents who said when I brought home an A minus on my report card, "Well, why couldn't that be an A plus?" My dad even said to me when I won a writing contest and I sent him a copy of the story, "They must not have had too many entries to pick yours." So I have this real sense of needing to prove something.

Figure 2.1. Cycle Of Overdoing It

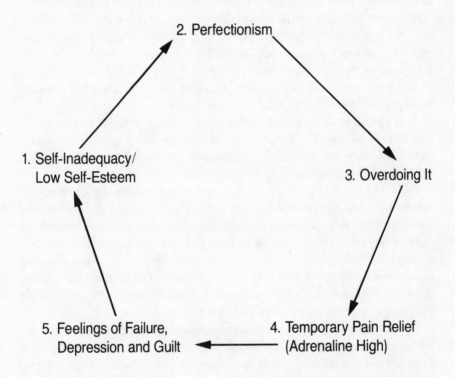

2. Perfectionism

1. Self-Inadequacy/
Low Self-Esteem

3. Overdoing It

5. Feelings of Failure,
Depression and Guilt

4. Temporary Pain Relief
(Adrenaline High)

The Cure Has Turned Into The Cause

Telescopic thinking happens when we set ourselves up for failure by comparing ourselves to the geniuses. We must be smart like Einstein, creative like Leonardo da Vinci, compassionate like Mother Teresa, witty like Joan Rivers, rich like Ivana Trump, sexy like Nick Nolte and play tennis like Boris Becker. Even if we excel in three out of four areas, we ignore the achievements and focus on the failure. We berate ourselves, although others may perceive us as outstanding. We continue to overlook our accomplishments and positive actions because we are focused on our shortcomings. Through such superhuman standards, we shower ourselves with self-criticism and self-contempt. "That was a stupid thing to do" and "I just can't seem to do anything right" are familiar rings to the ears of chronic overdoers.

People who overdo lack clear boundaries. With *blurred boundary thinking* we consider typical what others consider excessive.

Lyn Rhoden gives a good example in her own life: "I don't think I overdo it by my standards. Lots of times when I take on projects, other people's responses are stronger than mine. They see what I do as a bigger deal than I see it."

It's hard to realize we're biting off more than we can chew or to say no because we don't know where or when to draw the line. We often sacrifice our own needs by giving in to the demands of others, whom we perceive as more needy than ourselves. We are so used to doing what others expect us to do, we don't know what we really want or need to do for ourselves. This type of thinking leads to self-neglect until we either explode with uncontainable resentment or collapse with burnout.

Sometimes what others believe about us is more important to us than what we believe about ourselves, and we develop the habit of people pleasing. *People-pleasing thinking* makes us indecisive and overly agreeable because we use the opinions of others to determine our actions. We figure that if we can get others to approve of us, we'll feel better inside. It is impossible to please everybody and when we try, we lose our self-respect and don't know what we believe without someone else to tell us.

When we do get praised by friends or co-workers, our *pessimistic thinking* discounts it, and we continue to feel unworthy and unfulfilled. We unconsciously filter out the positive aspects of our lives and allow only negative aspects to enter. Our pessimism reminds us that nothing we ever do is good enough. This bad habit of selecting the negative and ignoring the positive eventually leads us to believe that everything is negative.

We engage in *catastrophic thinking* and believe we live in a fearful world where sooner or later there will be suffering, frustration, conflict, depression and illness. At the core of our fear is a deep feeling that we are failures, no matter how successful we are in the outer world. We believe we got where we are by luck or accident and that it's only a matter of time until people will know the truth about us, that we are inadequate and unworthy. Our catastrophic expectations can become self-fulfilling. When we carry the fear of failure, we unconsciously set ourselves up to fail. Our fear becomes a self-fulfilling prophecy, driving us so hard that we sabotage our own success. It ruins our physical and emotional health and cripples our relationships with co-workers, families and friends.

We feel helpless and unable to change our lives. When we engage in *helpless thinking* we view ourselves as pawns. We externalize our responsibilities and blame our problems on other people and situations. We blame the workplace for our work addiction, feminist ideology for the double bind of women today or our achievement-oriented society for its emphasis on competition.

Believing problems and solutions are outside of us puts us into a victim role. *Self-victimizing thinking* disempowers us because we relinquish our personal power to external forces and make ourselves victims of today's social trends, whether it's the dual-career household, workers trying to make it to the top of the corporate ladder or clergy trying to save souls in this era of materialism and consumption. We think that we have no say-so over our lives, that we are victims of fate, chance and other people, events and situations. Then we begin to behave that way, which reinforces our thinking.

The more victimized we feel, the more our resentment builds. *Resentful thinking* is expressed through bitterness and cynicism toward a fast-paced lifestyle. We feel trapped and see no way out, except to be angry and to vent our anger by complaining and blaming. We hold tightly to our resentments because we're afraid if we let them go there will be nothing left of us.

Resistance thinking causes us to perceive life as a struggle. We structure our lives by wearing too many hats and doing too many things. We keep pushing ourselves beyond human limits, refusing to take time for ourselves and determining to do it all. We straight-jacket ourselves into a lifestyle that doesn't allow for spontaneity or flexibility. We try to cram 48 hours into 24, to make life's natural rhythm conform to our needs to keep doing. We get frustrated in traffic jams and become annoyed with people who move too slowly. We waste a lot of emotional energy getting mad at the conditions of our daily lives, instead of accepting them and living within their boundaries.

We engage in *wishful thinking* — wishing we had more of something or someone to make us feel more finished, more complete. This type of thinking fans the flames of overdoing it to gain more. We want most what we cannot have, and we devalue or ignore what we already possess, simply because it is ours. Wishful thinking defines happiness in terms of lack and discontent. Focusing on what is missing keeps us feeling empty and incomplete, which encourages us to do more to fill up the hole. The solution to this never-ending cycle is to want what we already have, not what we think we want, and to express gratitude for the people and things that already enrich our lives.

Serious thinking tells us that life is all grim determination and that fun and joy are taboo. We forget to laugh at ourselves and see the humorous side of life. Many overdoers learned as children that life is serious business. Perhaps they did not get to enjoy the carefree world of childhood. Laughter and fun are looked upon with contempt because they conflict with the single-minded goal of getting the job done. Relaxing is often considered wasteful, and people who fritter time away by playing and having fun may be considered frivolous and foolish.

Overdoers experience *externalized thinking,* which focuses their attention on a concrete product. Our self-worth is attached to what we can produce, not on how we feel inside. The more we produce, the better we feel; the more worthy we are. Overdoers deliberately or unwittingly create work just to stay busy. One man who was obsessed with making lists that ran his life told me: "I always found a way to fill in any extra spaces or lines on my yellow pad with obscure chores so that it would look like I'm busy." Listmakers say that completing each item and checking it off provides them with indescribable satisfaction.

Making Responsible Choices

Do you feel like a prisoner in your own life? Are you condemned to never having enough time for yourself? When you discover that you're not living your life, that your lifestyle is controlling you rather than your controlling it, then you know you have a problem.

Viktor Frankl survived three years in Auschwitz and other Nazi concentration camps. He was separated from his family, deprived of food, stripped naked and exposed to harsh weather. Still, through all the suffering and degradation, each day he created choices for himself. Starving and freezing, he chose to relive in his mind a more pleasant moment with his loving wife or to recreate the memory of a warm spring day in a meadow. He sought meaning in his personal tragedy, and his power of choice gave him renewed purpose in life.

Hostage Terry Waite said he survived his captors in much the same way. No matter what they did in the physical world, they couldn't rob him of his inner essential being.

Frankl's and Waite's experiences can be an inspiration to all of us who are caught up in today's frantic-paced lifestyle. We see ourselves as victims of a lifestyle that we say we don't want. It is sometimes difficult for us to see that we *always* have choices. We can always decide what we think, how we feel and how we will act in spite of the limitations of our lifestyles. Those of us who overextend ourselves through work, caring, sports, grades or carpooling are making choices every minute of our lives, although we often see them as society-imposed, instead of self-imposed.

Lyn Rhoden views her inability to slow down as part of her culture:

> When Mark and I took a trip to France before I started college, I found that that culture helped me live in the present. I started entertaining the idea of living like that, where you didn't always strive for something to accomplish or achieve but live every day to the fullest. I don't think our culture helps us live in the moment. I feel like I would need to be in an environment that would be conducive to that

because I feel I can't maintain it in the American culture, in the city where your success depends on what you've achieved. But I wish I could be in an environment where I was somehow able to stay connected to the idea that my success was the quality of life being lived every day in its own moments. I think European cultures help people do that.

Stephanie Felder attributes her overdoing it to the supermom syndrome of the 1990s, where women are expected to do it all. These expectations, according to Stephanie, force women to overextend themselves in every arena of their lives in order to measure up:

I think the message from the women's movement is clear: Women can do it all. That's what they've been telling us. You can do it all. You're going to be considered a wimp if you just stay at home with your child. There was a time when I didn't have a job and I was embarrassed. I was a mother with two little babies and I'd go to a party and meet someone new and the first question they'd ask me would be, "What do you do?" I died a thousand deaths when I had to say I stayed home with the kids. I felt like the biggest loser and failure. So my career is really important to me, and I feel like I have to prove something. I have to show people that just because I'm a mother, just because I have other responsibilities outside of school, I'm not ever going to say no to any challenge, never fall down, miss a deadline or be late for anything.

While some of today's women view the many roles they must play as a hardship, others view them as liberating. Hillary Clinton, wife of Arkansas governor and presidential candidate Bill Clinton, told *The Charlotte Observer* about the choices women have available to them:

What I have tried to do to be a wife, a mother, have my own profession, plus be active in the community, is a balancing act that millions and millions of women of my age and younger have engaged in. And so we don't know what to expect these days because, when my mother was growing up and making her choices, they were more limited than the choices available to women in America today. And we have to understand that any woman who makes a responsible choice — whether it be to be a full-time homemaker and mother or to be a full-time professional or to do what most of us do, which is to juggle those roles — is exercising choices that were formerly not available.

Whether you are a juggling supermom, a struggling student or an ambitious corporate executive, you are exercising options whether or not you are aware of it. True. They may not be the choices you want to make, but they are choices nonetheless. I spent the majority of my life blaming my work addiction on high-pressured jobs or on the fact that I was brought up in an alcoholic home.

The truth of the matter was I chose that lifestyle, and I was the only person who could change it, regardless of cultural norms or society's expectations.

Lib Willis, once a dispirited wage earner, was able to stop blaming the workplace and accept responsibility for her job choices: "I have picked high-pressured jobs for my last three jobs. I wasn't aware of it going into them, but now I see that I am doing that. Nobody's doing that to me."

There is growing consensus that none of us can do it all. We can't give 100 percent to everything because it is not humanly possible. Trying to compete with modern technology is like signing your own death warrant; we are human beings, not machines. You are the only one who can change your situation. Because daily pressures will probably not vanish at the snap of a finger, your best bet is to accept that you cannot do it all and to make responsible choices about what you will do. Valuing this type of thinking as a strength instead of a weakness helps you feel better about yourself, makes you more efficient and keeps you more balanced and healthy.

Where you live and what you do for a living have little to do with whether you can lead a more balanced life. Nothing will change until you rethink your priorities and values. It is important to confront the characteristics of chronic overdoing and the faulty thinking that have become part of your personality. It is important to commit yourself to changing these habits and to stop blaming your family, the media, society, your job, the women's movement or the dog. The way to change is to change your outlook. As Anthony de Mello said, "Nothing has changed but my attitude; everything has changed."

It is not what life deals us that makes us happy or unhappy. We are given life, but we have the power to create our experience of life. The way we think about what happens to us creates our emotions and reactions, not the incidents themselves. When we think of ourselves as victims, we automatically imprison ourselves. When we focus on hardships and problems, we keep ourselves stuck in faulty thinking.

How To Think That Black Cloud Away

Sometimes critical messages blink in our troubled minds like neon signs. We stew over mistakes we make, worry about things we cannot control and expect the worst in every situation. In childhood we internalize messages about ourselves from adults. These messages — true or untrue — become our reality. Critical messages such as "Can't you do anything right?" or "You're always getting into trouble" or "You're such a failure" teach us that we are unworthy. In adulthood the mental dialogues we have with ourselves continue to remind us of who we are. Much of what we think and do is dictated by our refusal to let go of the critical voices of our parents.

The solution to overdoing it is to go straight to the source and become conscious of your critical thinking. For a one-week period, notice each time you have these inner dialogues and write them down, without censorship, in a daily log. At the end of the week look over your list and star the ones that occur more than once. You may be surprised at how often you call yourself "stupid" or "unworthy." These thoughts actually govern you; they are translated into bad feelings and self-defeating behaviors. They tell you what you think of yourself, how to behave and even how others see you. They prevent your life from working the way you want it to.

In your recorded dialogue identify the names you call yourself, the words that are shame-based (such as "should" or "must") and the put-downs. Now we are going to learn how to confront and challenge this inner critical voice. Draw a line down the middle of a sheet of paper, making two columns. In the left-hand column write the first faulty-thinking statement, and in the right-hand column rewrite it by substituting a re-evaluation or an affirmation. Go through your list one statement at a time. Here are a few examples:

Faulty Thinking	Positive Affirmation
"I must be thoroughly competent in all the tasks that I undertake."	"Trying to be outstanding even in one task is difficult. Achievements do not determine my worth. Regardless of what happens in the outer world, I am always succeeding within myself."
"I should be loved by everyone."	"It's unrealistic to expect to be loved by and to please everyone. My worth doesn't depend on everyone liking me, so I will try to please only myself."
"I can't do anything right."	"I am worthy and capable in all things."
"If only things were perfect, then I could be happy."	"Life is uncertain and people, myself included, are not perfect. I accept myself as I am with all my strengths and shortcomings."
"I cannot help the way things are."	"It is up to me to change the things I can because I am responsible for my life. I am in charge of my life; it is not in charge of me."

My father often told me, "You'll never amount to anything." That critical voice, echoing in my head and reminding me that nothing I ever did was enough, drove me deeper into overdoing it. Today I know that my father's criticisms, although directed at me, were a reflection of his own inner frustration, low self-worth and deep unhappiness, all of which he medicated with alcohol. When we know where the critical messages come from, we can give them back to their owners. I was able to give back the drugstore clerk's rude behavior once I realized it was about her, not me. I was able to give my father's critical messages back to him by saying, "Dad, I'm letting you have your feelings back. I know you felt like you never amounted to anything. Those feelings are yours, not mine."

Make a deliberate attempt to change your faulty self-talk. Work first with those messages that you most often send yourself, noticing what they are and, if possible, with whom they originated. Ask yourself what you can write or say to yourself to enable you to return faulty messages back to where they started. Practice your affirmations as often as you can during the day . . . in the morning as you look in the mirror, on the way to work, while waiting in line or before falling asleep at night. After a period of dedicated practice, you will begin to see a difference in your ability to think and feel more positively about yourself.

Making A Perceptual Shift

People who overdo it excel at tasks rather than relationships. Achieving allows them to avoid intimacy and gives them an excuse for remaining distant. While people are overdoing it, they are dying emotionally. Because of the external referencing, overdoers tend to suffer from spiritual starvation. They experience an emptiness that they try to fill up with activity.

A perceptual shift must occur for us to get out of the overdoing-it cycle. We take an internal, instead of an external, focus. We learn to use flexibility and to live in the process instead of trying to quantify our lives by pointing with pride to a product.

The shift happens by learning to define yourself, not by what you have or do, but by who you are on the inside.

You do this by letting something go to make room for yourself. Time for you is the only way out of the trap. You learn to take some of the energy you have been sending outward and redirect it inward. You develop a relationship with yourself and break out of the self-destructive cycle of trying to fill yourself up with overdoing it. You learn to take time for renewal and rest, for contemplation, for intimately connecting with that deeper part of yourself.

Putting Yourself In The Driver's Seat

It's time to put yourself in the driver's seat. When we put ourselves down, call ourselves names and use shame-based language, our minds are like small children who do as they wish. We can take charge of our lives by disciplining our minds as if they were unruly children. Here are some ways to restore order in your life:

• *Learn to identify your feelings and to accept the fact that you're angry or frustrated.* You may want to ship the kids off to relatives and disappear into a federal witness protection program. But a more realistic way to cope is to work on yourself on the inside. Listen to yourself. Pay attention to your thoughts and feelings, and get in the habit of writing them down in a journal. Ask yourself: What are my activities helping me to escape from? What am I afraid of facing? What resentments or hurts are unresolved? Face your feelings and feel them completely. Where does the voice that tells you nothing you do is good enough come from? Is it *your* voice, or as in Stephanie Felder's case, is it the voice of a critical parent or other adult figure from your childhood? Learn to stand up to the critical voice instead of letting it take charge of you.

• *Give yourself pep talks.* Whether you're taking a test, making a speech, starting a new job or struggling with parenthood, doubt and lack of confidence can flood your mind. You might tell yourself, "I can't do this. I might as well give up." Engaging in such critical thinking sets you up for failure. When you have these negative feelings, ask yourself, "What would I say to my best friend or child if they thought they couldn't do something? I wouldn't say, 'Of course you can't do it. You might as well give up.' " Your confidence in their ability would encourage them. Once we love ourselves enough to be our own best friend, we'll give ourselves that same encouragement. Pep talks bring self-assurance and success. Tell yourself, "Yes, I can do this and I can do it well." Look at yourself in a mirror as you give yourself encouraging messages. Before you get into a situation, image the best of outcomes, instead of the worst. Tell yourself, "I can do anything I set my mind to, and I can do it well."

• *Give yourself positive affirmations.* Keep a bulletin board with all the affirming letters, notes, gifts and sayings that people send you. Look at them often to remind yourself that others see you as a wonderful human being. Put messages on your bathroom mirror so that each morning you can look yourself straight in the eye and say, for example, "I am looking at the only person in the world who can stand in the way of my happiness."

• *Learn to accept your human limitations without feeling flawed.*
Learn to admit and accept your mistakes and to love yourself in
spite of them. Acknowledging and accepting your mortality, your
vulnerabilities and your limits strengthen your character. Begin
to think of yourself as a human being who needs nurturance,
rather than as a machine that can keep going. Stay away from
relationships that drain you, and surround yourself with people
who support, love and affirm you.

• *Strengthen relationships.* Everybody has bad days, but try not
to unload your anger or frustration on the people you live with.
Try to focus on the positive things loved ones do rather than
harping on the negative. In healthy relationships partners view
their lives together and the energy required to maintain these
bonds as a privilege and challenge — not as an obligation or
struggle. One of the best ways to strengthen relationships is to
spend time together. Preparing meals together and having pleasant mealtime conversations (without television) give a chance for
healthy communication. Take a genuine and active interest in
your partner's life. Listen to what they have to say. Find out what
they have been up to. If you have children, plan special times to
give them undivided attention. Save the newspaper for when
they are asleep. Spend time with youngsters by helping them
with homework, playing board games, scheduling weekend
outings or doing family projects.

• *Practice the rituals in your life.* Rituals are the glue that holds
relationships together. This glue is being lost in families that —
caught in demanding jobs or in single-parent roles — forego the
bedrock ritual of nightly dinners. Partners become virtual
strangers when they lose track of who is doing what and how
they are feeling about their lives. Research supports the idea that
rituals keep loved ones stabilized amid the chaotic life in the fast
track. Families that eat on the run or in shifts — instead of sitting
down together — are not so close as families that eat together.
Households that recognize and celebrate holidays, birthdays and
anniversaries have stronger relationships than those that don't.

Rituals help heal tensions and teach kids the importance of
togetherness and of having plans and seeing them through.
Rituals provide stability and dependability and give family
members something to count on. Families that value and practice

rituals generally have less anxiety and fewer physical signs of burnout. What rituals can you put back in your life to restore feelings of togetherness and heal tensions? Here are a few suggestions:

Have dinner together at a set time each evening without television.

Have a regularly scheduled time to meet with friends for a tennis game, a shopping jaunt, a talk over coffee or to pursue your favorite hobby.

Attend church, synagogue or meditation group on a specific day and time each week.

Have a special vacation place where the family goes each year to get away.

Read a book to the children each night at bedtime.

Celebrate Thanksgiving or Christmas in ways that become traditional and that family members can depend on.

• *Do something new and fun.* Increase the number of process-oriented activities in your life. Treat yourself to a hobby or activity that will allow you to enjoy its process rather than the product. Choose something that you can deliberately do "imperfectly." Getting involved in right-brain activities such as art, dancing and acting will take you out of your logical left brain and into your intuitive and creative side.

• *Learn to be in the present.* As long as we live in the future or dwell in the past, we miss the present. Hugh Prather said, "Every moment that I am centered in the future, I suffer a temporary loss of this life."

Yesterday is gone forever, tomorrow never comes; all we really have is now. You can combat overdoing it by learning to live in the now.

Pay attention to the people you are with and focus on your surroundings. *Carpe diem,* the Latin phrase for "seize the day," reminds us to live in the now because the present is the only time we really have. It advises us to live our lives fully, not fretting about what went wrong or worrying about what will happen. As we think of our own mortality and how fleeting life is, many things come to mind that need doing. Today is the day to tell someone we love them, make a confession or mend a relationship. We seize the day to do what we have left undone.

• *Develop an intimate relationship with yourself.* While we have guilty thoughts that it is selfish, wasteful and counterproductive to care for ourselves, the fact is the more we do for ourselves, the more we get done and the more efficient we are. Shakespeare said, "The greater sin is not self-love; it is self-neglect." Balancing busyness with a rich internal life can heal our stress and burn-out. Think about yourself as a bank account. If you're always making withdrawals, you're headed for spiritual bankruptcy. To stay "open for business," you've got to make deposits in your personal account.

Set aside 15 minutes to an hour each day for yourself and call it *internal time* or *daily deposit time.* Use it in any way you choose, to go within to collect your thoughts, to stay in touch with who you are, to nurture *you.* Get to know yourself, be kinder to yourself, be your own best friend and take better care of yourself. Develop your own inner values and beliefs and stand up for yourself. Write your feelings in a journal, meditate, pray, say self-affirmations, listen to soft music with eyes closed, read daily devotions or anything else that helps you stay in tune with yourself. As you practice this, you will find that you are more efficient at what you do. The more you give to yourself, the more you have to give to others.

• *Pamper yourself.* Set aside a block of time, no matter how short to start. Groom yourself or soak in a hot bath. Relax by a fire or on a cool screened porch, go for a walk or get a massage. Whatever you decide to do, be sure to block from your mind all work-related thoughts or to-do lists. This is a time for you. You may at first go through withdrawal and feel bored, restless or depressed, but don't give up. You may just want to sleep because of tiredness and that's okay too. You are not used to paying this much attention to yourself, so your mind and body might naturally resist. Feel the boredom or restlessness instead of numbing it with something to do. Sleep if you feel the need, walk, sit and stare into space — whatever feels right. Recognize and experience the symptoms and be aware of what your thoughts, feelings and body say to you. Remember to take it gradually, one step at a time.

• *Eat properly, rest and exercise.* To put your mind and body in optimal shape, eat right, get ample rest and exercise. Balance is the key. Eat balanced, nutritional meals instead of junk food. Eat three meals a day rather than one or two. Avoid eating while working, mealtime in front of the television and snacking between meals. Include rest and exercise into your schedule. You will think more clearly and creatively and have fewer health problems. Make sure your exercise regimen matches your health, age and physical condition as well as your interests. People who are inclined to overdo it with food, rest or exercise have to take extra care to maintain a healthy balance in the time they put into these activities so that they work for and not against them.

• *Recognize that less is more.* The key to stop overdoing it is to simplify your life, to appreciate how rich your life already is and to recognize that more things will not bring more happiness. Lower your standards and be more realistic about what's possible. You can relax your standards and still do a good job. Instead of taking on additional commitments, ask yourself what obligations or chores can be eliminated from your to-do list. Instead of purchasing more things, ask yourself what you can sell or give away.

I realized I transferred my faulty thinking that "more is better" from my work to my exercise and that no amount of exercising was ever enough. Finally it occurred to me that 15 *more* minutes would not make me feel like a *better* person. Today I live by the adage "less is more." It is liberating to leave in the middle of a workout class when I need to, without feeling guilty or bad about myself. Even though I do 15 minutes *less*, I'm taking *more* care of myself.

• *Work smarter, not longer.* Make your schedule work for you, instead of you working for it. Leave gaps in your calendar for something spontaneous and unexpected to happen. Delegate responsibilities at home, at work or at play. Assign errands and household chores to others with whom you live. Rely on outside help to get such things done around the house as windows washed, lawn mowed, house painted and rooms cleaned. Tell yourself that you don't have to do it all. Get up earlier or go to bed later to have extra time with loved ones. Remember, it's your life. You can be in charge of it, instead of letting it be in charge of you.

Whatever Happened To Spare Time?

Where does the time go? Why is there never enough time left over just for you, time for fun and relaxation? This exercise will help you understand better how you use your time and think about how you can rearrange your life in order to include time for yourself. Fill in the number of hours you spend *each day* in the following activities:

Hours Per Day							Activity
M	T	W	TH	F	SA	SU	
—	—	—	—	—	—	—	Sleeping
—	—	—	—	—	—	—	Eating
—	—	—	—	—	—	—	Household chores such as cleaning, cooking or washing dishes
—	—	—	—	—	—	—	Running errands
—	—	—	—	—	—	—	Preparing for work
—	—	—	—	—	—	—	Studying
—	—	—	—	—	—	—	Getting to and from work
—	—	—	—	—	—	—	Working
—	—	—	—	—	—	—	Taking care of other family members
—	—	—	—	—	—	—	Social/family obligations
—	—	—	—	—	—	—	Volunteer/civic work
—	—	—	—	—	—	—	Carpooling/chauffeuring people
—	—	—	—	—	—	—	**Total Hours Per Day (168)**

168 hours

___ Total Activity Hours Per Week

___ Spare Time

There are 168 hours in a week. Subtract your total activity hours from this number to get the number of hours left over for spare time to do the things that you really want to do. Then ask yourself the following questions:

1. What has this exercise told me about how I'm living my life?
2. How can I restructure my life for more *being* and less *doing?*
3. What do I notice about how I spend my time through the week?
4. How can I distribute my remaining hours over the week to give myself more spare time?

3
Warning Signs Of Overdoing It

On every level of life from
housework to heights of prayer,
in all judgment and all efforts to get
things done, hurry and impatience
are sure marks of the amateur.

— Evelyn Underhill

Sarah, who is 45 years old, approaches life in a compulsive way that affects practically everything she does:

I have a very strong compulsive nature, and I've always felt that I was excessive and intense. Part of my whole compulsivity is to do more than one thing at a time. For example, in getting dressed for work each morning, I have a definite routine. I'm very methodical because when I wake up, I'm a slow riser and slow communicator, but my mind is racing a mile a minute. I'm already so busy thinking that I have to depend on a routine to keep me on track and on schedule.

While I'm cleaning my contact lenses, I'm thinking, "What else can I be doing to get ready while I'm doing this?" Or when I'm brushing my teeth, I use a fluoride rinse that takes 30 seconds and my mind says, "Now, what am I going to do for 30 seconds?"

That scares me because I know it's so compulsive. I guess productivity is the key and the fact that I don't want to get bored. Another part of it is that staying busy keeps me from stopping to think what's underneath all the frenzy, like what am I running from?

Starting when I get in the shower in the morning and on my way to work driving, I already have my priorities for the day in my head. Of course, I'm very much wedded to my calendar. I really live by that, which I don't mind. My Day-at-a-Glance is perhaps the most significant tool at work. I take it home with me; it goes everywhere I go.

Part of my relationship with my calendar is that I like to plan in advance. I use it as an aid to schedule activities. If I lost my calendar, it would cripple me. The few times I have either left it somewhere or forgotten it, I don't actually panic but I'm extremely annoyed. It's as if I have to backtrack because I don't want to miss an appointment, let somebody down, hurt some-body's feelings, fall down on the job, be unproductive or fail to follow the rules.

I'm one of those people who works better without a break. If I interrupt work, I lose my momentum. I'm much more productive and get more work done if I work four or five hours at a time. So when I eat lunch, I usually grab something around 2:00 P.M. or after. I'm glad I have the kind of job where I set my own schedule.

I have a compulsiveness to accomplish — productivity-related accomplishments. Sometimes at stoplights I read, file my nails, apply my makeup, put on my lipstick or comb my hair, clean out my purse, balance my checkbook or anything — anything just to stay busy. When I don't go out to lunch, I'll go get a sandwich and bring it back to my desk. It usually sits there and I'll eat while I talk on the phone or write a memo.

I've always got some kind of work with me. I think it couldn't hurt to throw this report in with whatever I'm taking with me so that I'll have the security of knowing I will not get bored. Sometimes I get preoccupied with work and ask myself, "Did I already ask that?" I'm usually 60 miles ahead of myself on fast forward, thinking what I will be doing in the next ten minutes, the next meeting, the next encounter, or what I have to do next or what and how much I have to do tonight.

I always stay at work long after my co-workers have gone home for the day, sometimes until 8:00 P.M. or later. I get this momentum going once the phone has stopped ringing, people stop dropping in, my meetings are over and I have returned all my calls. Then I can concentrate on paperwork: reports, letters and policies. It's worth it to me to invest extra time, organization and energy after hours because the next day I'm prepared.

The last thing of the day is to make a list for the next day's priorities. I work long hours, sometimes on weekends. On my calendar I keep a tally of the hours I put in every day. My mentor at work told me when I started this job — because I was working 12- and 13-hour days — I was going to burn out. And I almost did. She said, "You keep track of those hours so that when you take 'comp' time, you don't feel guilty about it." I'm sure my overtime equals more than 40 hours a week.

I get scared when I get behind. I had a recent situation where I was asked to chair a committee. There was a timetable for the mission of this committee. I got a three- or four-month late start. I thought "We'll never get that done." The appointment came at a very busy time. Even though this committee was very important, I had to perceive my job responsibilities as more important. I had to prioritize and I couldn't delegate this.

I worried about it so much that one night I woke up at midnight in a panic, thinking, "I'm not going to get it done! They're going to think I've failed." It was terrible! It was the first committee that I'd ever chaired, and I was afraid they'd think I had made a mess of it. This thinking was all projection. I told myself not to panic. I decided to schedule myself an hour for the next day and go to a quiet place and think this whole thing through and that's what I ended up doing. And it worked out fine.

Nevertheless I had terrible anxiety about it, and it kept me from sleeping two nights in a row. But again, it's that message: Do a good job; be a good girl; follow the rules. Your reward will be . . . who knows? I don't know what the payoff for this kind of behavior is — maybe it's the sense of accomplishment. But I'm not sure. When you find out, let me know.

Recognizing The Insidious Signs

Growing up I always had a terrible fear of the dentist. Back in the fifties, painless technology didn't exist. To make matters worse, my dentist looked like Bela Lugosi and he was mean. Being in his chair was like being a victim in a grade-B horror flick. When children cried from fear, he actually yelled and sometimes even slapped them to calm them down. So you can imagine my terror of this drill-wielding, Dracula-look-alike heading toward my mouth and mumbling, "Open wide."

But there was one consolation for my fear. My father always stood by my side offering his big hand for my small, sweaty hand to squeeze as hard as I wanted. Somehow knowing he was there for me always eased the pain.

These memories rushed through me the day my father lay near death and the nurse called the family in to be with him. This time I held *his* hand in mine. He was too weak to squeeze it, so I did the squeezing for both of us. All I could do was tell him I loved him and that everything would be okay. We had traded places. I had become the comforter. When the flatline appeared on the monitor, I could only hope that my words and my hand wrapped around his limp sweaty one were as comforting to him as his had been to me.

Today these memories return every time I visit my dentist, who, by the way, I wouldn't trade for anything. My fear of dentists has subsided for the most part, but when it does rear its ugly head, I am able to be a strong father for that scared little boy inside. I try to be available for myself as my father had been for me and as I had been for him.

This type of self-care has been essential in getting me through lots of tough times — particularly when I neglect myself and begin to suffer the consequences of doing too much. All of us can nurture ourselves in our hearts this way. We can comfort that small child inside and reassure him or her that we will always be here. We can be emotionally available for ourselves the way our parents were once emotionally present for us. We can nurture ourselves even if our parents never did. We all have the power within us to endure any situation.

Before we can nurture our inner selves, we need to recognize the warning signs. Instead of drawing upon their inner resources for renewal and refueling, overdoers medicate their fears and emotional hurts in external ways:

1. Busyness and hurrying
2. Need to control
3. Perfectionism
4. Troubled relationships
5. Binging and purging
6. Difficulty relaxing and having fun
7. Brownouts
8. Impatience and irritability
9. Inadequacy
10. Self-neglect

The signs are hard to spot because almost everything over-doers attempt is top drawer. They look so good on the, outside, how could there possibly be a problem? The fact that our society values overdoing it adds to our denial that a problem exists. As we look underneath the veneer, however, we begin to recognize and then address each sign by developing a strategy that helps us to slow down, brings our lives into greater balance and nurtures our inner selves.

Busyness And Hurrying

People who overdo it lose perspective on the balance in their lives. They do not know their limitations and drive themselves beyond human endurance, putting themselves under abnormal pressure by overinvesting, overcommitting and overcompensating in careers, housework or schoolwork. Sarah said:

Things never move fast enough for me. That's why I'm always doing three or four things at a time. There have been times when I've asked my secretary to do something, and if she hasn't done it in the next 60 seconds, I have to catch myself because I think, "Why hasn't she gone to do that?" Then I have to tell myself, "If you want it done immediately, you have to tell her that, and you don't need it imme-diately." Just because it's on my agenda and it's my issue, doesn't mean it's hers or someone else's. It's not that I get mad at her, I just think,

"But why isn't she doing it?" Or I think about my supervisor and that I need to light a fire under him. "Why doesn't he see this as a priority?" Somehow I think if I dive in and do it my way, I'll do it better.

Nothing ever moves fast enough for people who overdo it. They are haunted by a constant sense of urgency and are always struggling against the limits of time. Kate said:

> As I go out the door at home ready to leave, I think I'd better feed the cat or take something out of the freezer. I just try to cram in one more thing. I look at my watch and realize I have ten minutes, so I'll put a load of clothes in the washer. While I'm in the basement, I'll pick up something and bring it upstairs. Before I know it, 15 minutes have passed and I end up being late.

Unless many things are going at once, overdoers are discontented. They usually have so many things to do there are not enough hours in the day. "The faster I can bathe, eat, get the kids to day care or clean the house, the more time I have to get other things done and the better I feel," said Moira. She also told me:

> I'll be talking to someone on the phone, filing my nails and thinking about what I'll wear to work the next day. I've read magazines at stoplights or studied for a test, drunk coffee and eaten breakfast while driving.

Overdoing it creates stress. Stress causes the body to produce adrenaline, which has an effect similar to amphetamines, or speed. Overdoers unknowingly stress themselves to get the body to pump an adrenaline fix. Addicted to the adrenaline rush, overdoers require larger doses to maintain the high. They thrive on stress, driving themselves beyond human endurance and pushing those around them to meet unrealistic deadlines.

Saving time is important. Overdoers take shortcuts wherever possible, sometimes even when it sacrifices the quality of their home life or relationships, just so they have more time to do. Kate said:

> When I realized I was away from home too much, I'd take work home. My kids used to take some responsibility at home, but they got tired of it. We used to have a neat and orderly house, even though it was never spotless. Later I forgot all that and the children lost interest

because I would never see it anyway. I've actually stepped over dog excrement on my floor for days because I didn't have time to pick it up, and the kids weren't going to pick it up.

The more overdoers can produce, the better they feel. A writer told his friend that he had signed five different book contracts. His friend looked at him in dismay and said, "You need to check yourself into a mental hospital!"

"Don't worry," the writer assured him. "They're not all due on the same day."

The friend thought the writer's behavior was strange. The writer thought his friend's reaction was silly.

People who overdo it manage time inefficiently by overscheduling and overcommitting so that they are constantly racing against the clock. When there's nothing to do, they manufacture something, such as cleaning closets, pulling weeds — anything to stay busy. They do not set priorities or put personal or family time in their work days. Sometimes they seem to take the most inefficient avenue for completing tasks.

Dennis, a 45-year-old school administrator, is a good example of someone who deliberately or unwittingly creates work just to stay busy:

> To an extent, I think I'm superhuman. I've always taken on more than I was capable of doing. It's not that I don't have the ability, but I just don't have the time. Physically within a 24-hour period, I don't judge my time well enough and always take on more. I'm obsessed with creating lists by which to live, finding ways to fill in any extra spaces or lines on my yellow pad with obscure chores so that it would look like I'm busy. By virtue of my lists, I cannot be content to accomplish something without laying the groundwork for something else. Fearing idleness, I have to be striving to accomplish some kind of goal or some block of work.

How Can You Slow Down?

Consider the ways you can slow down the pulse and rhythm of your life. For example, set aside a period of time to eat slower, walk slower and drive slower. Slowing down might mean saying no when you are already overcommitted. At work it could mean not imposing unrealistic deadlines or time limits on important assignments. It might mean prioritizing your tasks, eliminating those that are the least important. Or it could mean giving yourself extra driving time to arrive at your destination and leaving time between appointments so that you can have a conversation with a colleague or friend. The examples are endless, and our strategies are different because our lives and jobs are so varied.

As you read this book, keep a journal of your thoughts, feelings and goals for change. Write down the ways you think of to slow down at work, at home and at play. Keep adding to this list as new ideas come to you. Then put these ideas into action slowly, one by one.

Need To Control

People who overdo it are uncomfortable in situations where they are not in control. Trying to eliminate the unexpected and the changeable, they overplan and overorganize their lives. They have difficulty being spontaneous or flexible because the fear of losing control is too great.

Because of their need to control, overdoers cannot ask for help. They prefer to do things themselves rather than share the workload. Many employers who overdo it refuse to delegate authority because no one else can do what needs to be done as fast or as well as they can. Parents who do everything around the house get to maintain more control over the situation, rather than delegate household chores, because only they can do them the "right" way. Lucille in Columbus, Ohio, said she turns holidays into overdoing. Every Christmas she prepares a ten-course meal for 20 people, and won't allow anyone to help because she admits that this is her way of getting approval and self-esteem. Sharing the load might somehow diminish the amount of approval from others and her own self-importance.

Overdoers often get upset in situations when they cannot be in control or when things do not go their way. Being a part of a group where negotiation and compromise ensure that everyone's voice is heard, such as committee work, civic groups or friends deciding on a restaurant, challenges their need to control. As a result they are overworked, tired and overstressed. They often put co-workers in a double bind, first by denying them an opportunity to carry their share of the workload and then by complaining that they have to do it all themselves.

I once watched a colleague insist on doing all the planning for an annual conference of which he was chairperson. When other committee members volunteered to help, he ignored their offers. Once he became overloaded, he vented his anger toward the other members, charging that they sat back while he did all the work. The inability or unwillingness to ask for help assures quantity control but not quality control.

Because overdoers tend to be inflexible and rigid, they are uncomfortable in spontaneous and unpredictable situations. Weekend lulls, when nothing is planned, can be traumatic. Awash in a sea of errands, appointments and family obligations, overdoers pack their weekends full of busy tasks to escape from the anxiety of not being in control. Although planning their lives to the split second does assure some predictability, there is no room for those unexpected events that do erupt.

Martha, a 38-year-old executive for a major computer corporation, confessed, "I stay booked up three months in advance. I know when I do or don't have any free time. Usually I don't. That's good because I always know what's happening."

How Do You Exercise Control?

We all have at one time or other a need to control. The need can be expressed in a variety of ways: from the inability to delegate household chores to family members to the refusal to compromise on choosing a restaurant. In your journal list how your control needs manifest in your personal, professional and social life. After you have generated an exhaustive list, check each item you would like to change. Beside each checked item, write down in detail what you can do to make these changes.

Letting Go

Control comes in three forms: forcing, resisting and clinging.

Forcing is an *offensive* reaction in which we manipulate or impose our will on other people or situations.

Resisting is a *defensive* reaction in which we block the truth about other people or situations.

Clinging is an *avoidance* reaction in which we clutch the familiar and avoid change.

Are you a forcer, resister or clinger? Think of all the ways you have been forcing, resisting or clinging in your own life. You may be resistant to a life change or unwilling to try something new. In your journal divide a page into two columns. In the left-hand column list each aspect of your life that you are forcing, resisting or clinging to. In the right-hand column state what you can do to let go of and accept this part of your life.

Perfectionism

People who overdo it mercilessly judge themselves, colleagues and family members. Their tendencies to overdo it cause them to push and measure themselves, their children, other family members and colleagues against unrealistic standards. Underneath the perfectionism is often a deep-seated fear of failure and rejection. This fear drives them to be their own worst critic. When failure ultimately occurs, overdoers rebuke themselves and others for not meeting their standards of perfection. Sam said:

> Preferring to do things myself rather than asking for help is part of my perfectionist syndrome. It's like that old phrase, "If you want it done right, do it yourself." If I do it, I know it's been done, I know it's been done completely and I know it's been done the way I want it done. If I had an employee I completely trusted to do it the way I would do it, I would give up the task. I'd like to find a support person who could do as complete a job as I would do. I haven't found one yet, although the people who work with me are very qualified and talented.

There is no pleasing the perfectionist, no matter how hard you try. They complain about small things: "Why isn't the house clean?" or "Who left the cabinet door open?" or "Why isn't there any soap?" On the job, they are grumpy when little things are not exactly right. "You typed my name without my middle initial! You'll have to redo the whole letter," complains one compulsive worker. Another is concerned about more trivial things: "The door to the supply room should stay closed at all times!" They do not give themselves or others permission to make mistakes.

Martha's perfectionism gives rise to self-recrimination when she makes the slightest error:

I get upset with myself for making the smallest mistake. I learned a lot of this from my mentor. If something went wrong on the computer, I'd just die inside. It was like, how could you be so stupid? Now I'm learning to say, "Well, you screwed up. So what?" I get upset with myself because I think I should know better. If I screw up, I'll do it again. I cannot stand for that to happen. I'm a real perfectionist in what I do. It's difficult for me to leave things to someone else because I have the feeling that they're not going to do it right or they're not going to do it the way I would do it. Sometimes I feel that it takes so much time to tell them what I want to do it's easier for me to do it.

From "Should" To "Could"

Notice that Martha said, "I *should* know better." Overuse of the words "should," "ought" or "must" reflects our feeling that nothing we do is ever good enough. Overuse of these words is called shame-based language. Psychologist David Burns calls it "shouldy" thinking. These shaming thoughts make us feel bad about ourselves and the world and are a way of punishing ourselves because we were not perfect.

This exercise is adapted from Louise Hay. Write in your journal at least three things that you "should" have done today or yesterday or last week.

1. I should have _____.
2. I should have _____.
3. I should have _____.

One man's "should list" looked like this:

1. "I should have finished that report on Friday."
2. "I should have taken more time to listen to her problem."
3. "I should have cleaned the house before company arrived."

Now let's examine how this man's perfectionism makes him feel ashamed and guilty. If we ask him why he "should" have done those things, he would answer that his teachers always told him to finish what he started, his parents pounded into his brain that he should be sensitive to other people and his culture taught him that "cleanliness is next to Godliness." Shoulds are shame-based, perfectionist

messages drilled into us at an early age. They are barriers
to self-esteem.

You can turn those shame-based messages around by replacing the word "should" with "could."

1. "I *could* have finished that report on Friday."
2. "I *could* have taken more time to listen to her problem."
3. "I *could* have cleaned the house before company arrived."

Now look at your "shoulds" list. Substitute the word
"could" for each "should" and notice how it changes the
meaning of the perfectionist message you send yourself.

1. I could have _____.
2. I could have _____.
3. I could have _____.

The words you use to talk to yourself reinforce your
perfectionism and feelings of shame and defeat. Changing
those words can soften the blow and remind you that you
always have a choice and that you may decide not to exercise
certain choices.

Gratitude

Gratitude for the things we already have is another antidote to perfectionist standards. Accepting our failures along
with our successes releases us from the bonds of self-defeating perfectionism.

Close your eyes and get comfortable. Take a deep breath
and relax. Inhale and exhale a few times. Think of the many
things you are grateful for and that make your life worth
living. Visualize what is precious to you. See the things you
take for granted, things that would leave your life empty if
you didn't have them. You can include material items, such as
your car or house, as well as relationships with loved ones,
such as a child, spouse, partner or pet. Let your thoughts
come and visualize each one as vividly as you can. Acknowledge each important thought as it appears and feel the gratitude in your heart.

In your journal write down all the things in your life that you are grateful for. Practice this exercise regularly so that you begin to appreciate how positive and rich your life already is.

Troubled Relationships

Overdoing it is a sedative for some people. It keeps them so preoccupied they don't have to deal with conflict either within themselves or in close relationships. Kate describes how overdoing it took precedence over everyone and everything else and interfered with her intimate relationships:

> My husband complained about my working late at the office in the evening. So I bundled up all this stuff, took it home, closed myself in the bedroom and worked on it into the wee hours of morning. I'd fall asleep with work piled on top of me. My husband would come to bed and find his side of the bed covered with ledgers.
>
> Finally he quit coming to bed and slept on the sofa. It was two years before I realized anything was wrong. When we separated, I wondered why I was crying about the bed being empty on the other side. I'd tell myself how dumb it was because he had been on the sofa for so long anyway. I'd find myself almost falling off the bed, rolling over to try to find him there. I started purposely leaving books and stuff on his side of the bed, so there would be something there.

When friendships do exist, they often revolve around work or another narrowly defined interest as Martha suggests:

> I don't have many friends other than those at work. There's a family culture way of life in my company. Everybody knows everybody. So I know many people. I know I should meet others and should participate in outside functions, but I don't.

Sometimes overdoers are dependent on others outside the workplace — usually a partner or close family member — to enable their overdoing it. All their thoughts and energies go into busy activities, and little is left over for anything else. Work addicts, for example, are too busy to take the time to understand the small things that get them through the day. Having someone else do these things gives them more time to work. Learning to set a digital watch or to assemble a complicated toy seems bothersome because it takes precious moments away from more important tasks.

On his trip across Europe, Alvin left all decisions to his wife. She kept his wallet and passport. She managed their daily sight-seeing. She computed the exchange ratio from dollars to foreign currency and made the actual transaction. Alvin dutifully followed her lead.

Accomplished in their chosen fields, such people can be klutzy at home and in the social world. They have put all their energies into work and have developed few social skills and few interests outside of work. Either they discuss work or they remain silent during social events.

Co-dependence on a loved one or friend strains relationships. The wife of a compulsive overdoer told me she resented the fact that her husband prided himself on his work but neglected their home life:

> The issue of control is a battle all the time. He's a perfectionist about his business. His condos are in such beautiful condition and look like model homes. If he gets a drop of paint anywhere it doesn't belong, he'll work hours to remove it. But our house is a dump if he has anything to do with it. He will not pick up after himself, and he never cleans anything. Doing as little as he can, he doesn't even take out the garbage. If I ask him to help me with something he gets sullen and withdrawn.

The biggest complaint spouses have is about being neglected. A housewife told me, "I'm tired of sloppy seconds. After my husband finishes working, there's nothing but cold leftovers for me and the kids." Spouses feel jealous — and perhaps for good reason. They become suspicious that an affair is taking place because of long and late hours away from home. Even when no lovers are involved, spouses complain that there might as well be — the excessive work is just as hard to take.

The term "wedded to work" illustrates this condition, and it knows no gender boundaries. A female architect confided that she more than once had mentally worked on a client's plans during sexual intercourse with her husband. A gardener confessed that sometimes he, too, found himself designing landscapes while making love.

Overdoers put more thought, time and energy into busy activities than into intimate relationships with their families, socializing with friends or enjoying leisure and recreational activities. They forget, ignore or minimize important family rituals and celebrations, such as birthdays, reunions, anniversaries or holidays. They cannot stop long enough to participate fully because such events require total immersion of the person whose mind is usually on getting something accomplished.

Some overdoers even bargain to get released from family "obligations." They might tell a spouse, "I'll go to the family reunion with you next weekend, if you'll keep the kids out of my hair this weekend so that I can finish this report." Promises of cutting down on work or spending more time with the family are frequently broken. As the weekend approaches, there's more work to be done, accompanied by an apologetic refrain: "Sorry, honey. Looks like you and the kids will have to go without me."

When strong-armed into going on family outings or leisure activities, overdoers are dutiful but often begrudging. Their minds stay occupied almost all the way. They pull every trick to busy themselves during the outing. "Gotta make a phone call" or "I'll just read this report while we wait for dinner." Kate remembered how her compulsive overworking contributed to the demise of her marriage.

> My mind was constantly racing and I couldn't sleep at night. Finally, I put a yellow pad by my bed. Every time I had a thought, I'd turn the light on and write the thought down and maybe I could go to sleep. My husband constantly said, "You're working day and night. Can't you turn it off?" My overworking didn't cause our split, but it brought it to the forefront. He was unemployed and in my absence from home, he lost interest in doing his share around the house. He quit preparing meals or doing any household chores and got into activities I thought were morally wrong. Maybe some of the things that were going on at home were leading me toward workaholism. Maybe I was just escaping and that's why I became work-addicted, rather than the other way around.

Strengthening Your Relationships

Think of up to eight people who are important in your life: your partner or love interest, co-workers, friends, parents,

children or others. Write their names in the circles around
the "you" circle. Next draw a line symbolizing the nature of
your relationship with each person. Straight lines represent
solid, healthy relationships; jagged lines, bumpy or shaky relationships; spirals confused or uncertain relationships.

Your Relationships.

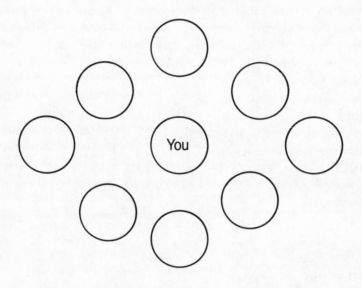

Solid Relationships = _____

Bumpy Relationships = /\/\/\/\/\/\/\/\/\/\/\/\/\/\

Uncertain Relationships = _llllllllllll_

Then, examine your relationships and how they have suffered because of overdoing it. Complete the following in
your journal:

1. I can strengthen my family relationships by _____.
2. I can strengthen my work relationships by _____.
3. I can strengthen my social relationships by _____.
4. I can strengthen my relationship with myself by _____.

Binging And Purging

Another sign of overdoing it is binging and purging. Many
overdoers, for example, fluctuate between highs and lows. They
may swing from frantic productivity to inertia. During the period
of my compulsive overworking, you would have seen tell-tale
signs of my binges had you dropped in without my having the
time to hide the clues. You would have walked into a work factory:
stacks of books, wastepaper baskets overflowing, pencils and pens
scattered around, reams of computer paper strewn over table-
tops. The typewriter would have been roaring, the computer
humming and I would have been on the phone and writing simultaneously. There would have been no place for you to walk, sit or
stand. I would have been so blissed out that I wouldn't have
recognized your presence; in fact, I probably wouldn't even have
answered the door. After binging I sometimes became a couch
potato for two weeks.

Household chores can turn into a binge when you clean nonstop for three days then sleep all weekend. The student who
crams for midterms and doesn't open a book again until finals is
binging and purging.

Overdoers rarely work eight-hour days, five days a week. They
are usually still plugging away after others have called it quits.
Their golden rule is "Do today what doesn't need doing until six
months from now." They have trouble spreading their work out.
They binge for days on a project until it is finished, rather than
complete it in small steps over a period of time.

Travis, a self-employed landscaper, works day and night for
three days until he completes a project, rather than spreading it
out over a four- or five-day workweek. Carol, a community college
instructor, used to complete all the work on her desk each day, no

matter how long she had to stay at the office. A healthy co-worker helped her rethink her compulsive attitude: "There will always be plenty of work to do. No matter how hard and fast I work, I'll never really be able to catch up. So I just relax, take it easy and work steadily rather than try to stay ahead in this business."

Everybody has to overwork occasionally to meet deadlines, and there are times when all of us feel overextended. But overdoers are often overextended because of self-imposed, unrealistic deadlines, not mandatory time frames. A report may not be due for six months, for example. But an overdoer completes it in a 12-hour marathon, rather than gradually over time. The sense of completion is satisfying, and having the assignment out of the way early leaves time to focus on other work items. Other overdoers postpone what they need to do for fear of not doing it perfectly. They take on too much, wait until the last minute, throw themselves into a panic and work frantically to complete the task. Either way — too early or too late — is an extreme work habit that is out of balance and prevents a smooth, paced approach.

An office manager told me:

> My supervisor needs a report by Friday, so I'd better have it done by Tuesday and typed by Wednesday. If I have changes to make or errors to fix, I can get them done and submit the report first thing on Friday and he won't have to call me and ask for it. I self-impose deadlines all the time. I'm rarely late because I usually give myself enough time to get where I'm going, even if it's across the street, with time to sit and read. If a meeting is at one, I'll get there five minutes early. But I don't think anything's wrong with that. When I have projects that I have to submit to someone else, I work very hard so that I can get them done on time. The price I have to pay for procrastinating is unbearable. I go nuts. I panic. I can't sleep I have such anxiety. Oh God! How will I get it done? Procrastination is a killer to me!

As the condition worsens, some overdoers conceal work from family and friends. It goes everywhere they go: in briefcases or luggage, under car seats, in glove compartments, in car trunks beneath spare tires, in dirty laundry bags or stuffed into pockets. Some overdoers become extra busy after a quarrel or a major disappointment.

Kate's work obsession became her "weekend lover." She lied to her family so that she could rendezvous with work at the office:

I would tell my family that I was going shopping on a Saturday and I'd end up in my office working. Or I'd tell them I was going to my girlfriend's house. After calling my girlfriend and not finding me, they'd call the office and say, "I thought you were going to Dottie's." I felt like I had been caught with my hand in the cookie jar.

Keeping An Even Keel

There are things you can do to learn how to abstain from excessive overdoing.

For example, you may:

- Establish a more steady work, study or exercise schedule with set hours, rather than binging for days or weeks at a time. Confine your work hours to eight hours a day, five days a week or whatever boundaries best fit your lifestyle and job.
- Refrain from self-imposing strict, unrealistic deadlines, and spread activities out over a longer period of time.
- Eliminate one responsibility that has lowest priority, perhaps the volunteer work you agreed to do.
- Set boundaries by learning to say no when you are already overcommitted and have a choice of accepting or rejecting a request.
- Delegate housework, yardwork or other household responsibilities to family members.

In your journal set your own goals for balance and moderation. Design a moderation plan that helps you set boundaries for each day of the week. After trying it out for one week, ask yourself the following questions: What things need changing for the next week? What part of the plan worked well enough for me to make a regular part of my life?

Weekly Moderation Plan

Use this form to design a weekly moderation plan for yourself that helps you set boundaries for one week.

Monday:

Tuesday:

Wednesday:

Thursday:

Friday:

Saturday:

Sunday:

Difficulty Relaxing And Having Fun

Restless and easily agitated, overdoers find it hard to slow down, relax and have fun. They feel the need to complete more tasks before resting, which results in constant, compulsive busyness. Martha confessed her difficulty relaxing at home:

> I'm never caught up. It's hard for me to relax when I'm not working. At home I feel very guilty because I've got tons of projects and the house is dirty. I feel guilty when I get home at 8:00 P.M. and become a couch potato. There are just so many things to do, I cannot lie around or rest.

Even in social situations overdoers are preoccupied and uneasy and have trouble letting go, as the following housewife describes:

> I always try to relax, but I don't relax very well. Sometimes when I'm exhibiting compulsive behaviors, I'll tell myself, "Why don't you just stop and enjoy the moment? Live for the moment. Try it!" And I don't know what that means. I'm always in fast forward. Maybe I think I would be bored.

Overdoers believe that relaxation and fun are counterproductive to getting a job done. They view play as a waste of time and as detracting from their single-minded goal of accomplishing many tasks. Rest is at the bottom of their priority list, and they are often tired and unhappy. Kate told me:

> I don't have any hobbies. I've done all kinds of causes and committees, changing the laws here and there, and picking up the cross and carrying it with a lot of things. But I don't paint, sew, draw, bowl or sing. I'm not very sportsy. When I'm not in my office, I read, usually professional journals and self-help books. I haven't read any fiction in 15 years.

Many overdoers report hearing a nagging voice in their heads when they try to relax. The voice tells them that they are being totally unproductive and wasting time. They start to feel guilty because they are taking it easy. Becoming restless and even shaky, they start feeling bad about themselves. They may even tell themselves that it is not their nature to sit still for very long. They usually end up "white knuckling it" until they can get back into busy pursuits. Preoccupied, they take themselves too seriously, seldom laugh or smile and have difficulty having fun.

A woman described her husband's inability to let go and enjoy himself:

> It's really difficult to pull him away from any of his work activities. He gets really anxious when he's not working, and then I feel guilty if I try to get him to do something with me. I wind up feeling as if I have deprived him of something.

What Helps You Relax?

There are many ways to unwind and have fun: stress-relief exercises, mind-relaxation techniques, physical exercise, yoga, meditation, prayer, massage, daily inspirational readings or hobbies.

Write three things in your journal you like to do that are fun and help you relax. Now remember the last time you did each one. Was it a day ago, a week ago, a month ago or years ago? Beneath each favorite thing, write how long it's been since you've done it. Then, answer the following questions: What does this information tell you about how you're living your life? Did you have trouble even thinking of three favorite things? Are you doing the things you want to do in your life? Or are you living your life for someone else? What enjoyable pastime can you plan for yourself?

Brownouts

A car swerves down the highway. The man behind the wheel is high, but not from booze. He's high on adrenaline. The man is a minister and he's writing his Sunday sermon as he zips down the interstate. You've seen him before: the motorist trying to read the newspaper, talking on the telephone or eating lunch as the car speeds to get somewhere. When behind the wheel, some overdoers actually put their own lives and those of others in danger.

People who overdo it suffer from something I call *brownouts*, in which they don't remember long conversations or trips because they were preoccupied with planning and rushing and doing.

Stephanie, mother of three children and full-time career woman, describes her "zoning out": "What happens is the times when I'm with my kids I'm not listening to them because I'm already thinking what I have to do next and where I'm going to be next.

The kids will say something to me, and I realize I haven't heard what they've said. I'm zoned out."

Brownouts are also a side effect of tuning out the present. Preoccupied with the next thing on their list, overdoers miss the here and now. They have learned that the now is scary, unpredictable and uncomfortable, so they live in the future.

Different from daydreams, brownouts result from stress and burnout. One man told me:

> My wife sometimes tells me she thinks I have Alzheimer's disease. But it's just that my mind is on my work and nothing else is important at that particular moment. I'll ask her a question. And rather than wait for an answer, my mind has already jumped to something else. I'll ask the question again, and she'll say, "Do you realize you've asked me that three times?" And I don't remember asking the question, much less receiving an answer.

One woman said her staff thought she had a hearing problem:

> They would say things to me while I'd be working on something. They'd be telling me about a concern and I wouldn't hear them. Because something else had my attention, I'd tune out everything around me. Many times I'll be driving somewhere else and end up at the office. Because my mind is on five million other things, I get in my car and put on the automatic pilot without thinking.

Another woman told me that while she was in bed she'd try to figure out how to solve a problem at work. Once, feeling thirsty, she went to the kitchen to get a glass of water. With her mind still on the problem, she returned to bed. Fifteen minutes later she heard the sound of the running water. She realized that in her stupor she had put her glass under the spigot, turned the water on and walked away without turning the water off.

Brownout Stress Profile

Brownouts often result from stress and burnout. If you are on the fast track, you are at risk for physical, mental, emotional and social stress. The Brownout Stress Profile* can help you identify where your stress comes from and help you eliminate brownouts.

---

*Source: Bryan Robinson, Bobbie Rowland and Mick Coleman, *Home-Alone Kids* (Lexington, MA: Lexington Books, 1989). Used with permission.

Brownout Stress Profile

Place a "1" in the space beside each symptom that you have noticed in yourself during the past month.

Physical Stress

_____ Headaches   _____ Teeth grinding

_____ Fatigue   _____ Insomnia

_____ Weight change   _____ Restlessness

_____ Colds or allergies   _____ Accident-prone

_____ Pounding heart   _____ Upset stomach

_____ Tension in muscles   _____ Increased alcohol,
        of neck or shoulders   drug or tobacco use

	Total Physical _____ **Stress Score**	*Add your scores. Write your score in the space to the left.*

Mental Stress

_____ Forgetfulness   _____ Errors in judgment

_____ Dulling of the   _____ Confusion at home
        senses
                                     _____ Poor concentration
_____ Decline in problem-
        solving skills   _____ Loss of creativity

_____ Lowered   _____ Boredom
        productivity
                                     _____ Mental exhaustion
_____ Negative attitude
                                     _____ Confusion at work

	Total Mental _____ **Stress Score**	*Add your scores. Write your score in the space to the left.*

Emotional Stress

_____ Anxiety   _____ Irritability

_____ Feeling "uptight"   _____ Depression

_____ Mood swings   _____ Nervous laughter

_____ Constant worrying   _____ Self-criticism

_____ Bad temper   _____ Crying spells

_____ Loss of interest in hobbies   _____ Easily discouraged

_____ **Total Emotional Stress Score**	_Add your scores. Write your score in the space to the left._

Social Stress

_____ Resentment of others   _____ Lashing out at co-workers

_____ Isolation   _____ Nagging others

_____ Loneliness   _____ Being impatient

_____ Lashing out at family   _____ Clamming up

_____ Lashing out at friends   _____ Using people

_____ Lowered sex drive   _____ Being vindictive

_____ **Total Social Stress Score**	_Add your scores. Write your score in the space to the left._

Scoring

Because we are unique, we have different levels of stress and different kinds of stress symptoms. To determine how much physical, mental, emotional and social stress you have, follow these steps:

1. Write your physical, mental, emotional and social stress scores in the blanks on the grid below.
2. Put an "X" on the line above each stress symptom that matches your score. For example, if your physical stress score is six, put an X on the vertical line that is across from the number six.
3. Repeat step 2 for your mental, emotional and social stress scores.

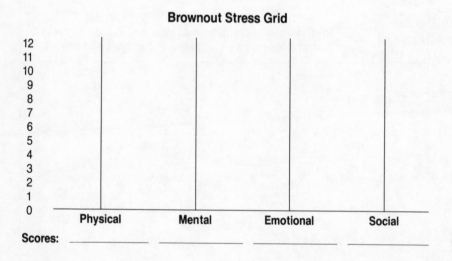

Brownout Stress Grid

	Physical	Mental	Emotional	Social
Scores:	_____	_____	_____	_____

Interpretation

Review your stress scores on the grid. What stress symptoms are most common? Compare your scores to those of your family members. Plan a family meeting to discuss the different levels of stress within your family. Consider the reasons for your stress and the ways to reduce it. Stress-reducing classes are offered through local community colleges and universities, mental health centers, churches and county cooperative extension offices.

Impatience And Irritability

Time is the most precious commodity to overdoers. They do not like to be kept waiting. They are easily annoyed and cannot tolerate delays, as Laurie explains:

> I have angrily left carts of groceries at supermarkets because they didn't have enough checkout people. Then I have to shop again later. I don't tell people off but if the line is too long, I won't wait.

Many are deliberately late or get routines down to a science so they won't have to wait. A salesman who lives in Atlanta and whose sales territory is in Alabama told me how he times to the minute the trip from his house to the airport to prevent waiting. He leaves his house an hour before flight time. It takes 30 to 45 minutes for him to get to the airport and 10 to 15 minutes to park his car and check his bags. With this system he can walk up and be the last person on board because he "hates sitting and waiting for things." Instead of leaving an hour earlier to prevent stressful hurrying, he says there are too many other things he has to do. So he takes his chances that he will not get tied up in traffic.

Another corporate supervisor told me that she deliberately developed a pattern of being late so that instead of waiting for someone, she could cram in more work:

> I'm always late. There have been so many times in my life when I've been on time and had to wait for people. In order to be on time, I had to stop something else that was important. I started consciously deciding to go five minutes late because I figured my appointment wouldn't be ready for me anyway. My first day on this job, I made it a point to be on time and ended up waiting for 10 minutes. I don't think I was ever on time again in six years.

I realized I needed help the day I jumped down the librarian's throat about a book that had been checked out by a faculty member. On my second special trip to the library just to get this book, I was furious when I was told it was still unavailable. I demanded that the librarian search the computer and tell me the person's name so I could talk with him. She searched and gave me a strange look. "We're not supposed to give out that information, but in this case I think it's okay."

"Well?" I demanded impatiently.

"It says *you* have the book already checked out, sir."

Needless to say, I was speechless and embarrassed beyond belief. The book had been in a huge stack of other books in my office for six months and I didn't even know it.

Some short-tempered overdoers interrupt others in mid-sentence to respond to questions or concerns that have not been fully verbalized. But if *they* are interrupted in the middle of work, it's a different story.

They even get restless and depressed after a day or two without an activity to keep them busy. Stephanie said:

> When I'm alone at home, it makes me nervous. A couple of times my husband took the kids to the beach for a weekend and left me at home by myself. I thought, "Oh boy! I'm just going to be in the house alone and read nonstop." After an hour, I started to get freaked out, and I called a friend and went to a movie.

Overdoers get grouchy and cranky and may bring a black cloud home that can affect everyone around them. Still, irritability and impatience are not always vented through full-blown anger. A woman described how her husband sometimes expresses hostility in passive-aggressive ways:

> He has a lot of passive-aggressive behaviors. His anger is indirect. He doesn't admit to being annoyed but instead acts sullen, with a facial expression that looks troubled. When I ask him if he's bothered, he says no. Then he'll do something spiteful not very long after — something he knows upsets me — and then deny having done it to manipulate me.

Impatience can lead to impulsiveness. Important decisions can be made and projects launched before all the facts are gathered, all the options are thoroughly explored or all the phases are finalized. The results can be disastrous when the compulsive doing outruns careful thought and reflection.

Kate had a reputation at her job for moving too fast without thinking things through and then going back and cleaning up her tracks:

I do that all the time. An idea will come to me and I'll say, "Ah! This is great!" And I'll jump in and go with it. I'll have it moving and be way ahead of everyone else. They're sitting back and taking it all apart and thinking through everything, and I'm way ahead of them. It took us two years to clean up the billing mess. Our billing proce-dures were behind because we were working so far ahead of our-selves. But I get high off it. "Why not make it happen, then we can go back and fix it" was the way I thought about it. We have to keep the ball in the air or it'll die. If you let it go back to committee 15 different times, you've lost your spark and it's not the same.

The Patience-Impatience Thermometer

On the Patience-Impatience Thermometer below, color in red how much patience you ordinarily have. Then use anoth-er color to show how much patience you would like to have.

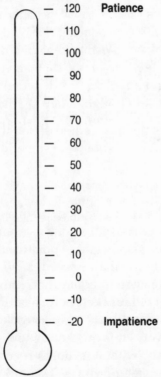

	120	**Patience**
	110	
	100	
	90	
	80	
	70	
	60	
	50	
	40	
	30	
	20	
	10	
	0	
	-10	
	-20	**Impatience**

In your journal write the ways you can think of to develop more patience.

Inadequacy

As I discussed in the previous chapter, a sense of inadequacy and poor self-esteem leads to a strong emphasis on production. People who overdo it often seek approval and affirmation through their accomplishments. Emphasizing productivity as a manifestation of their self-worth, they want something to show for what they do. The overimportance they assign to the product versus the process provides affirmation:

> I like to see progress. If I work really hard on a report, a letter or some type of document, it always looks better when it's completed. I like to see the finished product. I'm very result-oriented, which is definitely tied in with approval from the world and myself. I used to say that I didn't care what people thought about me, but I really do.

Overdoers are often more interested in the outcome of work than in the process. Said one, "The only time I felt good about myself was when I was producing *things* so that I could constantly prove that I was okay." Despite repeated accomplishments, overdoers continue to feel bad about themselves. Doing gives them a temporary high and a feeling of self-worth. But one achievement after another is never enough. They are like alcoholics who drink to feel better. They continue to push themselves harder and harder, thinking that eventually they will be able to stop or at least slow down.

Seeing The Positive Side

You will need a watch or clock with a second hand to time yourself on this exercise. In your journal write the numbers from one to five. Then list five positive traits about yourself that you can describe in one word. How long did it take?

Now list five negative traits that you can describe in one word. How long did it take? Compare the time it took to list the positive traits with the time it took to list the negative ones. Almost always it is quicker to name the negative things because those are what overdoers focus on. When you can find the positive side of yourself as quickly as the negative, you will know that your life is becoming balanced. Do this exercise from time to time as you work on positive feelings and see what changes occur in the lapsed times.

Affirmations are positive statements that help you recognize your inner worth and start to feel good about yourself. Examples are:

I can stand up for myself.
I am good enough just as I am.
I deserve the best life has to offer.

Repeating affirmations makes you feel more positive about yourself. Writing them down helps them become a part of you. Complete the following sentences in your journal:

Things about me I like are _____.

Some positive traits about me are _____.

Self-Neglect

Overdoing it leads to self-neglect, a host of psychological complaints and physical problems. It takes its toll as overdoers neglect themselves in order to push and get the job done. Overcommitted and spread thin, they suffer from stress, emotional exhaustion and spiritual starvation.

Sometimes overdoers seek tension and crisis and then complain about the results. This is most commonly observed when they overcommit themselves or set unrealistic deadlines. They end up grumbling that they are overworked and have no one to help out, even when they refused to delegate or share the load. Overdoers like Sarah are super-responsible when it comes to getting the job done but are super-irresponsible when it comes to taking care of themselves and staying healthy:

I don't feel productive unless I'm working. When I get depressed, I get immobilized and paralyzed, just can't do anything and feel helpless. At work you can't say, "I didn't sleep last night or I can't work today, I'm depressed." I've always had an insomnia problem, and there have been many times when I've gone three or four nights without sleep, but I still have to go to work. It makes me cranky, uncomfortable and grouchy, but nobody's going to say, "You don't have to go in to work today; you stay home and sleep." That's not the way the world works.

People who overdo it tend to ignore their own health. They neglect themselves physically (nutrition, rest and exercise) and mentally (play and recreation). Those who work in sedentary jobs are especially at risk. They may not get enough exercise, particularly if they binge for 12 or 15 hours a day. Poor nutrition results from eating fast foods in order to keep working through lunch. Accompanying addictions, such as chain-smoking, coffee-drinking and occasionally drinking alcohol, contribute to health problems.

Overdoers tend to ignore anything that distracts them from work, including warning signs of physical illness. When symptoms do appear, they are likely to deny their existence or minimize their importance. They ignore aches and pains that could be telling them their body is tired or even in danger. Although a part of their mind is aware of the problem, another part doesn't want to take the time to stop and think about it, let alone have it checked. Left unattended, these health hazards could cost them their lives.

The compulsive overdoing of an insurance company supervisor caused her many health problems, but her story has a happy ending:

> I always had allergies and headache problems. Two years ago I developed this devastating stomach pain with irritation and indigestion. I took the whole gamut of tests, and there was nothing there except damage to the lower end of the esophagus from gastric juice. My stomach hasn't hurt since I started walking in the evening two months ago. That's made a significant difference for my stress management. I understand myself better and see what happened to me. I used to drink coffee all day long, but now I only drink one-and-a-half cups a day.

Martha has also changed her ways and is learning to listen to her body:

> I've had chest pains that have moved down into my arm. A few weeks ago I was out of town doing some training. I thought I was going to have to stop because I started getting heart palpitations. I've had indigestion, stomach pains, stress in the muscles in my back and in my sciatic nerve down my leg. When I'm under a lot of stress, ailments get worse. My body is sending me lots of messages that I need to listen to.

Paying Closer Attention To Yourself

One of the best ways to slow down is to pay attention to yourself through meditation. There are many types of meditation: prayer, inspirational readings, relaxation exercises, quiet reflection, yoga or guided meditation. This guided meditation exercise is designed to help you slow down and pay closer attention to the needs of your body, mind and spirit:

Guided Meditation

In a quiet and comfortable place, close your eyes and get comfortable. Feet flat on the floor, back straight. Clear your mind of cluttered thoughts and focus on your breathing. Take deep breaths during the meditation, inhaling through the nose and exhaling through the mouth. Inhale and exhale a few times. Let your body become completely relaxed from head to toe. Continue breathing and relaxing until you are in a totally relaxed state.

When you are relaxed, visualize yourself going through your day at a slow pace. Pause now and then to vividly see and feel through your mind's eye as you go through your daily routine from the time you rise until you go to sleep that night. See yourself getting out of bed, having breakfast, talking to and caring for loved ones, getting dressed and going to work.

Take yourself through your daily routine, all the while slowing yourself down. See yourself eating slower, driving slower and doing one thing at a time. See the events of the day, and imagine the smallest details of each one. Release any images you have of hurrying. Notice how you begin to feel as your routine slows down. How do others around you feel?

Pay close attention to your body. What does it need that it hasn't been getting? Pay attention to your mind. What does it need that it doesn't get? Pay attention to your spiritual needs (or feelings). What have they been missing? Next, think of how you can nurture your body, mind and spirit. Then visualize yourself attending to the needs of your body, mind and spirit.

Conclude your meditation by imaging going to bed that night. How do you feel as you drift off to sleep? Don't be discouraged if you initially feel discomfort or even anxiety.

Remember, you're changing habits that you've had for a long time. Giving yourself attention and slowing down take time, practice and patience.

Repeat this exercise as often as you feel the need. Each time you complete this meditation, record your feelings and thoughts in your journal. Notice how your feelings begin to change with practice and how you feel more comfortable with taking a slower pace and nurturing yourself.

4
Origins Of Overdoing It

Larceny is not a
difficult crime to condone
unless your childhood
was the item stolen.

— Pat Conroy, *Prince of Tides*

The last time Kate saw her father, he was leaving one afternoon and said, "Come tell me good-bye, I'm going to the hospital."

She was roller skating on the sidewalk and said, "Are you sick?"

He replied, "I'm going in for some tests. When I come home, I'll buy us a TV." She kept on skating and her father never came home again. During the night, he was accidentally given a lethal dose of a sedative.

At that point Kate gave up her childhood. Her mother took a second job. She was gone from early in the morning until late at night. Kate was 13 and had two brothers, age 11 and 6. Her little brother became her child. She got him up every morning, made sure he had his lunch, made sure he learned to read when he came home from the first grade every afternoon. After she got home from school, Kate also made the beds and put on a pot of beans. If there was any time left over, she went outside to shoot a few baskets with the boy across the street — her first boyfriend.

Three weeks after her dad died, Kate's basketball friend committed suicide. Said Kate, "I just kept on trucking, doing all these things to keep my family going. Mother would come in at suppertime, eat, tell me it was a good supper and go to her second job. One day

I made a birthday cake for one of her friends, and they were so
impressed with my ability to do so much at such a young age."

Kate, *now a 50-year-old nurse, sees her early caretaking as boot*
camp *for her life today.*

I just sort of knew things had to be done and I did them. I had
lost my dad, my boyfriend, my grandmother and my uncle
all in six months. My world was falling apart around me and by
grasping on to those duties, I was able to gain control over my
life. I could take care of my brother, clean the house, make the
cake and do those chores that would make my world stable.
And I have been doing them all my life. I have been through
crises that people wouldn't believe. People ask me how I keep
my sanity when my whole world is falling apart, but that's the
way I kept on going, to do what I could do well.

Out of a desire to do great things, I was a public health
nurse. I would see patients, but I was bored. I thought, 'Is that
all there is?' So I got interested in kids in foster care and gave
up my job. Day and night I was burning the midnight oil doing
things for kids in foster care, writing letters to legislators,
going to the general assembly, speaking in front of the Senate
subcommittee on foster care — all of which consumed me with
a fire. I was feeling good about doing it.

We adopted a couple of kids. Once they went to school, I
started nursing again. I was stuck behind files of backed-up
work two feet on both sides of my desk and on the floor
around my desk.

People were pecking at me all day long, 'Can you do this?' or
'What should I do about that?' I helped people solve problems
while all the paperwork piled up. Then I started staying after
5:00 P.M., trying to make a difference in the stacks. Some days
I'd work from 8:00 A.M. until 11:00 P.M. I thought the house and
my two kids (one in the third grade and one in the eighth)
could handle my absence. I started working late because I wanted to get all this work done. Then after a while, it became the

accepted practice. I didn't feel good not doing it. I never resolved the stacks. They were still there when I left that job.

My marriage completely fell apart. One child lived with my husband and my 15-year-old with me. One year later she decided to leave after an argument over rules we had. She went to live with her father, thinking the grass would be greener. One day after leaving my office, I went home and there wasn't a thing in the house to remind me of my family — no pictures, no nothing. She had taken all the little reminders. Then I fell apart.

I was as close to being shipwrecked as I'd ever been in my life. But I was totally devastated because no more could I control anything. I was so physically exhausted that I started giving people at work the authority to do the things they knew how to do already. When I became so emotionally drained that I had to detach from all of my responsibilities, I was afraid my super-achieving wouldn't mean anything to me anymore. After all, doing and producing were what had saved me for so long. I was scared that, because I had removed myself from it a little, it might abandon me as everyone else in my life had.

From Bart To The Beaver

As a child my dream of what a healthy family "should" be like was what I learned from television of the 1950s. I set out to live the life of June and Ward Cleaver. I was determined that my family would live on a tree-lined street, everything would be perfect, no one would ever get angry, everyone would do what they were supposed to do and smile and be happy. What could be more simple?

Many adults like myself who grew up in "The Addams Family" or the "Simpsons" household have unrealistic images of what a healthy family "should" be. We use the Andersons of "Father Knows Best" or the Donna Reed family as a model for our adult lives. We swing from one extreme to the other — from the imperfect family of Bart Simpson to the perfect family of Ward Cleaver — and then feel frustrated and confused when we discover the perfect family "ain't what it's cracked up to be." Growing up with "Donna Reed" moms and "Ward Cleaver" dads can be just as dysfunctional as growing up in the Simpson family. Although dissimilar, Bart and the Beaver illustrate two types of family dysfunction that lie on opposite ends of a scale. Both extremes provide an environment where the seeds are sown for overdoing later in adulthood.

Families that operate in these extremes are off balance. They have either rigid rules or none at all, boundaries that are too thick or too blurred, lifestyles that are chaotic (imperfect) or overorganized (perfect). These families are often characterized by conflict — open or subtle — poor communication, lack of nurturance and inconsistency and unpredictability. These families often have secrets of "don't talk, don't trust, don't feel." Self-esteem needs are unmet, and some type of compulsive disorder is usually present in one or both parents. We tend to think of alcohol- or drug-addicted families as dysfunctional, but these substances do not have to be present.

Dysfunctional families can grow out of other types of trauma: mental illness, work addiction, religious obsession, parental perfectionism, compulsive gambling, eating disorders, compulsive spending or violence, where sexual, emotional, or physical abuse are present. A death or divorce in the family that is never talked about can create the kind of tensions among members that lead to dysfunction.

Looking Good: The Perfect Family

On the surface problems are less conspicuous in perfect or "looking good families." But when we examine conversations between Donna Stone and her daughter Mary (mother and daughter characters from "The Donna Reed Show"), the unhealthy messages slap us in the face. When Mary wonders how to get that certain boy interested in her, for example, Donna might say, "Did you ever hear of feminine charm? You must laugh at his jokes and make him feel superior. To get anywhere in this man's world, women must be charming." On another occasion, when Mary tries to get boys to compete for her around prom time, Donna says something like, "It's wonderful to be popular and attractive. But you must learn to use that power kindly and gently."

The messages here are that Mary must learn how to manipulate men to get them to like her. It is implied that these are secrets that build coalitions between mother and daughter against father and son and all members of the opposite sex. Emphasis is on people-pleasing, perfectionism and gentle manipulation.

Looking good and putting up a happy front are traits of dysfunctional families. The message is clear: Say and do the right thing, pretend everything is okay even when it isn't, don't talk about your feelings and don't let people know what you're like. Donna Stone often baked cookies dressed as if she were on her way to church. When the kids wanted to do something "scandalous," like have a loud party, Donna preached something to the effect, "People expect a doctor and his family to set an example. All of us in this family have a responsibility to uphold that image."

Being in control, being perfect, doing what others want you to do and measuring your worth by what others think are character traits of children from perfect families. They become "perfect" candidates for overdoing it because they learn that self-esteem means being good, doing right, doing well and never failing.

Irene, one of my clients, is an example of how children get caught in this no-win cycle that evolves into overdoing it.

Irene remembers that there was a sense of something missing as a child, despite the fact that her parents, Jack and Lib, both raised in alcoholic homes, were determined that Irene and her brother would not have to live through the kind of hell they did. Alcohol was never around as Irene and her brother grew up, but Jack was a work addict who held high standards for himself and for his family. If he could do his best, then everybody else "should" do their best too.

There were lots of "shoulds" in Irene's family. Her father was a traveling salesman, and because he was working most of her life, Irene only saw him on weekends. Jack gave Irene a dollar every time she read *How To Win Friends And Influence People.*

Says Irene, "That book emphasizes the people-pleasing stuff — tuning into others and making them feel important. Now I understand that underneath all that kind manipulation is the basic need to control how others feel about me. The message I got was that I wasn't okay as I was. I needed to be whatever it took to get people to like and approve of me."

Irene's parents never wasted time and were forever busy and doing. Everybody in the family was always trying to do everything right — anticipating and avoiding anything that could create trouble or conflict. Nobody talked about their feelings, and everybody pretended things were okay: "When my dad got angry, he got cold and sarcastic. I didn't know how to deal with it. I would have rather been beaten."

As a child Irene wished there had been more closeness in her family and thought it was her fault she was so unhappy:

> My dad was a good provider, a regular churchgoing man. My parents worked hard to provide for us and to send us to summer camp. They wanted to be Ozzie and Harriet, and they tried real hard to be. But I never felt loved and accepted, even though I know my parents meant well. So with such a perfect upbringing, there had to be something wrong with me for wanting to have intimate, feeling conversations and relationships, and for feeling like I wasn't loved or accepted.

Jack and Lib's household required family members to follow the consistent and often subtle rule of being perfect, doing what others wanted you to do and measuring your worth by what others think. Feeling she could never measure up, 42-year-old

Irene spent much of her life being accommodating to others to avoid conflict. Being accepted became so important to her she was willing to forfeit her own wants and needs. Caught in this no-win cycle, Irene was still trying to do it right, be perfect and achieve enough, hoping that eventually she might gain her critical father's approval.

Inconsistency And Unpredictability: The Imperfect Family

On the other side of the scale are overdoers who develop their habits to cope with a topsy-turvy childhood. Inconsistency and unpredictability during early childhood are often at the root of compulsive overdoing in adulthood. All children must wrestle with some degree of emotional adjustment as they grow up, but for many overdoers the seeds were sown when there was constant family confusion and disruption or when they became caretakers of younger siblings or a disabled parent. Others take charge of a life that is crumbling around them. They learn that their absolute control over people and situations was essential for their survival.

Examples are adults who grew up in families where there was mental illness, alcoholism or other types of dysfunction. My own upbringing in an alcoholic home, where I was caretaker of a younger sister and overly responsible for the emotional tone of my family, led me to use housework, schoolwork and homework as groundwork to my adult work addiction that almost killed me.

Author and feminist Gloria Steinem chronicles in her best-selling book *Revolution From Within* what it was like as a child caring for an invalid mother who vacillated from wandering the streets to sitting quietly:

> I remember so well the dread of not knowing who I would find when I came home: a mother whose speech was slurred by tranquilizers, a woman wandering in the neighborhood not sure of where she was, or a loving and sane woman who asked me about my school day. I, too, created a cheerful front and took refuge in constant reading and after-school jobs — anything to divert myself (and others) from the realities of my life.

The unpredictability and inconsistency of these types of families lead children to make the unpredictable more predictable, the inconsistent more consistent. They learn that being overly controlling, super-responsible and perfectionistic provides them with a more stable and secure life. Because they are under emotional construction, these traits become permanent parts of their personalities. Carried into adulthood, these behavior patterns take the form of overdoing it, superwoman syndrome, careaholism and work addiction.

Parents fan the flames of overdoing it when they use perfectionism, criticism, ridicule, rejection and mixed messages with their children. Deidre's mother beat her from the time the child was four years old.

> While she hit me, she'd say, "You're a good little girl." How could I believe that? I remember she was on the couch and sandwiched me between her feet and the coffee table, pushing me hard against it with her feet and the whole time she was telling me what a good girl I was. I remember thinking, "Well, why are you doing this if you think I'm a good girl?"

Parental inconsistency and unpredictability can put children in a cyclone of confusion. They learn early about the Dr. Jekyll/Mr. Hyde syndrome because their parents are notorious for making and breaking promises and for extreme swings in mood.

Nine-year-old Molly learned the hard way. Her mother would beckon her with open arms: "Come here, sweetheart, and give me a kiss. Mommy loves you so much!" Expecting to be comforted in the security and warmth of her mother's arms, Molly was met instead with a sharp slap across her face and a belligerent reprimand, "You are a bad little girl!" Molly never understood what she had done wrong or what her mother meant.

Children often learn to cope with parents who have multiple personalities. They walk on eggshells and desperately try to second-guess parental expectations. But the consistency and orderliness they see in the outside world are absent at home. Rules, when they do exist, are changed daily so that children never know what to expect.

Many children from dysfunctional families have witnessed their parents out of control or violent. Children have been slapped, hit or thrown around. They live in constant fear of what will happen next. The seesaw upbringing arouses anxiety in children who do everything in their power to change in order to make their lives stable, predictable and manageable.

Trena said, "I thought that if I just tried to take some of the burden off my mom, she would stop drinking. I thought that if I worked a little harder to keep my room clean, to make good grades and to help around the house, things would get better. But they didn't. Nothing changed."

Grappling For Control

Children naturally make sense and order out of their world as they learn, grow and develop. When everything around them is falling apart, their inclination is to latch onto something that is stable and predictable — something that will anchor them and keep them from drifting in a sea of chaos, turmoil and instability. Out of their confusion and desperation, youngsters begin to seek control wherever and whenever they can.

For some kids that anchor is drugs or alcohol. For others it becomes food or relationships. For many it is productivity, usually schoolwork, housework or supervising younger siblings. They overinvest in schoolwork, housework, competitive sports and ultimately job-related work to overcome these feelings of inadequacy to make them feel better about themselves and to give them a sense of security and control over their lives.

Arlene was enslaved by the compulsion to overdo at a young age:

All my life I was conditioned by my parents. And when they stopped influencing me, I took it over myself — telling myself, conditioning myself. I've been compelled all my life to be a good girl, follow the rules, do the right thing. You gotta make A's, gotta get a good report. And now I hear that echo in my head on the job: Do a good job, do the best you can, make sure it's in on time. Make sure it's the most comprehensive and complete document you can provide. Make sure everyone is pleased with it. It's definitely tied into the "do the right thing and do it perfectly" syndrome. The deep fear is that somebody would tell me that I don't deserve to be manager, or to get my paycheck, or that people are disappointed in me. Boy, that's the big one. Or my supervisor will say, "Gosh, I thought you were doing such a good job. Now look what you've done!" I can't imagine that would ever happen. But my compulsive voice tells me that it could, so I'd better look out for it. Fear of failure, fear of looking stupid, fear of not being taken seriously, are all carryovers from my childhood.

In order to "feel" stabilized and balanced, children put an over-abundance of their energies into doing. As they begin to feel more secure, they clutch it tighter and tighter. Afraid to let go for fear of losing control, they become obsessed and compulsive. As children, they have embraced one disorder, that of overdoing it, in an attempt to escape from another.

Young Overdoers

Many kids show signs at a young age of compulsive overdoing it. Characteristics of young overdoers are:

1. They overextend themselves with adult responsibilities for keeping the household running smoothly — cooking, cleaning and paying bills — before they are developmentally ready.
2. They assume the role of caretaker for the physical well-being, safety and nurturance of younger siblings or of a dependent parent or both.
3. They are forced to deal with grown-up emotional worries and burdens.
4. They exhibit compulsive overdoing it in sports, schoolwork, extracurricular activities and civic organizations or in all areas of life.
5. They demonstrate precocious leadership abilities in the classroom and on the playground.
6. They strive to be perfectionists in their social behaviors and to gain adult approval by being "a good girl" or "a good boy."
7. They are serious, with little if any relaxation, play, fun or enjoyment of the world of childhood.
8. They develop early health problems that are symptoms of stress and burnout.
9. They become overly responsible for providing their family's self-worth and identity and for solving their family's problems.
10. They are rushed to grow up faster than they are developmentally ready for.

Young overdoers feel inadequate. No matter what they do, it never makes a dent toward alleviating the problems. Nothing is ever good enough, so they keep plugging away to do better. Parents, who are consumed with their own problems, never have time for them except to say, "Keep up the good work," "Do it right" or "I'm depending on you." Or parents might suddenly and unpredictably switch personalities and make promises that are always broken. Children feel guilty and blame themselves. Embarrassed in front of friends by the family's tainted image, they internalize the shame as part of their personal identity. Shame and humiliation become part of their self-concept, culminating in low self-worth.

Young overdoers are often the oldest children in the family. I worked with 14-year-old Fran who had the look of a child who carried the burden of the world on her shoulders. She and her eight-year-old sister were frequently left alone by their cocaine- and alcohol-addicted parents at all hours of the night. Fran, who had become the parent of the whole family, spoke openly about her parents' addictions:

> It makes me sick to my stomach when they get high. They smile and ask me if I want some too. I feel like they don't really love me because they'll let me do anything I want. I can go anywhere and do anything and stay out as long as I want to. But I don't because there wouldn't be anybody to take care of my sister. I feel like I have to do it because they're too drugged out.

Nina, one of two siblings in a children's group that I led, was ten going on 35. I asked her how things went during the Thanksgiving holiday. "Not so good," she replied. "My momma and uncle yelled at me because the turkey didn't turn out right." Asked to explain, she said, "I cooked the turkey too long, and it was too dry, so they fussed at me. I just went into my bedroom and closed the door and hit my bed and cried."

I responded, "That's a pretty big job for a ten-year-old."

She looked at me as if I were half crazy. "I always cook Thanksgiving dinner 'cause my momma's too drunk!"

Not only did Nina cook all the meals, she also looked after her six-year-old sister and got them both off to school every morning.

She made breakfast, cleaned the house, did the laundry and did any other chores that were necessary for her survival.

Nina and Fran are not children but they are overcompensating adults in children's bodies. Bereft of any sense of security and safety, they have become the adults that everyone in their family relies on. They are likely to grow into people who are envied by everyone: responsible, achievement-oriented, able successfully to take charge of any situation. At least that's how they will appear to the outside world. Inside, they will continue to feel like little kids who never do anything right, while holding themselves up to standards of perfection without mercy, judging themselves harshly for the most minor flaws. Convinced that they can never depend on anyone, they will bring a sense of isolation into their adult relationships. Sadly, Nina might end up spending many nights crying in her bed, pounding her pillow over things far more serious than dried-out turkey.

Sam, a 39-year-old man, never knew what it was like to be a child. His father was a physically abusive alcoholic, and his mother was addicted to prescription drugs. As the oldest child, Sam was the only responsible person in the house. From the time he was nine years old, Sam took care of his little brother. His father made him and his brother work at the gas station he managed. They didn't get to play or have much of a childhood, and on top of that the household was at war most of the time. As an adult Sam doesn't know how to enjoy himself. He cannot be playful, he has no favorite foods, he doesn't read the newspaper, he doesn't enjoy any kind of entertainment and he doesn't even enjoy sex. He doesn't have a good time doing anything. He's so stiff and rigid most of the time and his need for control is so great that he avoids situations where he has to behave spontaneously or act on the spur of the moment.

Hurried Children

Dressed in makeup, heels and blouse and skirt, five-year-old Heather walked into McDonald's with her grandmother and ordered a hamburger. An onlooker remarked, "Look at that midget!" When Heather was six, her teacher expressed concern to Heather's father that the child was not paying attention because she was constantly putting on her makeup and primping during class.

At ten, Heather is on a diet so that her tight designer jeans will fit a more shapely figure. A tall, large child, Heather looks more mature that she is. Her designer clothes, carefully manicured and painted nails, coiffed hair, jewelry and perfume and penchant for MTV and Madonna mask her age and provide her with a veneer of sophistication that hides her childlike confusion. She keeps a lot inside, according to her grandmother, and she appears very pensive, as if she were harboring secrets she will not share, yet she cannot handle them either.

Exposed to things that many kids her age never experience, Heather had to grow up fast. At 18 days of age, she started her whirlwind growth when she was flown from place to place — she lived with her grandmother in North Carolina for a year and then her grandmother in Virginia until she was three. Heather's parents, involved in their careers and in fast-track living, didn't set up a home until the child was three, when they moved into a Washington, D.C. condominium. After a year, the parents divorced, discussing the impending split in front of their four-year-old, who appeared to take it in stride. In the absence of her parents, however, Heather cried uncontrollably in her grandmother's arms. At four she routinely flew alone to various relatives on the East Coast.

Academically Heather is pushed to read. Her parents buy books to teach her to read rather than for enjoyment. The ten-year-old has difficulty playing with others her age, and when she does, she takes the adult role of director, telling her friends what to do rather than playing like most other school-age children. From the time she was two, Heather was in nursery school and since school age has spent after-school hours caring for herself at home alone.

Heather's story illustrates the problem of what psychologist David Elkind refers to as *hurried children* — youngsters forced to grow up too fast. They are pushed to take on adult responsibilities before they are developmentally ready for these burdens. Most adult overdoers have a childhood history of some kind of adult responsibility, from caring for baby brother to making sure the electric bill gets paid. Like Heather they are thrust into a

grown-up world with which they are emotionally and intellectu-
ally unprepared to cope. Not only do they acquire adult responsibilities, but they are recipients of the stress and tension that
come with them.

The pressure from taking on grown-up responsibilities — such
as calling in sick to a drunken father's employer or paying monthly
bills so utilities are not disconnected — can cause severe childhood
burnout. Children who assume the role of parent to a younger
sibling or to a parent become little adults with all their worries
and burdens. Ultimately they miss childhood altogether.

Hurried children often have what medical scientists call Type-
A personalities that lead to physical health problems. Paul Visin-
tainer and Karen Matthews of the University of Pittsburgh have
traced the origins of Type-A behavior and its association with
coronary artery and heart disease to childhood. Type-A children,
through their overdoing it, often become compulsive overachievers. They attempt to control others and suppress fatigue; are
impatient, competitive and achievement-oriented and have a
sense of urgency and perfectionism. Healthwise, this compulsive
need to achieve in children is linked to such cardiovascular risk
factors as fluctuations in blood pressure and heart rate. Visin-
tainer and Matthews observed Type-A characteristics among
schoolchildren as young as five years of age, and these traits
endured over a five-year period.

Carl Thoresen in his research at Stanford University found
that Type-A-personality parents pass their behavior on to their
children. Parents who were rated as high Type-A tended to be
more controlling and dominating and to give specific directions
and criticism to their kids. Their children turned out to be more
competitive, angry and stressed out than children whose parents
did not pressure them to succeed. Although Type-A children
struggled and worked harder, they did not accomplish any more
than children who approached tasks with a calm and more relaxed
style. Overall, Type-A kids were more anxious and unhappy with
themselves and their relationships than were non-Type-A children.

The box on page 103 contains the Matthews Youth Test for
Health (MYTH), which was developed to distinguish school-age
children with Type-A behaviors from those with Type-B behaviors
(youngsters who do not exhibit Type-A traits). The child is rated

on a scale from 1 (extremely uncharacteristic) to 5 (extremely characteristic). Possible MYTH scores range from 17 (extreme type B) to 85 (extreme Type A). This test allows you to check a child for any early compulsive overdoing habits.

The Matthews Youth Test for Health*

1. When this child plays games, he/she is competitive.
2. This child works quickly and energetically rather than slowly and deliberately.
3. When this child has to wait for others, he/she becomes impatient.
4. This child does things in a hurry.
†5. It takes a lot to get this child angry at his/her peers.
6. This child interrupts others.
7. This child is a leader in various activities.
8. This child gets irritated easily.
9. He/she seems to perform better than usual when competing against others.
10. This child likes to argue or debate.
†11. This child is patient when working with children slower than he/she is.
12. When working or playing, he/she tries to do better than other children.
†13. This child can sit still long.
14. It is important to this child to win, rather than to have fun in games or schoolwork.
15. Other children look to this child for leadership.
16. This child is competitive.
17. This child tends to get into fights.

---

*Reprinted from K. A. Matthews and J. Angulo. "Measurement of the Type A Behavior Pattern in Children: Assessment of Children's Competitiveness, Impatience-Anger, and Aggression." *Child Development*, 51, (1980), 466-475. Used with permission of the Society for Research in Child Development.
† The scale is reversed for these items.

The Invulnerable Child Myth

During the 1980s social scientists identified and began studying
the phenomenon of "invulnerable children" — those reared under
the most dire circumstances who somehow develop remarkably
well despite their disadvantaged surroundings. Also known as
"resilient children," the most common characteristic of these kids
is their ability to cope and handle stress in exceptional ways. Even
though they are reared in extremely traumatic dysfunctional
homes, they are described as stress-resistant and are said to thrive
in spite of these disadvantages.

Resilient children are said to share a number of common traits.
They have good social skills. They are at ease and make others
feel comfortable too. They are friendly and well liked by class-
mates and adults. They have positive self-regard. And they have
a feeling of personal power for influencing events around them.
This contrasts with the feelings of helplessness that vulnerable
children experience.

Not only do invulnerable children feel in control, they also
want to help others needier than themselves. They are successful,
usually receiving high grades in school. And as adults, they become high achievers in their careers. Their early family misfor-
tunes, instead of destroying their intellectual and creative potential, help motivate them. Invulnerable children, in fact, are said to
thrive on the early turmoil in which they live.

Invulnerable children sound like carbon copies of young overdoers. On the surface these kids appear to function exceptionally
well, despite their dysfunctional upbringing. Outwardly, they appear to have it all. They may be the most attentive, the most
dependable, the smartest and the most popular child in school.
They follow the rules, make the best grades, always finish their
schoolwork on time, and are often leaders in school governments
and extracurricular activities.

But they are by no means invulnerable. Underneath the facade,
a different story unfolds, and herein lies the danger of the invulnerable child myth. Many cases of invulnerability are disguised
inner misery that children are compelled to hide. Since they are
more adept at most things, it is only natural that they would be
more skilled than most children in hiding their pain. These resil-

ient kids may, in fact, be in greater need of help than kids who show their vulnerability.

Their childhoods are filled with serious issues ordinarily reserved for adulthood. While their friends are playing and being children, young overdoers dwell on their family's dysfunction and welfare. Their resiliency also conceals their feelings of inadequacy and low self-esteem. Underneath their success and achievement is an obsessive drive to excel at everything and a compulsive need for approval, deep-seated unhappiness and a poor sense of self-worth. These children browbeat themselves into being perfect and refuse to allow themselves to make mistakes. They are overly serious and judge themselves unmercifully. To keep their world from coming unglued, they learn to control everything around them. Their invulnerability becomes their compulsion and prevents them from becoming intimate with others.

Because achievement and competition are so highly valued in our society, these children not only go unnoticed, they are, in fact, rewarded for their compulsive overdoing. The myth of the invulnerable child encourages children's overdoing it, and instead of helping them learn to lead a more balanced life, perpetuates their dysfunction.

I used to think I was an invulnerable child, called myself that during public-speaking engagements and was even written up as a classic case in two textbooks on child development. But that was before I knew I was the child of an alcoholic. Accolades from teachers, neighbors and relatives who admired and rewarded my invulnerability only drove me further into self-misery, feelings of inadequacy and eventually work addiction.

I always thought it strange that I could be so perfect in everyone else's eyes and still feel miserable inside. The truth is I was not invulnerable at all. I was just clever and made everybody think I was. My success actually came about as a result of my overdoing it from the time I was ten years old (see my story in Chapter 10).

Accessing Your Inner Child

It is important to make an inventory of our lives to determine how and when we filter our present experiences through a lens from our past, causing us to confuse today with yesterday. Getting in touch with our inner child helps us to do that.

All of us have an inner child, the playful, spontaneous care-free part that gets stifled by our need to be overly responsible, controlling and perfect as children. The inner child is the part of you that longed to come out as you were growing up but couldn't for one reason or another. This exercise helps you to get in touch with that undeveloped part of yourself that missed its opportunity to flourish and that you may have thought was long gone.

One of the techniques many therapists recommend to access the inner child is left and right handwriting. Using your dominant hand, write a letter to your inner child, saying how much you value him or her. Let this child part of you know that you will always be there for him or her. Your letter can be as long or as short as you want. Here is one I wrote to my inner child:

Dear Little Bryan:

I have missed you all these years. You and I have been together a long, long time, but I feel we are strangers. I know you've always been there, but I've neglected you because I've been so busy rushing and hurrying to get things done. I want to know you better and have you teach me a whole side of my life that I've missed. I know you have tried to come out before and that I have been telling you to wait for a long time. But I promise you that I will not make you wait anymore.

Love,
Big Bryan

Now let your inner child write a reply to your adult self. Think about what things it would say to you that it longs to do. How would he or she want to express himself or herself? Write this letter using your nondominant hand. If you're right-handed, use your left hand, and if you're left-handed, use your right hand. This technique allows you to bypass the serious, logical and overly responsible adult part of your brain that can interfere with the process.

As your inner child writes, let the words flow without worrying about spelling or legibility. You are interested in the process, not the product. Below is a letter from my inner child. After you have finished writing both letters, read them out loud to yourself or to another person with whom you feel safe. Pay attention to what you're feeling and be sure to feel and process whatever comes up.

Dear Bryan:

I want to come out. I've been waiting a long time. I miss you and am very lonely.

Please love me and accept me into your life.

Love,

Little Bryan

Self-Parenting

Joe spent half his adult life complaining that he never had two "real" parents who could give him the kind of love and care his friends had. As early as Joe could remember, his father awakened him with, "Get your lazy ass out of bed!" then jerked the covers off his bed. Until he was 38, Joe perceived himself as shiftless and unproductive, even though he was a compulsive overdoer determined to prove his father wrong. As he started to heal, Joe learned that he had developed a mental picture of himself as reflected through his father's critical eyes. Self-parenting helped Joe see himself through healing eyes as the worthy, competent and lovable person he really is.

Self-parenting helps us do the healing for ourselves that we never got from parents loving and nurturing us in childhood. Now that we are grown, we can change our perceptions by taking responsibility for ourselves. We can give ourselves the love and caring we missed as children. We can nurture ourselves, be good to ourselves and expect the best that life has to offer.

How we start the morning sets the tone for the whole day. How we start our days in childhood sets the tone for the rest of our lives. When you were a child, how did your parents awaken you in the mornings? What did they say? What did they do? Try to recall what mornings were like. Maybe they didn't awaken you and you felt abandoned or uncared for. Perhaps they were hostile like Joe's father, and you felt angry or hurt.

Imagine what you would have liked your parents to say and do; then say and do those things for yourself. Perhaps they were loving and gentle, and there's nothing you'd change about your mornings. If so, awaken yourself with that same loving and gentleness that you received when you were young. Close your eyes and create it in your mind. See the situation and hear the words. Experience the feelings that come up. Talk about them with someone close to you, or write them in your journal.

Learning To Play

Sometimes overdoers must learn how to have fun. We can do this by getting in touch with our playful inner child.

Visualize the little boy or little girl inside yourself. What fun things did your inner child want to do in childhood that he or she never had a chance to do?_____

_____

_____

How did missing out on these opportunities make your inner child feel?

_____

_____

_____

It's never too late to get in touch with our playful child — whether we walk barefoot in a rainstorm, go skating or build sand castles at the beach. Imagine as many playful things as you can to release your inner child. Then do them. Don't let your self-consciousness or fear of being silly stand in the way.

After you've done the things you've always wanted to do, how do you feel?_____

_____

_____

_____

5
Compulsive Overworking

*They intoxicate
themselves with work
so they won't see how
they really are.*

— Aldous Huxley

Dennis Stratton of Houston is 45 years old and is recovering from work addiction.

This is his story:

I have two jobs and I spend the majority of my waking hours taking care of the responsibilities and duties for both of them. This is a pattern of behavior I've followed for years. But I've had no reason to change, even though I know something's wrong. I know I do things better, faster and more efficiently than most people can.

Most people with whom I have come into contact don't care or have the degree of concern for their jobs as I do. They don't view work or the responsibilities at hand as seriously as I do. Of course, I probably take them too seriously. If people are not going to do as well as I'm going to do, I might as well do the work myself.

Even in elementary school when a teacher would give an assignment, I would do more than what was required. If a report was to be five pages long, I'd do ten. If the teacher wanted me at school at seven in the morning, I'd be there at

6:30 A.M. If the teacher wanted me to help with the erasers, I'd straighten the desk, do a bulletin board, help correct papers and stack textbooks too. I'd stay until the teacher went home, even if it was five in the afternoon. That was okay because I was doing what was right. I had to be the most outstanding one who did any task assigned to me. Then I could get the recognition that I felt I deserved for being the best and for all of the hard work and sacrifice I'd done.

As an only child, I never could predict what was going to happen. Because my father drank heavily on weekends and my mother drank all the time, I felt the need to overcompensate. I didn't want my life turning out as unpredictable and chaotic and lacking in direction and goals as theirs. I wanted mine to be more structured so that when all was said and done I would have accomplished more than they did, and no one would view me as I view my parents.

From early childhood, whether I was playing the piano, preparing a meal or giving a lecture, I had to be the best. If I made mistakes, I would find ways to punish myself so that I'd do better the next time. When I made errors, I wanted to make sure I suffered for them so that they wouldn't happen again.

I must *always* be in the process of being productive — *all* of my waking hours. I cannot relax, but I wish I could. I like to see an effect that has come about as a result of my work because I know what I've done has paid off and was worthwhile.

I've allowed myself to take on more than I can reasonably do in the waking hours of the day, making me feel I am always behind. There are just not enough hours to accomplish things to the degree they need to be accomplished. I don't want to just scratch the surface of a task. I want to do it to the best of my ability. Although I know it's wrong, work always comes first and my personal needs and activities always go to the bottom of my "list." I need to work on this weakness.

I'm a very goal-oriented person. I try to make the process bring about a better final result than what happened in the past. I like to take a situation, such as the method we used to take attendance in our 61 homerooms. I want to take last year's way of doing it and fine tune it so we can get faster and more efficient results from the roll-taker of homeroom teachers. By working harder in the present sometimes you can limit the amount of work to be done in the future, and that will give you more time to take on more projects.

I sit at my desk in the mornings opening mail; my secretary brings in letters to sign; I have to dictate to her; I take care of several phone calls that come in while she and I are talking or shuffling paperwork; or another teacher will come to the door. At the same time I will drink my coffee, eat a snack and fill out a report that's due in the county office by noon. When I'm at home, I'm usually sitting at my desk, paying bills, talking on the telephone, eating dinner, running the computer and having the typewriter and computer printer going all at one time. It's just like a work factory.

I want people to leave me alone when I'm in a work mode. For example, I don't like to have discipline problems brought into my office while I'm in the middle of writing a memo. I want to do it at my time and at my pace. I have a tendency not only to do what's on my job description, but to create new duties and responsibilities to make it better than what the other administrators are doing. Down the road I get mad at myself for taking on more than was expected of me or more than I'm being paid for. Always doing more than is asked of me, I end up despising the job and everybody around. I have created a situation by taking on extra tasks that I don't need to do. I have lost control of my life, and when people ask me to go out, I am so bogged down with work that I cannot do both. I can't be social and be a work person. I cannot find the balance.

There's something in my body and my mechanism that keeps me moving. When I am fatigued and have had only three hours of sleep after staying up all night at the computer, something keeps me moving, even when there's no energy left. It isn't easy for me to give up, no matter what the clock says. I take a break to eat and try to work out once in a while. But I usually don't stop until 11 or 12 o'clock at night, and many times not until two in the morning. Because I want to bear down on myself, I tend to put too much on my list, stay up past the time I should have and do projects that really could be done the next day. I want to make sure that I put forth some blood, sweat and tears so that I will remember that I've done the work and I did not come by it in any easy way.

A human being cannot accomplish all that's expected in education. As an administrator I give more paperwork to my teachers and have to evaluate them based on it, as well as their classroom teaching. My job is overwhelming, frustrating and high pressured to the extent that I'm now looking for a way out. Having backed myself into a corner, I wish I could find a less stressful work situation. I have headaches almost every afternoon to the extent that I'm keeping Extra Strength Tylenol in business. I'm tired all the time, but I don't allow the kind of rest I need. I haven't made time for it because there's too much work to be done.

I try to make everybody else do it the way I do it — to the degree of perfection that I do it. But people will only change to the degree to which they care about accomplishing the task. If someone rings up my groceries the wrong way, I let them know irritably that they have inconvenienced me by causing me a delay. I'll walk right out of the store, leaving the items on the checkout counter. On the other hand I am usually the one to cause other people to be late. That's another pattern of behavior I really cannot explain. Even though I will go in early to do an assignment for someone else to gain recognition, get ahead or be successful, I have not been careful in controlling my own time when I arrive and when I depart. I have kept other people waiting many times because I have overscheduled myself.

Frequently I have fallen asleep with my eyes wide open, looking straight at my secretary or another school colleague. I know they're talking, but my mind and body have gone on a short vacation. It's almost like I'm out of my body. Because I've overlooked my body, it says, "Hold on. I'm going on automatic pilot for a while." It's a funny feeling.

My work has brought about the end of several relationships because after the newness wears off I get back into my work. Although work has caused problems with my spouse, she understands and realizes my weaknesses when it comes to work. With unconditional love she accepts that this is the way I am at this point in my life. We both acknowledge that I need to change. I certainly prefer not to be work addicted, but I'm sure there's a solution. It's going to take a lot of time to get myself out of the situation that it took a lot of time to develop. Admitting the problem is the first step.

What Is Compulsive Overworking?

In March 1988 I stepped onto the stage, making my acting debut at 43 years of age. The extent of my acting experience had been as a butterfly in the third grade. As head butterfly it had been my job to flitter around and wake up all the sleepy little flowers. Now 35 years later I donned my powdered wig and hit the boards again. This time I played John Rugby in Shakespeare's *Merry Wives of Windsor*. I debuted not only my acting abilities but also my new life in recovery from compulsive overworking.

Dramatically speaking, it was a small part — only three or four lines in three scenes. But in the drama of life it was my biggest role ever. The experience was a humbling one, to say the least. I played a servant who was beaten, pushed, pulled, kicked and ordered around. I was a "slack" servant at that — someone who always tried to avoid work. No typecasting here. My character was the complete opposite from the true me who was resistant to authority and addicted to work.

Although I was not the "big cheese" I was accustomed to being, the role symbolized a turn of events — a life without hurry and without a concrete product to show for my efforts, a life of comfort in an unfamiliar role. I was *actually playing* a role in which I had to separate myself from the character, be spontaneous and flexible and let go of my stiff and stodgy persona. And all the while I was supposed to be having fun.

My need for control and predictability was challenged as my lines were cut in some places and added in others. Scenes were changed, and I was put in some and dropped from others. I had entered a world that required fluidity. It was a process where you try things out that might fit and see what works. Gradually I learned to let go, do as I was told and go with the flow.

"Try things," the director said. "Play with your character."

In rehearsals when I'd miss a cue, I felt devastated. I was harder on myself than the director was. "Relax," she'd say. "Everybody misses a cue once in a while. This is supposed to be fun!"

At first I took my small role too seriously, as I did everything in life. I approached rehearsals as I had approached my work. Eventually though, I learned another part of who I am and what

I can do. I discovered that living is not a series of projects to turn out like an assembly line and that the process can be meaningful and satisfying. I truly felt whole, as if my life had shifted and become more balanced.

During our final bows, I felt sheer exhilaration. I had just accomplished one of the most important roles in my life, and neither the audience nor the cast knew the significance of this small part in my recovery from work addiction and my path toward self-discovery.

Compulsive overworking is the most accepted and encouraged of all the compulsive behaviors. It draws cheers from onlookers as the overworker dies a slow painful death, both psychologically and physically. Ironically compulsive workers create more problems than their co-workers. They are generally not team players and often have difficulty cooperating to solve problems, negotiate and compromise.

On a trip through Scandinavia and Russia I met and traveled for a month with a couple from New York. Because of his failing health, Alvin, the husband, had been told by his physician to slack off work. "You cannot change work habits," the doctor told him. "But you can take long weekends and vacations." What this physician did not know, however, was that Alvin is a compulsive overworker. Long weekends or trips to faraway lands are no antidote to a deeper problem in which work addicts literally carry their addictions with them wherever they go.

Alvin's wife, Dolores, says:

> He's embarrassed for people to know it, but he has lugged his files all over Europe. But both he and I know that they will never be opened. I will not allow it! But he feels better just knowing they're there. He still hasn't unwound from the trip. He's been very uptight and compulsive the whole time. He works constantly. Even when we go to our mountain home in the Adirondacks, he must carry a portable phone with him in the boat when he goes fishing. He is in direct and constant contact with the other attorneys in his firm in New York.
>
> It's been a constant source of conflict in our marriage. When we'd take the children on picnics, I'd carry the blanket and picnic basket and he'd carry the briefcase. On trips I hit the museums alone while he works. It gets lonely.

Work As Medication

Compulsive overworking is the only lifeboat guaranteed to sink. It saves you as a child when you are drowning in your family's dysfunction. But it insidiously holds you hostage and forces you to pay the price.

From the time he was seven years old Neal learned to connect to the hum of the family air conditioner when his "rageaholic" mother "went ballistic." He stuffed his fear, anger and hurt. Today, incapable of expressing feelings, Neal medicates them with excelling, producing and compulsive activities on and off the job. Forty-eight years of age and faced with a crumbling marriage, he is in therapy to learn to express his emotions.

Compulsive overworkers use work to deaden their feelings somewhat like medication. When things get bad, the natural inclination is to get busy overdoing to dissociate from facing painful feelings. A survival skill that pulled Neal through an emotionally troubled childhood, overworking kept him detached from his feelings and from facing himself and intimate relationships with others.

Compulsive overworking can be as ravaging and insidious as alcoholism or eating disorders. How many times have you been told, "Keep up the good work"? And then there's, "Boy, is she dedicated!" or "What a go-getter!" We all hear these accolades from time to time on the job. Compulsive overworkers take them to heart. Work is the drug of choice for many adults because excessive work numbs emotional pain and makes them feel better. It represses rage, hurt, fear, guilt, sadness and just about any emotion.

Compulsive overworkers get hooked because work anesthetizes them from dealing with unpleasant feelings stored in their bodies since childhood. They suffer some of the same symptoms as alcoholics. They have similar denial systems, reality distortions and needs to control. Careers zoom and marriages and friendships falter because of compulsiveness, self-absorption, overindulgence, mood swings and highs and lows. Compulsive overworkers get high from work, go on binges and get hangovers as they ultimately start to come down. The downward swing is accompanied by withdrawal, irritability, anxiety and depression.

Compulsive overworkers will never be fully happy until they face their neglected inner feelings. The fact that Alvin was embarrassed about carrying a suitcase of work across Europe says a lot. He knew something was wrong. Instead of admitting it, he tried to hide it from others — everybody, that is, except his outspoken wife. Keeping the secret of work addiction is often part of the disorder. It's really no different from alcoholics who hide bottles.

A university professor told me that she remembered leaving her office one Friday afternoon after a long hard week. With butterflies in her stomach, she wondered what she would do during the weekend. At that point someone handed her an announcement that grant proposals were due in one month. Exhaling a huge sigh of relief, she knew she had something to carry her through another weekend and calm descended over her. She was like an alcoholic, bottle under her arm, who was assured of plenty to drink.

> For me work was an anesthetic. It was tranquilizing. It numbed the pain, calmed me down, helped me forget and made me feel good. Folding that 3-inch-thick computer printout under my arm made my adrenaline flow. That bundle was my security, promising to fill the hours and give me purpose, meaning and self-esteem. Knowing what I'd do that weekend, I was in full control. But after the proposal was written, the emptiness, unrest and depression returned.

Work addicts often have more impenetrable denial systems than those suffering from other addictions because overwork is rewarded at every level of society — especially in corporate America. Work addiction destroys relationships and kills people. Amid praise and cheers marriages break, friendships dissolve, work effectiveness ebbs and physical side effects and health problems appear. No one, least of all the compulsive worker, understands what went wrong. Amid their crumbling world, work addicts drown their sorrows by rolling up their sleeves and digging their heels deeper into their jobs.

Accompanying Addictions

Patterns of work abuse often include the use of other drugs, such as caffeine and cigarettes, to keep the body going. Stronger drugs, such as alcohol and marijuana, are also used to relax and bring relief from accompanying withdrawal symptoms. An ad-

Bryan Robinson

The Work Addiction Scale

Early Stage

The Progression of the Disease

Middle Stage

Late Stage

- Rushing, busyness, caring, rescuing

- Inability to say no

- Constantly thinking of work

- Compulsive list-making

- Exaggerated belief in one's own abilities

- No days off

- Hours per week exceed 40 consistently

- Increase in other addictions begins:
  Food, alcohol, relationship, money, etc.

- Social life diminished or nonexistent

- Begins giving up relationships and
  relationship obligations

- Attempts to change fail

- Physically worn out, difficulty sleeping

- Periods of comatose staring into space

- Blackouts at work, on the road

- Chronic headaches, backaches,
  high blood pressure, ulcers, depression

- Stroke, serious illness, hospitalization

- Emotional deadness

- Moral and spiritual bankruptcy

- Death

Table from *Working Ourselves to Death* by Diane Fassel. Copyright 1990 by Diane Fassel.
Reprinted by permission of HarperCollins Publishers.

Progression of Recovery

- Joyfully alive, living a day at a time
- Intimacy with self, others, work
- Secondary addictions confronted
- Boundaries set appropriately
- Compulsiveness diminishes in all areas
- All decisions made with awareness of priority of recovery
- Ability to distinguish between being into compulsive overworking and when not
- Reawakening of feelings
- Sense of humility; realistic about abilities
- Family obligations met
- Relationships re-established
- Sleeps regularly; food and exercise integrated in healthy manner
- Gradual recovery of physical health
- Limits hours at work; takes time off
- Spirituality returns
- Develops work plan; uses tools of recovery program
- Feels optimistic about possibilities
- Feels grief at loss of addiction
- Begins attendance at 12-Step program
- Seeks treatment
- Open to support; input of others
- Actively seeks help
- Admits having a disease
- Understanding disease concept of work addiction
- Admission of powerlessness

dicted worker for a major corporate sales force confessed how he used drugs as a crutch to help him balance a workday:

> I go home at night, frequently uptight and wound up about everything. I want to quit, to stop working. I'm home now — let's leave it behind. I'll pick it up tomorrow morning when I get to work. My release is to have a drink and mellow out a little bit.
>
> I don't see mine as an addiction yet, but I see that it could be if I continue to allow the stress to get to me. I could see myself getting home and having two or three drinks to completely forget and unwind.

A long-standing body of research has linked work addiction to the release of adrenaline in the body. Most work addicts describe a rush or surge of energy pumping through their veins. They often identify their euphoria from work excitement as an "adrenaline high." Adrenaline is a hormone produced by the body in times of stress and it has a similar effect as amphetamines, or speed. Some researchers believe work addicts unconsciously put themselves under stressful situations to get the body to pump such a fix. Addicted to adrenaline, work addicts require larger doses to maintain the high that they create by putting themselves and those around them under stress. Adrenaline addiction, in effect, creates a need for crises so that the body will produce the hormone. On the job work addicts' managerial style is to create an uproar that they must resolve. Crises, which require the body's adrenaline flow, are routinely manufactured and doused. Another way they create stress is by driving themselves and pushing others to finish assignments within unrealistic deadlines. While work addicts get high, co-workers and subordinates caught in the unpredictability experience many of the same emotions as children of alcoholics, notably, confusion and frustration.

Work Bulimia

Jenny would work for two or three days straight and then sleep off her work high for two days. She would collapse, sleeping in her clothes, just like an alcoholic sleeping off a drunk. Work addicts often promise to cut down on work but break their promises and may even resort to hiding their abusive work habits.

Work addicts bounce between total immersion in work and paralysis and procrastination because of an inability to work steadily and within healthy boundaries. We call this *work bulimia* — out of control work patterns that swing from one extreme to another.

Procrastination and frantic working are two sides of the same coin of work bulimia. Underneath procrastination is the fear of not doing it perfectly. The work addict may become so preoccupied with perfection that he or she cannot start a project. So they engage in behaviors that divert them from the task while simultaneously obsessing over getting the job done well. Outwardly a work addict may appear to be avoiding work, but in their minds they are working very hard.

During Workaholics Anonymous meetings members, who outwardly appear to be participating, can find themselves working in their heads. When this reaches the level of an individual's awareness, it can be shared and processed within the group.

Switching Addictions

As an adult child of an alcoholic, I prided myself that I never became addicted to alcohol "like my old man." Many adult children from dysfunctional families fool themselves into believing they have mastered the family alcoholism or dysfunction when, in fact, it masquerades as work. They often sense that something is wrong but cannot put their fingers on it. They may even boast, "I don't drink like my mom. I spend my time constructively, making worthwhile contributions on my job. I'll never be a drunk like her." Although many adult children convince themselves that they are in control, they are unaware that all addictions are part and parcel of the same disease, co-dependence. Transforming an addiction into work is a good camouflage, yet it is an action for which little help is available.

Alvin left the dinner table and went to his room saying he would return. He didn't. After a half hour, Dolores started getting uncomfortable. "I'd better go see what happened to my husband," she said despondently. She found Alvin back in their hotel room feverishly slaving away over his files. For the remainder of the trip, Alvin grabbed work in his room as often as he could.

After two weeks, he was still tense and anxious and only felt "right" when he was able to get to the suitcase of files that he was dragging with him all over Europe.

Type-A Behavior, Work Addiction And Workaholism

Work addiction is denied more frequently in our society than any other form of addiction. If you check some dictionaries, you won't find "Type-A behavior," "work addiction" or "workaholism." We have not developed the language to refer to the problems of work dependency, and it has not been accepted into the official psychiatric and psychological nomenclature.

Even with the identification of the Type-A behavior pattern, nomenclature was a problem. Cardiologists Meyer Friedman and Ray Rosenman, in their groundbreaking book *Type A Behavior and Your Heart*, described the Type-A person as hard-driven, competitive, hostile and hurried. They invented the term because it was a new research area, and it got them grants to study the phenomenon. Type-A behavior is considered a personality type that has most commonly been linked to heart disease. By contrast, Type-B behavior types are relaxed, easygoing and not overly ambitious or irritable.

In some ways the Type-A personality pattern and the work addiction syndrome overlap. They certainly share the same high stress level and the resulting physical and health problems. Both take a hard-driving, urgent and impatient approach to life. Many Type As are doubtless also work addicted, although there is no way to know how many. The greatest difference comes in how they are conceptualized. Rosenman insists that Type A is not an illness and that it is a perfectly normal way for some people to behave. Work addiction, on the other hand, is a condition from which the dependent can recover. The work-addicted learn their addictions over the course of years as alcoholics do, and they can unlearn them through a similar type of recovery program.

Although the term "workaholism" was invented to create an analogy with alcoholism, it is used in such a way that it minimizes the severity of the problem and perpetuates society's denial. The word is tossed around the office. People proudly refer to themselves as workaholics at social gatherings.

Workaholism is separated from other addictions because it is viewed as a positive trait; whereas alcohol and drug dependency, gambling and eating disorders are often considered character defects. It is even sometimes fashionable to be a workaholic.

Because correct terminology is important for discussing addiction as a disease, I have chosen "work addiction" and "compulsive overworking" rather than "workaholism," which has assumed an air of normality that is disturbing. It has even been hailed as a positive addiction by some management consultants, and newspaper ads frequently recruit for workaholics.

"Work addiction" more adequately conveys the seriousness of the disorder. Real work addicts will not brag about it. Although they cannot cut down, people who overwork, no matter how successful or happy they appear to be, are inwardly miserable.

Intimacy Problems

Intimacy is a major problem for work addicts. The barriers that protect them from intimacy are hard to penetrate. They have few or no friends, and they immerse themselves in their jobs to fulfill intimacy needs.

In 1992 I conducted a study of 107 self-identified work addicts from across the United States and Canada. Results indicated what therapists have been observing for years: Compulsive overworking interferes with intimate and social relationships and leads some work addicts to re-create dysfunctional families in adulthood that are similar to the ones in which they grew up.

Their relationships were characterized by poor communication, unclear family roles, lack of affective involvement and low general family functioning. It is clear from these findings that work addiction is not just an individual problem; it negatively affects the entire family.

Seeing how Dolores and Alvin were still struggling after 40 years of marriage, I casually introduced the term "work addict" one night after dinner. It helped Dolores see her husband in a different light.

"Work addict you call it? That sounds as if my husband's a sick man. That gives me a whole new way of looking at him — with more compassion and understanding," she said softly, looking into his eyes through the candlelight. Alvin seemed far away and never responded.

Healthy Work Habits Versus Abusive Work Habits

Most people at some point in their lives overeat, overwork or drink too much. Work addicts cannot be diagnosed by how much they work, alcoholics by how much they drink or food addicts by how much they eat. Just because the department store clerk puts in three or four hours of overtime a week, for example, doesn't mean he or she is a work addict. The amount of time is part of the overall puzzle, but it is not the whole picture.

Many factors are involved in diagnosing work addiction because it is a general approach to life that consumes the abuser's time, energy and thoughts. The major difference between abusive (or compulsive) work and healthy (or constructive) work is the degree to which excessive work interferes with physical health, personal happiness or intimate and social relationships.

Healthy workers give an amount of time and thought to their work that is proportionate to their other activities. They enjoy their work, are productive and generally are effective in what they do, but they balance their lives with social and leisure activities, hobbies and personal and family time. Compulsive overworkers cannot control their compulsive work habits and even use different words that reflect their feelings about "the great divide" between work responsibilities and family obligations.

In general constructive workers think about and enjoy the now. They're not thinking about work during off times. Compulsive workers think about work all the time; it takes precedence over and interferes with all other areas of life. The compulsive worker is interested in "quantity control" while the healthy worker is interested in "quality control." The quality of work does not improve just because addicts spend more time at it. Quality, in fact, can be diminished by overworking.

All recovery programs require abstinence from the substance of choice. For the chemically dependent, that means total sobriety. However, because compulsive overworkers have to work and compulsive overeaters have to eat, abstinence for them requires avoidance from compulsive *overworking* or excessive *overeating*. Abstinence in these cases essentially means balancing the time and energy devoted to these addictions with the other areas of life.

Symptoms Of Work Addiction

Physical Symptoms	Behavioral Symptoms
Headaches	Temper outbursts
Fatigue	Restlessness
Allergies	Insomnia
Indigestion	Difficulty relaxing
Stomachaches	Hyperactivity
Ulcers	Irritability and impatience
Chest pain	Forgetfulness
Shortness of breath	Difficulty concentrating
Nervous tics	Boredom
Dizziness	Mood swings (from euphoria to depression)

How Do I Know If I'm A Compulsive Overworker?

The following questions were developed by Workaholics Anonymous Worldwide Service Organization. Ask them of yourself to determine if you or someone you know could be addicted to work.

1. Do you get more excited about your work than about your family or other things?
2. Are there times when you can charge through your work and other times when you can't get anything done?
3. Do you take work with you to bed? on weekends? on vacation?

4. Is work the activity you like to do best and talk about most?
5. Do you work more than 40 hours a week?
6. Do you turn your hobbies into money-making ventures?
7. Do you take complete responsibility for the outcome of your work efforts?
8. Have your family or friends given up expecting you on time?
9. Do you take on extra work because you are concerned that it won't otherwise get done?
10. Do you underestimate how long a project will take and then rush to complete it?
11. Do you believe that it is okay to work long hours if you love what you are doing?
12. Do you get impatient with people who have other priorities besides work?
13. Are you afraid that if you don't work hard you will lose your job or be a failure?
14. Is the future a constant worry for you even when things are going very well?
15. Do you do things energetically and competitively, including play?
16. Do you get irritated when people ask you to stop doing your work in order to do something else?
17. Have your long hours hurt your family or other relationships?
18. Do you think about your work while driving, falling asleep or when others are talking?
19. Do you work or read during meals?
20. Do you believe that more money will solve the other problems in your life?

If you answered yes to three or more of these questions, there is a chance you are a compulsive overworker or well on your way to becoming one.

Recovery From Compulsive Overworking

Compulsive overworkers feel a void in their lives, which they try to fill by staying busy. Work is used to fill a spiritual hunger that only recovery can satisfy. Although compulsive overworkers can and do recover, self-sabotage is their biggest threat because personal healing requires more work, the very thing that addicted persons are trying to overcome. Their natural inclination will be to approach recovery the way they approach everything else — to hurry up, cram it in your schedule and rush through it. This approach is self-defeating: Recovery cannot be rushed.

Abusive work habits do not begin at age 21 or 30; they start in childhood. Don't expect to reverse your early patterns in a day, a week or a month. There is no such thing as a "quick fix." My favorite poster is a breathtaking picture of the Grand Canyon that has a caption saying, "Things Take Time."

Give yourself plenty of time for recovery and give yourself credit for the small gains you make. Don't focus on all that needs to be done; pat yourself on the back for your steps along the way. It takes time to change patterns that took 30 or 40 years to develop. It is important for you to remember this so that you won't become frustrated and sabotage your healing process.

If you are aware that you are addicted to work, recovery has already started. Don't give up. Allow the process to unfold, and approach it as an exciting new adventure. There is a whole unexplored world waiting for you to experience.

The Balance Wheel Of Life

As recovering persons reorganize their lives to allow more space for growth, work becomes proportionate to life's other commitments. Achieving and maintaining balance are goals of those who want to develop their full potential. We function as harmonious and whole human beings when balance occurs in four major areas of life: healthy work, family, play and self.

Healthy work habits include being effective and productive on the job, enjoying what we do for a living and working moderately. Family includes positive communication and communion with your partner and other loved ones. Today "family" means many different things to different people. Your family can be a spouse; it can include both a spouse and children; it can include unmarried partners (both homosexual and heterosexual) or adults who reside with older parents or siblings. The play area involves our need for social relationships with others outside the family. The self area includes attending to such personal needs as spiritual nurturance, nutrition and physical exercise.

Achieving this balance is sometimes difficult. One way to image it is to see it as a wheel with four spokes: one each for work, family, play and self. If each spoke is valued and gets equal attention, your wheel keeps its shape. If one is left unattended, the wheel starts to deflate, loses its shape and becomes unbalanced. Nobody is perfectly balanced. But the closer you come, the fuller, more centered and more alive you feel.

Life Inventory

The following will help you discover where balance is missing. This knowledge will help you to develop your personal recovery plan.

Using the rating scale of 1 (never true), 2 (seldom true), 3 (often true) and 4 (always true), put the number that best fits you in the blank beside each statement.

Your Balance Wheel Of Life

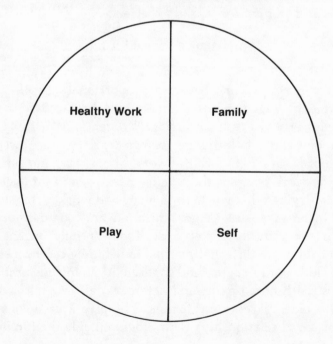

Area 1: Healthy Work

_____ 1. I have many interests outside work.

_____ 2. I spend as much time after hours with family and friends as I do with co-workers.

_____ 3. I enjoy my work today as much as ever, and I am productive and effective at what I do.

_____ 4. I work overtime only on special occasions.

_____ 5. I am able to leave my work at the workplace.

_____ 6. I am good at organizing and pacing my work time so that it doesn't interfere with other commitments.

_____ 7. I work moderately, pace myself and confine my job to regular working hours.

_____ 8. I spend an equal amount of time relaxing and socializing with friends as I do working.

_____ **Total Work Score**

Area 2: Family

_____ 1. I communicate well with the members of my family.

_____ 2. I take an active interest in the lives of my other family members.

_____ 3. My family spends quality time together.

_____ 4. My family plays together and takes family outings regularly.

_____ 5. I participate actively in family celebrations, traditions and rituals.

_____ 6. I have good interpersonal relationships with other family members.

_____ 7. I enjoy spending time with my family.

_____ 8. My family and work life are in harmony with each other.

_____ **Total Family Score**

Area 3: Play

_____ 1. I socialize with friends who are not co-workers.

_____ 2. I enjoy social gatherings.

_____ 3. I like to unwind with friends.

_____ 4. I go out socially with friends.

——— 5. My social life and work life are in harmony with each other.

——— 6. I enjoy inviting friends to my house for dinner.

——— 7. I like to play and have fun with others.

——— 8. It feels good to laugh, have fun and get my mind off work.

——— **Total Play Score**

Area 4: Self

——— 1. I plan time each day just for me to do whatever I want to do.

——— 2. For fun I have a hobby or recreation that I enjoy.

——— 3. I take time out each week for my spiritual development, either church or synagogue, inspirational readings, meditation or a 12-Step program.

——— 4. I eat nutritional, well-balanced meals.

——— 5. I make sure I get adequate rest.

——— 6. I do physical exercise daily.

——— 7. I send myself positive mental messages and try to look at the best in myself.

——— 8. I make sure I get my personal needs met.

——— **Total Self Score**

Scoring

Using the Balance Wheel Of Life that follows, put an X on the number in each that corresponds with your total score in that area. Draw a line from that number to the center of the circle. Then darken the entire area from your total score back to the number 8. For example, if your *total self score* is 16, put an X over the number 16 in the *self* area. Draw a line from 16 to the center of the circle; darken the area between 8 and 16. Repeat these steps for all four areas of the wheel. That part of the wheel that has the largest shaded area is the area in which you are most balanced. The part that is least shaded is where your life needs attention.

The Balance Wheel Of Life

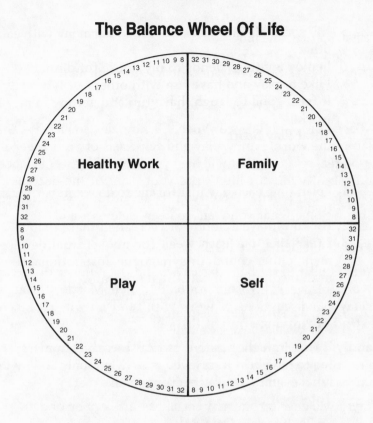

Recovering From Compulsive Overworking

The following points will guide you toward personal recovery:

- Slow down your pace.
- Learn to relax.
- Work in moderation.
- Strengthen family ties.
- Celebrate life's rituals.
- Get back in the social swing.
- Live in the now.
- Build social networks outside of work.
- Develop social pastimes.
- Pamper yourself.
- Eat, rest and exercise properly.
- Affirm yourself.
- Mourn the loss of your childhood.

- Seek spiritual healing.
- Attend a 12-Step program.
- Apply the 12 Steps of Workaholics Anonymous.

Developing A Self-Care Plan

Based on your Balance Wheel Of Life, develop a self-care plan in the work, family, play and self areas of your life. For each area, set goals that will help you achieve greater balance and serenity in your life. Write your plan for the upcoming week in your journal. After you try it out for a week, revise it by deciding what you want to keep, delete or add.

Example Of Self-Care Plan

Work: I plan to set boundaries around the number of hours I work this week. I will aim for 8:00 to 5:00, Monday through Friday. No discussions of work with family. I will eat lunch instead of working straight through.

Family: I will limit the amount of time I work at home. Plan extra time to have fun with loved ones. My family and I will start having evening meals together again.

Play: I will develop one new social pastime, hobby or activity, that is totally unrelated to work.

Self: I will practice stress relief exercises. I will meditate for 15 minutes each morning. I will begin an exercise program and get more rest. I will contemplate my spiritual life and take steps to expand it.

Workaholics Anonymous*

Workaholics Anonymous was started in April 1983 by a New York corporate financial planner and by a school teacher who had been "hopeless" work addicts. They founded WA in an effort to help others who suffered from the disease of workaholism and to stop working

---

*Information on Workaholics Anonymous in this section was reprinted by permission of Workaholics Anonymous World Service Organization, Inc., Copyright 1991, by WA World Services, Inc.

compulsively themselves. They were joined in their first meeting by the spouse of the planner, who started Work-Anon, a program of recovery for those in a relationship with a workaholic.

The only requirement for membership in Workaholics Anonymous is a desire to stop working compulsively. There are no dues or fees for WA membership; it is self-supporting through member contributions. WA is not allied with any sect, denomination, politics, organization, or institution; does not wish to engage in any controversy; neither endorses nor opposes any causes. The primary purpose is to stop working compulsively and to carry the message of recovery to workaholics who still suffer.

The Tools of Workaholics Anonymous

WA has developed tools of recovery which supplement the suggested 12 Steps. The tools are guidelines for living happily, joyously, and free from work addiction one day at a time.

LISTENING. We set aside time each day for prayer and meditation. Before accepting any commitments, we ask our Higher Power and friends for guidance.

PRIORITIZING. We decide which are the most important things to do first. Sometimes that may mean doing nothing. We strive to stay flexible to events, reorganizing our priorities as needed. We view interruptions and accidents as opportunities for growth.

SUBSTITUTING. We do not add a new activity without eliminating from our schedule one that demands equivalent time and energy.

UNDERSCHEDULING. We allow more time than we think we need for a task or trip, allowing a comfortable margin to accommodate the unexpected.

PLAYING. We schedule times for play, refusing to let ourselves work nonstop. We do not make our play into a work project.

CONCENTRATING. We try to do one thing at a time.

PACING. We work at a comfortable pace and rest *before* we get tired. To remind ourselves, we check our level of energy before proceeding to our next activity. We do not get "wound up" in our work so we do not have to unwind.

RELAXING. We do not yield to pressure or attempt to pressure others. We remain alert to the people and situations that trigger pressure in us. We become aware of our own actions, words, body sensations and feelings that tell us we're responding with pressure. When we feel tension, we stop to reconnect to our Higher Power and others around us.

ACCEPTING. We accept the outcomes of our endeavors, whatever the results, whatever the timing. We know that impatience, rushing, and insisting on perfect results only slow down our recovery. We are gentle with our efforts knowing that our new way of living requires much practice.

ASKING. We admit our weaknesses and mistakes, and ask our Higher Power and others for help.

MEETINGS. We attend WA meetings to learn how the fellowship works and to share our experience, strength and hope with each other.

TELEPHONING. We use the phone to stay in contact with other members of the fellowship between meetings. We communicate with our WA friends before and after a critical task.

BALANCING. We balance our work involvement with efforts to develop personal relationships, spiritual growth, creativity and playful attitudes.

SERVING. We readily extend help to other workaholics, knowing that assistance to others adds to the quality of our own recovery.

LIVING IN THE NOW. We realize we are where our Higher Power wants us to be — in the here and now. We try to live each moment with serenity, joy and gratitude.

Applying The 12 Steps Of Workaholics Anonymous

The 12 Steps have worked for millions of people with a variety of addictions, including alcohol and other drugs, food, gambling, shopping and co-dependency. The Steps will also help those who are committed to a program of spiritual recovery from a life of compulsive, uncontrollable and harmful work habits. The Steps are vehicles for healing work compulsions and establishing a more meaningful and fulfilled lifestyle.

I have applied the Steps to work addiction. Suggested ways you can apply them in your daily living follow:

Step 1: We admitted we were powerless over work — that our lives had become unmanageable.

The first step is the key to giving up control of abusive work practices. The work abuser admits powerlessness over the ability to manage compulsive work habits. Building on this base, the work abuser admits that compulsive work habits are out of control and uses the support of others who have made similar admissions as a source of strength from continued work abuse practices. The roadblock of know-it-all superiority is removed through the admission of powerlessness. Through this admission, human fallibility and humility are acknowledged. This is the basis for admitting you are only human, you cannot do everything by yourself and you are allowed to make mistakes.

Step 2: Came to believe that a Power greater than ourselves could restore us to sanity.

As you let go of your control and perfectionism, you start to view your life differently. You realize your attempts to control your addiction only made your life even more unmanageable. This is the beginning of surrender. You realize your way is not *the* way and that only a greater source can restore your sanity. You reinterpret some of your old behavior patterns of overcontrolling as sick, even insane. You see that your insatiable drive was mad, crippling and made inhuman demands on yourself and others. Realizing your own human limitations and imperfections awakens the need for help from a Power greater than yourself. As you put your faith in a Higher Power, you will discard these unhealthy behaviors and achieve clarity, soundness of mind and inner peace.

Step 3: Made a decision to turn our will and our lives over to the care of God as we understood God.

Turning your will and life over to the care of a Higher Power means many things. God can be the synergistic help you receive from a support group, a sudden insight you have during an inspirational reading or the realizations received when listening to another group member. The point is that you have surrendered. You have reached for other sources outside yourself for help and support. Your omnipotence is tempered through this simple act, and you stand face to face with others, communicating through a common spirit of humanity. Your ability to interact and enjoy the company of others improves, and that empty void inside starts to fill.

Your willingness to let a Higher Power guide you through your inability to control excessive work habits will also carry over into other areas of your life. You will see that you are powerless over everything and everyone in your life, and that attempting to control other people and situations only creates stress, frustration and further unmanageability. Putting this admission into daily practice on the job, at home and in social settings paradoxically frees workers of addicted patterns, allows them to develop healthy work practices and positively alters their relationships with co-workers, family members and friends. As you turn your work habits and life over to a greater force than yourself, work quality improves and inner knowledge spirals. Worries, concerns and frustrations are resolved through self-insights and inspiration.

Step 4: Made a searching and fearless moral inventory of ourselves.

This step helps you identify your weak points and strengthen your strong ones. It helps you realize the traits that are conducive to your growth and the growth of others, as well as those traits that impede growth. For instance, you may identify your inability to delegate work to subordinates or peers, knowing deep inside that many co-workers could perform the task as well as or better than yourself. You may realize that your standards of perfectionism are unrealistic and unfair to those with whom you work, live and play. You will see how intolerance and impatience of those who do not keep the same pace and rigid adherence to your way as opposed to other possible viewpoints, hurt business associates and loved ones.

Essentially, all other disturbing character traits related to your work addiction are unearthed, stare you in the face and compel you to pinpoint behaviors that you want to change. As you take personal stock, you are not putting yourself down or devaluing yourself in any way. You are merely making an objective assessment of the reality of how you thought and behaved when you actively abused work.

Step 5. Admitted to God, to ourselves and to another human being the exact nature of our wrongs.

Along the path of life, all of us make mistakes now and then because we are human. Admitting when you are wrong permits you to be human with all its imperfections. Sharing your imperfections with a loved one, a close business associate or a group of recovering adults liberates you from self-degradation and from the need to justify, rationalize, minimize or attack. We will never be perfect, no matter how hard we try. But we can strive for excellence and try to become the best that we can be. It is important to expect and permit ourselves to make mistakes, and to stop beating ourselves up when we do.

The day will never come when we will not make mistakes. Being able to acknowledge our wrongdoings by saying, "I was wrong; I apologize; but after all, I'm only human," is healing. Permitting ourselves to make mistakes does not mean we become complacent or throw excellence out the window. The goal of self-insight is important only as long as we build in margin for error. When you begin admitting you are wrong you make giant strides in becoming real, genuine and authentic. As others reciprocate their admissions, you find that you are not nearly as bad as you thought you were.

Step 6: Were entirely ready to have God remove all these defects of character.

Having recognized and admitted your character defects, you are now ready to let them go. That means giving up all the securities you have clung to since you were a youngster. Actually, it means letting go of that sinking life raft — the need to control, to be perfect and to be on top — that no longer works anyway. It means opening yourself up to a new way of life with all its possibilities of change and having faith that everything will work out better without your control of it. This is a true test of self-security because it means ridding yourself of comfort and complacency, and facing the new and unknown. As you give up your old patterns, new, more healthy and mature ones replace them.

Step 7: Humbly asked God to remove our shortcomings.

Once ready to have character defects removed, this step prepares you to ask for help. At this point, you ask for imperfections, which you have acknowledged, to be removed. Making a *humble plea*, rather than a *strong demand*, goes against the grain of the addicted worker's temperament and presents a true challenge to the abuser's humility.

As old shortcomings evaporate, you will begin a metamorphosis of who you are. Work associates, family and friends will marvel at the change in "the new you." They, in turn, will begin to respond to you in new and more approving ways. You will attract new and interesting people in your life through social and business contacts. The quality of work improves along with your ability to interact with others on an equal basis. Your old relationships will undergo change. Some of them will become more intense and close-knit. You will discard others because, for the first

time, you can see them for the dysfunctional relationships that
they are.

*Step 8: Made a list of all persons we had harmed and became willing to
make amends to them all.*

This step takes you on a life review of sorts and actually suggests that you write down all the family, friends and colleagues
you have harmed by your abusive work habits. Perhaps you'll list
a time you jumped down the secretary's throat for forgetting to
mail an important letter; a time you worked late and missed your
daughter's first piano recital; or the many times you scolded a
loved one, who in begging for a portion of your attention, interrupted your train of thought.

Addictive work habits cause neglect of family, insensitivity to
the needs of others, suppression of love from those you really
care about, rejection of anyone who cannot meet your high standards, or belittlement of those who do not conduct business or
bake bread as fast or in the exact way as you. You accept your
past self-righteous behaviors, without guilt, and commit yourself
to changing them. As you make your list, you forgive yourself as
well as promise to make amends to everyone who was hurt in the
aftermath of your work addiction.

*Step 9: Made direct amends to such people wherever possible, except when
to do so would injure them or others.*

The mistakes of the past can never be totally erased, but they
can be mended. From all the people you have hurt through your
addiction, now is the time to ask their forgiveness. One of the best
ways to mend past injuries is to change old behaviors. The moment
you tell family and co-workers that you are in recovery from work
addiction, the process of making direct amends has begun.

Making amends can be done without guilt or obligation, and
out of desire and commitment. You spend more quality time with
your family because you enjoy it; you are patient and courteous
to the supermarket cashier whom you ridiculed for being "too
slow" because she is doing the best she can; you recognize and
compliment co-workers for a job well done because they deserve
it; you advise employees to slow down and take it easy because
you care about them; you pay attention to your own personal
needs because you are worth the attention; you apologize to
colleagues for pushing them too hard because you regret it or

you help your family with household chores because it is your responsibility to do your part.

During the amendment process, you will suddenly realize that the little child inside of you has grown up and that you are a more mature and responsible adult. You have restored your self-respect and the respect of others.

Step 10: Continued to take personal inventory and when we were wrong promptly admitted it.

Maintain a climate of honesty and openness at the factory, at the office and at home. Get in the habit of continued self-examination, admitting mistakes and imperfections, and allowing others to make mistakes too. Learn to forgive yourself and others, establishing work schedules and deadlines that are reasonable, and that reduce stress and improve productivity. You understand that no one ever arrives at perfection, and that life is a series of lessons and mistakes from which to learn. Self-maintenance is a continual life-long process of self-examination and self-insights that keeps all of us on track.

Step 11: Sought through prayer and meditation to improve our conscious contact with God as we understood God, praying only for knowledge of God's will for us and the power to carry that out.

Your spiritual development becomes just as integral as work and family. And you include it in your daily life. A spiritual life can be accomplished through organized religion, as well as through such themes as the golden rule, meditation, world peace, environmental harmony and a committed value system. Finding and living a spiritual life nurture your inner needs. Going with the flow of what truly feels right inside leads you to avenues of life that yield excitement, adventure and fulfillment. Your spiritual awakening makes you feel centered, grounded and self-confident. Self-affirmations replace seeking approval from others. Through self-examination, meditation and prayer you become connected with the past, present and future through a Higher "Knowing" — one that knows who you are, where you are and where you are headed. And you allow that Power to guide you in the right direction.

Step 12: Having had a spiritual awakening as the result of these steps, we tried to carry this message to work addicts and to practice these principles in all our affairs.

This step is a culmination of the others as you return to the universe what you have received. You give freely of yourself not out of obligation but out of love. You may get involved with an employee assistance program at work, start a discussion group to prevent burnout on the job, take a new employee under your wing or become someone's sponsor who suffers from work addiction, or you may live your life by example.

Putting all the principles into practice helps you connect from the heart, instead of from just the head. Relationships become healthier, and positive people come into your life. You will radiate and attract people through your deeds and actions, and become a positive role model for others. Many nonrecovering friends or co-workers might want to know how they can also have whatever you have discovered. You will have opportunities to share (without preaching, lecturing or advising) your spiritual growth with those who want to know. The best forum for such sharing is in a 12-Step program where people assemble willingly out of a committed desire to change.

As you share your message with others, you touch and help them transform their lives as you did yours. You will be spiritually strengthened by their message as well. The cycle perpetuates itself. As you share your spiritual awakening, you send out positive energy that helps others transform their lives; this, in turn, comes back to enrich your own life a thousand-fold.

6
Overcaring

Care is no cure,
but rather corrosive, for
things that are not to
be remedied.

— William Shakespeare

"What do you mean, I don't care?" he raged at the top of his lungs. "If anything, I care too much!"

Stephen M. Smith, an ordained minister, shouted those words at his wife in a desperate attempt to justify his emotional and physical unavailability. His inner pain, shame and loneliness generated enough rage for everyone, especially him. Those words haunted him for many years and today are still gentle reminders of his tendency to care too much and the destructive consequences it had on his life. An Episcopal priest, Stephen was available to everyone but himself. This is his story of care addiction:

These days I will often (with tongue in cheek) identify myself with, "Hi, my name is Stephen, and I'm a recovering priest" just as others would identify themselves as a recovering alcoholic. But the humor in that identification is bittersweet, if only because it is true and because it is so true. In many ways I am recovering from a false perception that I and many others have of the priesthood and the church — unrealistic expectations of both. I've carried these false assumptions most of my life,

supporting, reinforcing and even exploiting them over the last
ten years of ministry.

Growing up, I was "available" as counselor/confidant to many
people and, without boundaries, absorbed other people's pain
like a sponge. People left me feeling great, and I walked away
worried about their problems. That naive vulnerability spelled
trouble even then.

Later in life, at the height of my addictive patterns of caretaking, I was working 70 to 80 hours per week and still feeling
guilty for not working hard enough. I made myself available to
church members 24 hours a day and felt indispensable and
desperately lonely. That loneliness drove me to extend myself
even more. My caretaking gave me my greatest sense of self-
worth. It felt good to help people, and like so many others, I
assumed that if more and more, you did what was seemingly
appreciated by others, then more and more people would express their appreciation more and more, thus providing a constant source of "feel good."

But just the opposite happened and the law of diminishing
return was activated. For all the long hours, interruptions,
mountains of need and my costly attempts to meet them, I felt
less appreciated, more exhausted and taken for granted. If
anything, my high visibility in ministry only increased the demand for "someone so sensitive to the needs of others" and "so
helpful." That demand, people's genuine neediness and my desperate need to be needed, set me up for the Messiah Trap. I
bought into the belief system that whispered to me that I was
the only one who could solve these particular problems or
meet these special needs because I was the professional caretaker. I had the degrees, the experience and faith, to be a man
of God — privy to the mind of Christ and Holy Scripture.

Therefore I felt privileged, required and eager to make this
treasure available to others without thought to my own needs
for rest, nourishment, exercise or intimacy. In fact I usually
interpreted Scripture in ways that left me feeling that I was
just not dedicated enough. I felt called to present my body as a
living sacrifice to God, and did so to the extreme, becoming a
sacrificial "lamb."

Such an interpretation of the Scriptures washed me constantly in a flood of work-shame. Feelings of inadequacy, selfishness and laziness nipped at my heels driving me to try more, work harder, study the Bible more, pray more, listen more. MORE, MORE, MORE, the words resounded in my mind until I literally became sick and tired most of the time. Added to this were my wife's addictions, financial insecurity and my other compulsive attempts to numb the pain through food and sex. All the while I "put on a happy face" for my flock. *After all, I told myself, they need me to be strong.*

I was well aware that there was just too much to do, but I found other ways to stay busy, way beyond anyone's expectations except my own. I did not accept help until I realized that all my attempts to fix my mate had failed and I had become a walking shell, emotionally drained of all inner resources. I could see other ministers around me, seemingly happy and successful, so I thought my stress was unrelated to my job and that I was not off balance in my caretaking. Instead, the shame voices inside my head were saying, *Stephen, you are just not good enough. You just don't have what it takes to serve the Lord with gladness; you are defective. What makes you think God could use you? You must not be a real Christian.*

Finally I slid to the bottom of my own desperate agony and lifted an emaciated, trembling hand for help. I felt defeated. My faith, my ministry, my experience and my desire to minister burned off like morning fog. Instead, I fantasized about getting into the car, throwing away all identification and just driving until the car ran out of gas, leaving it and getting a job somewhere, living another life. I felt trapped. The emotional roller coaster I had been riding for years had finally rattled to a stop with a thud, and I felt too weak to even step off.

It was then that I admitted that I was powerless over work and the driving need to control others by helping them. No matter how well intentioned or prayerful my attempts to care for others were, I finally faced the reality that I was desperate, sick and spiritually bankrupt. It was only then that I raised my hand for help, and help came. Through other professional caregivers who had walked this road, I came to learn about "slow hope," as a 12-Step recovery has been called. Only then was I willing to attend some of those "secular" anonymous programs, and there rediscovered a God that could not love me more and who will never love me less. And it was at a treatment center that I discovered that truly I am a precious, worthwhile, lovable, fallible child of God. I came to believe that God loved me scandalously, unconditionally and without reservation. My very attempts to reconnect with people by caretaking and compulsivity, in fact, separated me from God. In my head I was trying to control life, not accept it on its own terms. Today I am relearning that I am beloved, not based on what I do or don't do, but based on God's character and my own preciousness. I have believed that for years. Now I am living into it, one day at a time.

Chronic Caretaking

I heard the sounds of whimpers that grew into a crescendo of moans and wails coming from behind the closed bathroom door.

"Are you okay?" I asked my houseguest.

"Yes," she sniffled. "I'll be out in a minute."

I was too exhausted to express my true concern, having chaired a two-day conference at the University of North Carolina that had ended the day before. I had got up at 5:00 A.M. for the last two mornings to drive speakers from hotels to their speaking engagements, had listened to strings of complaints from conferees, hosted a dinner party for eight people at my house and acted as all-around troubleshooter for last-minute glitches.

It was now Saturday morning. The conference had ended, but the real stress was just beginning. My houseguest, Carla Wills-Brandon, a conference speaker, was a close friend of mine who, along with her husband and five-year-old son, stayed at my house instead of at a hotel.

The wailing continued. Carla had just realized that she wasn't pregnant. She emerged from the bathroom in tears and collapsed in my arms. My heart broke for her, and I comforted her as best I could. My soothing comments were interrupted by a telephone call from my friend Brian. I reached for the portable phone with one hand, my other arm around Carla.

"How's it going, Brian?" I asked.

"I'm really bummed out, man," he replied sullenly and proceeded to tell me how he had just broken up with the woman he had planned to marry in two months.

With Carla crying in one ear and Brian lamenting in my other, my lhasa apso, not to be outdone, stood on hind legs begging to go outside to pee. As I glanced out of the window I saw the frantic and impatient beckonings of my partner, who had been waiting in the car for the past 15 minutes, holding up a watch and mouthing, "We're already 30 minutes late." We were leaving to pick up another guest across town at the Holiday Inn and spend the day at the largest flea market in the southeast.

Paralyzed, I stood there thinking, "How did I get into this mess?" and "Whom will I have to hurt or disappoint to get out of it?" The answer was, of course, myself. Grin and bear it. I must say, the thought of wading through throngs of people after dealing with 400 conference participants did not appeal to me. In fact, I would have much rather spent the morning in bed. But these were my guests and I wanted them to enjoy their stay.

I remember feeling totally out of control and angry. "What about me?" I asked myself. I loved and cared for my friends, but I needed someone to put their arms around me and tell me it's going to be okay. I wasn't in any condition to be there for anybody. But, I consoled Carla as best I could. I told Brian I just couldn't talk and had to bite the bullet to do that. I felt frustrated and guilty that I couldn't be emotionally present for both of them at the same time.

That evening I was at a neighbor's house for dinner. Every time his wife left the room, he grabbed my arm and pleaded, "What am I going to do? Our marriage is going down the tubes! I don't know how much more I can take." I consoled him and gave him advice.

I ended up spending the entire week overcaring — taking care of everybody but myself. My fear was that they needed me, they needed me now and I was the only one who could help them. If I didn't come through for them, they'd think I was unreliable, and they might not like me anymore. I saw Brian later in the day, and he said he was great. Great? I asked myself in shock. How dare he feel great! He's supposed to be upset! We hadn't even talked about his problem. How could he possibly feel great?

This attitude is disrespectful of Brian and myself. Somehow I thought I was the only person on this planet who could be there for him at that moment. This attitude fuels the flame of overcaring and compassion burnout. I was in no shape to help anyone that weekend because I was so strung out. I learned an important lesson. Like a magnet, I attract people in need of emotional support. I was angry at myself for acting as a therapist to my friends, instead of setting appropriate boundaries. My confusion and frustration dredged up resentment from within me.

Careaholism is compulsive overdoing veiled in noble intentions.

I was feeling burned out and resentful. But in truth nobody was to blame but me. It is up to me to set those boundaries between friendships and therapeutic relationships. Don't get me wrong. I want to be there for my friends and loved ones. But I had developed a pattern of encouraging them to use me as their therapist.

I had to ask whose needs were being met with my overcaring. My friends? Or mine? The honest answer was that much of my around-the-clock caring was out of my need to fix others, not out of their need to be fixed — out of my need to feel better, not out of their need to feel better. As I looked back over my life I realized how overcaring had motivated me since I could remember. I had spent my life as a partner, friend, therapist, professor and writer who had been caring too much.

Do You Care Too Much?

Before Valerie took her first vacation in two years to visit her sister, she cooked, labeled and froze meals for her family. She arranged notes around the house to help husband and kids limp through daily routines during her two-day absence. She washed all their clothes, cleaned the house from top to bottom and arranged her children's outfits and carpool. She spent her time away from home worrying that her family could not manage without her. She found it impossible to be emotionally present with her sister and to have a good time because she felt guilty for being away.

Valerie's overcaring leads her to make herself indispensable to her family. Because she believes that only she can do for them what needs to be done, she overdoes it around the house, and her family is so dependent on her that in her absence they cannot function.

Careaholics are so addicted to taking care of others, they seek out people to help either in their professions or in their personal relationships. They have a compulsive need to be overly responsible for others, to feel the feelings of others and to overdo for them. Those of us like Stephen Smith who are chronic caretakers often suffer from a *messiah complex* — the illusion that we are all-powerful, all-knowing and capable of solving everyone's problems. In her book, *When Helping You Is Hurting Me*, Carmen Renee Berry offers the following questions to help you figure out if you have fallen into this trap and, if so, what kind of messiah you are.*

---

*Excerpt from *When Helping You Is Hurting Me*, by Carmen Renee Berry, copyright 1988. Reprinted by permission of HarperCollins Publishers.

1. Do you spend your time at social gatherings making sure everyone is having a good time? Are you a Pleaser?
2. Was your evening at home again interrupted by the call of a friend in crisis and you dropped everything to run out and help? Are you a Rescuer?
3. Did you agree to help a friend move on your only free Saturday this month? Are you a Giver?
4. Were you up late again last night listening to someone struggle with his or her problems but this morning could think of no one you felt could listen to yours? Are you a Counselor?
5. Did you try to help a couple of friends work out their differences, get caught in the middle and they both turned on you? Are you a Protector?
6. Are you overwhelmed by the number of groups you are leading, presentations you are making and study or preparation that has to be done? Are you a Teacher?
7. Do you find yourself so driven to fight for a worthy cause that, between the committee meetings, newsletters, and fundraisers, you are about to drop from exhaustion? Are you a Crusader?

The Helping Professions

Career-development studies indicate that some professions draw more careaholics than others. A higher concentration of adult children of dysfunctional families is found in the helping fields than in other occupations: nursing, counseling, teaching, social work, psychology, psychiatry, the clergy, and the substance abuse treatment field.

The clergy is one of the highest risks for care addiction because there are few boundaries in this area. It is possible to caretake 24 hours a day because someone is always in need.

Stephen Smith is not unlike many ministers, rabbis, nuns and priests who feel drawn to their professions by a special calling from God. The church encourages the notion that people who do more are better than people who do less. A nun said, "I believe that some religious persons often seek salvation through the number of souls they save and sick they attend to; thus the more they do, the better human beings they are."

One Methodist minister believed that every person who came into his life was sent by God. This justified his overdoing it. Even when overloaded with congregation members, hospital visits and pastoral counseling, he had difficulty saying no because his guilt told him it was God's will that he help each and every person, even when his phone, mounted on the headboard of his bed, rang in the middle of the night.

One morning, after a full and hectic week, he got a 2:00 A.M. call about a death. He told family members he would be right over to the hospital, rolled over for what was to be a brief second and reawakened at 7:00 A.M. By the time he got to the hospital, the family was furious. Guilt-ridden and overburdened, it took the pastor ten years to recover from his feelings of failure and inadequacy that followed this traumatic event.

Careaholics try to become other people's Higher Power. They think, feel and act as if they are omnipotent and can take care of everybody's feelings and problems.

Ram Dass said, "If you need to be helpful, you'll look for someone to be helpless." Not only does this line of reasoning hurt us, the caretaker, but it damages the people we are trying to help. The relationship between the helper and the helped when carried too far, is potentially destructive. Many co-dependent people are more than willing to entrust their lives to another person and when they give their power to another, they keep themselves helpless. Our overcaring can keep people dependent on us and unable to move forward with their own lives.

Careaholics prevent others from taking care of themselves and from experiencing pain, hurt and other healthy emotions that can help them grow. By overidentifying with clients, friends or family, careaholics can rob others of their ability to empower themselves by working out their own problems. The one receiving the help becomes emotionally dependent upon the careaholic.

Careaholics are often happy only when they're helping others. This keeps the focus off themselves and gives them a type of high. A careaholic dentist told me that she didn't feel good unless she was helping or doing something for someone else. She worked full time, cared for a husband and two children and volunteered full time in her church, where she helped the needy and traveled to third world countries to help the poor. She wondered why she was burning out.

There is no end to this type of guilt-tripping mindset. Those of us who use it on ourselves can consider the possibility that God may have sent certain people to us to teach us to share and delegate responsibilities, to set boundaries with overcaring, to say no more often and to learn how to take care of *ourselves.* This perceptual shift is often helpful for those of us who use guilt to drive our excessive need to overcare. Helping professionals who overload themselves not only contribute to their own stress and burnout but also dilute their desire and ability to help.

Some careaholics actually overdo just to get strokes from clients, friends or colleagues. If others tell them they're doing well, then they must be okay. Careaholic therapists, for example, have trouble saying no to additional clients even when their client load is too high, especially if a client says, "But you're the only one who can help me." The therapist who needs that ego stroking often takes on the new client. There are plenty of other good therapists who are not overloaded and who are looking for more clients. It is careless and naive to burn ourselves out in the name of God or to presume that God wants us to destroy ourselves for each other.

The following story is told by Beverly Rodgers, minister's wife and therapist, who has been caring for others all her life — everyone that is but herself:

> I was born to an alcoholic mother who was also born to an alcoholic. My brother became chemically dependent during his teen years. With three generations of addiction, it's no wonder I became an overdoer.
>
> I was the family hero, always doing what it took to make the family look good and to make life somewhat livable. I caretook my mother and my brother, not to mention my two younger siblings.
>
> In order to prove our family wasn't so sick, I studied hard, made good grades and stayed involved in every extracurricular activity I could find. It was as if I was having a contest to single-handedly get more activities listed after my name than anyone in the school yearbook. I thought I could gain self-respect; sadly, it only fed my self-doubt.

I'd spend all day at school, come home and clean the house, cook supper, do the dishes, baby-sit my younger siblings while studying compulsively to make good grades. Falling into bed every night, I'd cry myself to sleep wondering why I felt so worthless.

Caretaking got me attention. It got me noticed. I felt accepted, loved and needed. This was the only way I could feel valuable. I became addicted to it. I needed my regular fix, the high of making someone feel good, of being there for them, of helping. I became a careaholic. Because of my careaholism, I couldn't set appropriate boundaries with those I felt responsible for.

My personal relationships were disastrous, with my playing the role of doormat. I chose social work as a career, leaving me wide open for boundary violations from clients and their families. I thought it was my duty to care. I was just a girl who couldn't say no.

Careaholism was a spin-off of my work addiction but with the noble and conscientious twist of helping that in my mind would make it more okay. It wasn't okay. While it seemed altruistic and compassionate, it was still a fix, a high — an addiction.

Addiction is anything that keeps us from feeling our pain, and careaholism did just that for me. If I was helping, I didn't have to feel the pain of my lost childhood. Giving up my careaholism is one of the hardest things I've had to do. In the past whenever I'd struggle with feeling worthless, I'd just perform some humane act and get high off feeling wonderful.

I now have days when I feel miserable and worthless, but I no longer medicate through overcaring. I have no choice but to feel my original pain. It's hard work, but it is worth it. Boundaries are the hardest of all. As a family therapist now, I'm having to learn to temper my helping, to care for others not out of a high but out of a genuine desire to help. It is hard to tell a desperate hurting family that I have no time to work with their teenager right now. They will have to wait or see someone else. I still have pangs of feeling mean and not valuable, but I'm learning to love me even without all the hype of being a careaholic.

Feeling my pain is one of the hardest things I've ever done. I actually thought at times that my original pain and sadness would kill me, but I am surviving. I don't want to go back to the addictive way of thinking. Journeying toward the light of loving me, and knowing that I'm loved by God no matter what, is the best thing that has happened to me. I am now willing to do whatever it takes to be free.

There is a difference between constructive help and enabling. When the following situations apply, you may be caring too much:

When helping leads to your own self-neglect.

When your need to help outweighs your concern for the person you're helping.

When you begin to show signs of burnout from not taking care of yourself.

When your self-esteem is wrapped up in successfully solving other people's problems.

When you have a childhood history of caretaking a younger sibling or parent.

When you feel the feelings of those around you instead of your own.

When you believe you are responsible for making others happy.

When you believe that you are the only person who can help a certain person.

When you don't feel okay about yourself unless you are helping someone else.

When you get high from solving other people's problems for them.

When you feel resentful from sacrificing your needs in order to help someone else.

Helping can be done in two different ways, one of which involves CARETAKING and the other CAREGIVING. This distinction illustrates the difference between overcaring and healthy caring.

Caretaking Versus Caregiving*

Do you enjoy taking care of others? Do you get satisfaction from doing as much as you can for your family, friends and clients? Do you take pride in anticipating the needs of others and meeting them before they ask? Do you believe that if a little giving is good, more giving is better?

How can you tell if you are helping others or if you are really serving your own need to be needed? What is the difference between being a caretaker and a caregiver?

---

*This section was written by Marilyn "Sam" Price and excerpted from the *To Life Newsletter*, copyright 1991. Used with permission of the author.

Caretakers believe that they are responsible for others and that they know what is best for them. They do more and more because, "I care about you so much!" Their type of caring encourages others to become dependent on them so that they can be indispensable.

On the other hand caregivers are people who care for others by assisting when needed without taking away their ability to care for themselves. Caregivers are responsible *to* others rather than responsible *for* others. Caregivers are facilitators, guides, helpmates — people whose caring results in other's growing ability to care for themselves. Caregivers will give only as much help as is really needed — allowing, encouraging and perhaps teaching the other how to care for themselves. With children, this may consist of teaching them to do tasks like cleaning up their rooms or tying their shoes instead of doing it for them. With friends, it may be by listening and supporting rather than by offering advice.

Why do we become caretakers rather than caregivers? There are several factors that may contribute to this condition. Patterns and messages acquired in childhood, unresolved personal issues and cultural values may help explain why we smother others with our care.

Caretaking may be used as a way of avoiding our own pain. Taking care of others can be an addiction that serves to distract us from dealing with our own issues. If we are focused on taking care of someone else, we don't have to think about ourselves. And if we have unfinished business of our own, we may not allow someone else to struggle with their own process.

Cultural values encourage caretaking. The caretaking of others is valued in our society as an expression of love. Women have traditionally been conditioned to see themselves as the caretakers of their families. While this may be slowly changing, many people mistakenly see caring for others as proof of their self-worth.

What if you see yourself as a caretaker rather than a caregiver? How can you move from a style that encourages dependence to one that empowers others?

Recognition of the pattern is the first step. Ask yourself if you are doing for others what they could and need to be doing for themselves. And if so, why? Does your caring come from a desire to feel needed or to feel important or from a genuine desire to help? While generosity and giving are qualities to be valued, caretaking is not.

Who are the caretakers in our society? Anyone and, at times, almost everyone. The person who ends up running most of the carpools in the neighborhood, the parent who joins every committee at school because "If I don't do it, who will?" The worker who feels taken advantage of. The friend who gives advice and gets angry when it is not taken. The spouse who always does for the partner but doesn't feel appreciated. And yes, even people who have a difficult time saying no.

Therapists, health-care workers, teachers, stay-at-home moms, anyone in a helping profession may be especially susceptible to the caretaking/caregiving dilemma. In fact many believe that people choose a career as a helper because of a need to take care of others. This need to be needed becomes a problem. It interferes with the process of developing self-reliance. If the helper is caretaking rather than caregiving, they may sabotage moves toward independence. The result can be a therapist whose clients are all long term, a health-care worker who insists on unnecessarily frequent checkups, the teacher who gives answers before the students have had time to struggle with the questions, the friend who gives advice rather than listening, the parent who overprotects a child or is so emotionally overinvolved that it is difficult to let the children solve their own problems.

These are the caretakers who assume responsibility for others and who may try to fix, protect, rescue and control others by their helping. The key question is, "Whose needs are being met?"

If you do see yourself helping yourself at another's expense, gather support from others who may also be struggling with this issue. Enlist the help of friends, family, co-workers. Explore ways of caring for and nurturing yourself. Begin to realize that while helping others does feel good it is not what defines your worth. If unresolved issues are interfering, therapy may be needed.

Realize that moving from caretaking to caregiving is a process. Be patient. Change requires hard work and commitment — the commitment that is the ultimate act of caring — for yourself and others. Bereavement counselor Marilyn "Sam" Price shared how the process of moving from caretaking to caregiving developed in her own life:

> I guess I've been involved with caring for others for most of my adult life. I have been a teacher for 25 years and a parent for 16. In both of those roles I've always thought of myself as a facilitator — someone who helps others learn how to be independent instead of dependent. I believe in the saying "Give me a fish and I will eat for today. Teach me to fish and I will eat for the rest of my life." As a parent I tried to encourage my children to do things for themselves — like tying their shoelaces even if it took too long. It took patience

to wait for them, but I believed that allowing them to do whatever they were able to do was healthy parenting. So I never considered myself to be a caretaker. Not until I was confronted by a friend did I realize how I had been caretaking in my relationships. Under the guise of caring, I was giving to friends to meet my needs rather than theirs. If a friend was having a difficult time, I would send cheery notes, call often, buy gifts, make food, etc., even if they didn't ask or want any of it. And I believed I was the best friend ever for my caring. If a little giving was good, a lot was even better!

What I didn't realize was that I was really caring for myself, giving to my friend what I wanted and secretly hoping they would need me and realize what a loving friend I was.

As I ignored what they needed I ignored them. For me it is this more subtle caretaking in relationships that has been more difficult for me to recognize and change. I still feel less than friendly when I don't act on those impulses to give. But I'm getting better at figuring out whose need I am trying to meet.

An Overworked Pastor Learns To Slow Down*

There were no limits to the confident dreams of the Rev. Joe Brown that Sunday in 1990 as he told his Hickory Grove Baptist Church congregation he was turning down a job offer in Alabama.

"Realizing it is the destiny of Hickory Grove Baptist Church to take the city of Charlotte for Jesus Christ, I hereby recommit myself to be your pastor," Brown announced to shouts and tears of joy. "The days ahead will be long. The days will be hard. But we will win this town for Jesus Christ."

As it turned out, Brown was right. The days were long as he helped build Hickory Grove into one of the Carolinas' largest Southern Baptist congregations — a conservative church with 7,200 members, 45 staff members and an annual budget of $6 million. The days were hard. And partly because they were too long and hard, the mile-a-minute pastor's dream of winning Charlotte for Jesus will have to wait.

Last week, a less confident but much more realistic Joe Brown told congregants he must slow down on doctor's orders.

"After a visit to my physician last week, he insisted that I 'come aside' for a period of time," Brown, 43, wrote in the weekly church bulletin.

---

*Reprinted from "Overworked Pastors Need A Break; Give It To Them," by Ken Garfield. Copyright 1992, *The Charlotte Observer*. Used with permission.

"Since I was 13 years old I have been employed. During my tenure at Hickory Grove Baptist Church, I have taken few days or nights to relax at home with my family. Now the Lord is saying through my body, 'It is time to come aside, and spend more time with Me.'

"Beloved church family," he confessed to his congregation, "I am physically exhausted."

Though still delivering sermons at three Sunday services, Brown will no longer preach on Wednesday night. He's doing much of his work at home while cutting back on the blizzard of appointments that keep clergy snowed under.

He's had his home telephone changed to an unlisted number, and administrative assistant Nancy McDowell is so determined to protect her boss she refuses to give it out.

"Pastors are not superhuman," explained McDowell, politely but very firmly. "They're like all of us."

What a beautiful lesson for Brown to learn — and for his staff to enforce as they eagerly pick up the slack. Though inspired to do God's work, pastors must recognize their human frailties and realize no one can run full-speed forever no matter how righteous the race.

God might call pastors to the task — and to the next board meeting or hospital visit — but it's up to fragile men and women to listen to their hearts and minds when they cry out to slow down.

But it's not nearly enough for members of the clergy to learn this about themselves. Congregants must learn it, too, if churches and synagogues are truly to become humane places.

"People understand pastors need time — unless people need something," said McDowell, recounting a conversation surely repeated in other church offices. " 'Yes, I understand Dr. Brown is not making appointments now, but my daughter really needs to speak with him.' That isn't just Hickory Grove. That's everywhere."

It's easy to say we understand the impossible position in which we put our clergy.

"We're supposed to save everybody and make everything well," said the Rev. Joe Mulligan of St. Luke Catholic Church, after a recent forum on pastoral burnout.

But it's difficult and painful to break an age-old habit in which we put pastors on a pedestal and expect them to do what we often aren't able to do for ourselves — make life easier and better.

We lean too heavily on clergy who yearn to support us, and sometimes the weight is too much for them to bear.

That's the lesson to learn from Joe Brown, who asks only that we allow him time and space to make his life easier and better before he resumes full time the task of doing the same for others.

Honoring the request is the least we can do for Brown and other clergy facing the same burdens.

Are You Overcaring?

Here is a self-test to help you find out if you care too much. Read each of the 25 statements below, and decide how much each one pertains to you. After you have answered all 25 statements, add up the numbers in the blanks for your total score.

The higher your score, the more overcaring you are. The lower your score, the less overcaring you are. The following key will help you interpret your score:

A score from 25 to 49 = You are not overcaring.
A score from 50 to 69 = You are mildly overcaring.
A score from 70 to 100 = You are highly overcaring.

Care Assessment Risk Evaluation (CARE)

1 Point = Never True
2 Points = Sometimes True
3 Points = Often True
4 Points = Always True

_____ 1. I get overly involved by taking on other people's problems.

_____ 2. I feel overly responsible when bad things happen and that it is my role to make them better.

_____ 3. I overidentify with the feelings of others by feeling their emotions as if they were my own.

_____ 4. I have an ongoing urge to take care of other people.

_____ 5. I neglect my own needs in favor of caring for the needs of others.

_____ 6. I take life too seriously and find it hard to play and have fun.

_____ 7. I have a need to solve people's problems for them.

_____ 8. I have a lot of painful feelings from my past that I have never dealt with.

_____ 9. I feel unworthy of other people's love.

_____ 10. I never seem to have enough time for myself.

_____ 11. I criticize myself or put myself down.

_____ 12. I am afraid of being abandoned by those I love.

_____ 13. My life always seems to be in crisis.

_____ 14. I don't feel good about myself if I'm not doing something for someone else.

_____ 15. I don't know what to do with myself if I'm not caring for someone.

_____ 16. Nothing I do ever seems to be enough.

_____ 17. I have dedicated my life to helping others.

_____ 18. I get high from helping people with their problems.

_____ 19. I have a need to take charge of most situations.

_____ 20. I spend more time caretaking than on socializing with friends, on hobbies or on leisure activities.

_____ 21. It is hard for me to relax when I'm not caring for others.

_____ 22. I find myself experiencing excessive fatigue and compassion burnout.

_____ 23. It is hard for me to maintain emotional boundaries by saying no when someone wants to tell me their problems.

_____ 24. I have developed health or physical problems from stress, excessive worry or burnout.

_____ 25. I seek approval and affirmation from others through people-pleasing and overcommitting myself.

Genuine Caring

We have been taught that self-sacrifice is a great virtue. Lewis Carroll wrote, "One of the deep secrets of life is that all that is really worth doing is what we do for others." But always putting ourselves last is just as detrimental as always putting ourselves first. Genuine caring begins with the way we care for ourselves. Here are some ways to avoid careaholism and to develop genuine caring.

• *Set a good example by living a balanced lifestyle.* Give yourself equal time. It is important to distinguish between self-care and selfishness. John Roger and Peter McWilliams write in *You Can't Afford the Luxury of a Negative Thought:* "Those who have given to others and found it depleting have not taken the time to give fully to themselves first. Always give to others of the overflow, and if you're giving to yourself unconditionally, the overflow will always be more than enough." The way you treat yourself will set an example for others to follow. You can teach others how to treat you and themselves by the way they see you treating yourself. Ask yourself if you practice what you preach. Are you kind to yourself? Do you care for yourself as well as you care for others? Do you care for yourself in the same way you tell others to care for themselves?

• *Know where to draw the line.* When you already are overloaded and need time for yourself, let that be a sign that you're in no condition to take on more helping commitments. Every time you say yes when you mean no, you do yourself and the other an injustice. If you cannot say no, you are not choosing freely in your life. Even when you say yes, you are doing so unfreely because many yeses are really noes in disguise. Until you can say no once in a while, you can never offer a genuine yes.

• *Set limits on what you can do.* Develop a healthy attitude about what is humanly possible for you. Remind yourself that you cannot save the world. You can bite off a small piece, but you cannot take care of everyone else, especially when you're not nurturing yourself. Tell yourself there is a limit to what you can do and that this is the best you can do. Do only that much and put the rest out of the picture. Start to see this attitude not as a weakness but as a strength. Once you are able to limit what you agree to do, you are freer to give more genuinely and more effectively.

• *Set emotional boundaries through detachment.* Avoid overidentifying with the feelings of others, and don't take other people's problems home with you. Leave them with the person who owns them. By detaching with love, you can let others care for themselves, and you can spend time caring for your own neglected life. Learn to feel your own feelings, not someone else's, and allow others to experience the outcomes of their actions, instead of trying to save them from the consequences. Stepping aside can be one of the best gifts you can give another person. Tuck the following phrase away in the back of your mind, and carry it with you in your relationships:

Detachment and caring are twins, not enemies

Sometimes the best way to care is not to get emotionally involved with and try to fix someone's problems because it can rob them of the benefit of learning to do it on their own.

• *Evaluate your own motivations for your need to help.* It is important to let people go when they are ready to fly. Where you have long-term relationships in which you are the helper, ask yourself if you are having trouble letting go because of your ego needs to have this person in your life. This is especially important for helping professionals who have long-term clients or parents who cannot sever their children's umbilical cords.

• *Assess what needs healing in your own life.* Ask yourself if you are focusing on other people's pain to keep from facing something in your own life that is unresolved or needs healing. Do you believe in your heart that fixing others will fulfill a greater need in you than in the one you're helping? If the answer is yes, you could examine the unfinished business in your own life that you might be projecting onto others with your need to care for them. Avoid projecting your unresolved issues onto others to the point that you cannot separate your problems from theirs. Before you embark on a helping campaign, get yourself healthy *first*.

Establishing Healthy Boundaries

Those of us who are chronic caretakers can begin to draw boundaries and stop feeling responsible for whatever happens around us. We stop blaming ourselves when situations go haywire, and we have no control over them. We stop apologizing for things that are not our fault. We don't feel like failures because we haven't saved the planet. We don't feel the emotions that someone else needs to feel, and our self-contempt and guilt over not being superhuman evaporate. As we allow ourselves to be human with all its fallibilities and strengths, we practice the art of self-care.

Think about the relationships in your life in which you caretake instead of caregive. They can include your parents, life partner, children, siblings, colleagues, friends or clients. Do you enter relationships to rescue people? To feel more complete? To take refuge from the world?

Using two circles, one for you and one for a significant person in your life, (1) draw a picture of what your relationship looks like with that person *now* and (2) draw a picture of what that same relationship would look like *after* establishing healthier boundaries. I've given some examples on page 170. Use your journal to draw your own pictures and then answer the following questions:

1. What kinds of people surround you in your life?
2. Do any of these relationships fill a great emptiness within you?
3. Are you overly responsible for any of these people?
4. Do you need any of these people to be dependent on you so that you feel more secure?
5. Is your overcaring robbing any of them of their own independence and individuality?
6. What do these pictures tell you about your relationships?
7. Would you like to change any of these relationship patterns?
8. If so, which ones and how can you accomplish this change in a positive and healthy way?

Types Of Relationship Boundaries

Separate Boundaries

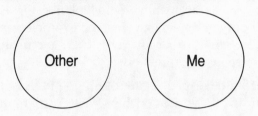

Closeness and Caring

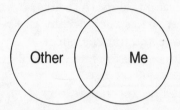

Loss of Personal Boundaries In Overcaring Relationships

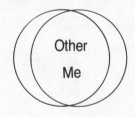

Intimacy

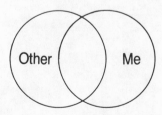

7
Friendly Fire: Living With A Compulsive Overdoer

You're home from school, you have things to say,
And you find that I'm not there.
You have some problem and need to talk,
But I'm still at work somewhere.
Oh, how I'd love to have shared those times.
Somehow it doesn't seem fair.
That the only times I now regret
Are the times I wasn't there.

— George E. Young

Maureen describes her experience of living with a work-addicted husband:

My husband's work is more important than anything else he does. The main problem living with him is that it makes me feel secondary. He's involved in some aspect of work 12 to 16, sometimes even 20 hours a day, seven days a week. Aside from his full-time job with the city, he owns two houses and three condominiums that he manages. He takes care of all the repairs on the units. He is also president of one condominium complex. So he goes to those meetings and does the books. He'll get up, go to work and work eight hours. When he comes home, he goes straight to his study and works from six o'clock to 11:00 or 11:30 at night. After a couple of hours of sleep, he'll wake up at one or two in the morning and work until five o'clock. Then he'll go back to sleep for another hour, get up and go to his regular job for another eight-hour day.

He's always busy and in a hurry to get things done. To me it seems compulsive. I think it's just the process of being involved in the work that gives him adequate distraction so that he doesn't have to reflect on himself or face other issues. I think it's a smoke screen. I think he's really depressed and doesn't know how to deal with it. He's worked compulsively all of his life, and it's a form of escape. He's not getting ahead financially, although he claims he's overworking for money. He savors every moment of the work process so that it never ends. When he's balancing books, he'll do some figuring or tabulating in eight hours that most people could do in one. I don't know how much he's accomplishing. Sometimes I look at what he's done, and it doesn't look like he's really produced anything. For all I know he's adding up the same column of numbers day after day. It seems bizarre to me. Like people who eat too much, he has the same sort of intoxication with work that they do with eating.

Wherever we go or whatever we happen to be involved in, he's in a tremendous hurry to leave or stop doing it so that he can get back to work. His work cannot be measured from start to finish. The more he works, the more he wants to work; the more he does it, the more he feeds his need to continue. When it bothers me, I've said, "I wonder if you realize you worked 22 hours yesterday."

He'll think about it and say, "Well, maybe it was 18." When I present him with this information, he'll deny it even though it's plain as day. I've told him before that I feel real lonely. He never talks to me, he's real withdrawn. I don't feel like he loves me, and I'm basically unhappy about it. He'll say that he's sorry that I feel that way, but these are things that he has to get done, and if he doesn't do it, who will?

He's got a semivalid argument for doing whatever he does. But it's only because work is an accepted activity. He tells me that he was raised Baptist with the Protestant work ethic, which isn't something I would know about (because I'm Jewish and because my father always had money). I guess putting the attention on my lack of understanding is his way of avoiding the problems.

One time, while upset and crying, I told him that I thought he was addicted to work. He said that there may be some truth to that. That's the closest he's ever got to admitting it. He thinks that working 20 hours a day and taking work on vacation are normal. He thinks that these are his responsibilities and he's got to take care of them.

He spends so much time alone. At night he sleeps on the carpeted floor of his study. He says that he does this because it's too hot in the bedroom, even though the fan blows on him. I think it's just easier for him to get up in the middle of the night to work without bothering me. That way I won't know whether he's working or not. I think he realizes to some degree that his behavior is abnormal and excessive.

He looks for justification to help him deny his extreme work habits. When we go on vacations, he'll stay indoors and work, while I'm out by myself at the beach. I bring books to read, and he compares his working to my reading. It's like saying, "If you read books, then I can do work." I tell him I read to amuse myself, and he says his work is a hobby for him. So I don't argue with him past that because at that point I realize I cannot win.

He doesn't know the first thing about relaxing. He's very fidgety. He drinks a lot of coffee. When he doesn't have caffeine in his system, he gets a migraine headache. The headache gets so bad that it will cause him to vomit. His foot is always moving, and he cannot sit still. He's often tired, but he doesn't sleep much either because of insomnia. He's impatient with anyone or anything that stands in the way of his work, showing it through sullenness. He's especially impatient when I ask him to help me with something around the house. He's bored when he does anything that's not work-related.

He ignored our first wedding anniversary. I gave him a card and asked him why he didn't get me a card. He said he didn't think it mattered to me. He doesn't pay any attention to other people's birthdays or special events. It would never occur to him to give someone a gift unless it was a season like Christmas. There is no such thing to him as a day without work, including Christmas and every other holiday.

He forgets things that he told me and that I told him. Probably he didn't even listen to me when I told it to him the first time. He's just very senile-acting sometimes. Other times he has responded to me in a way that is so inappropriate that I wondered if he was hallucinating. I have even asked him if he was hearing voices because his response was so inappropriate.

I thought too that maybe he had a hearing problem. For example, frequently I make an observation about something, and his answer has nothing to do with the subject, but addresses something in a totally different context. I think he's distracted and 99 percent of the time he's not paying attention. He has disciplined his mind so that it stays on work as much as possible. He's always fantasizing about how he's going to do this report or that plan. His saying he has some thinking to do means he's preparing to withdraw.

It's All In How You See It

Many of the feelings we have about ourselves and others are simply illusions. A good example of this occurred while I was waiting for a bus near a busy intersection in Honolulu. A traffic cop was talking to a woman who was stopped in the middle of the street. Traffic was tied up and horns were blowing. A woman standing behind me complained loudly and obnoxiously about her disdain for law enforcment officers.

"If he wants to give her a ticket, why doesn't he pull her over to the side? That's what makes me sick about cops! They have to throw their weight around. He's got traffic tied up for miles!" The woman continued to blast the officer as she walked off waving her arms in protest, carrying her misperception of that event with her forever.

The police officer raised the hood of the car, sat in the driver's seat and tried to start the engine with no success. My perception was that the car had stalled in traffic, and the officer was trying to help. Obviously this woman's perceptions were influenced by her past experiences with policemen.

I then watched the driver of the car go into a telephone booth while the policeman lay across the front seat looking under the dashboard. As my bus pulled up and I got on board, one of the passengers said, "Look! Someone abandoned their car in the middle of the street! What's this world coming to?" A third perception of the same event was offered by a passenger, new on the scene. There are many different ways to look at the same situation.

One of the fundamental problems in families is that overdoers view their behaviors very differently than their partners do — not necessarily rightly or wrongly, just differently. This different way of looking at things causes many rifts in relationships because family members exhaust themselves trying to get the overdoer to *see* it their way. "Can't you see what you're doing?" is a common refrain from family members, the answer to which is often no because many overdoers are in denial. They cannot *see* the forest for the trees.

Challenging overdoers' perceptions undermines their belief that they are in control. Sadly the more partners or children try to convince or force the overdoer to *see* it their way, the more threatened the overdoer feels and the more tenaciously he or she clings to the compulsive overdoing. The overdoers' perceptions belong to them and only they can change them. Their healing comes as they begin to look more objectively at their lives, change their outlook and reinterpret their world from a different standpoint. As they change the way they use their minds, they can overcome fears and worries and shed limitations that separate them from their families. That's not to say that there's nothing the family can do or that the family is to blame. Partners and children need help too as they get caught in the dance of overdoing it, but their help comes by taking the focus off trying to change the overdoer and by changing themselves.

The Dance Of Overdoing It

Maureen's marriage is a testimony to the fact that families of compulsive workers suffer too. Unfortunately, Maureen left her husband after six years of living with his work addiction. The children of overdoers, both small and grown, are wounded too. Nell, now 35 years old, lamented that while her executive father lay dying in intensive care, she smuggled memos and contracts into his hospital room. "He died with a pen in his hand," she said through tears. "If he had been an alcoholic, I would never have enabled his disease by sneaking drinks to him. Now I live with the guilt of speeding up his death."

Nell's behavior is typical. In the work-addicted family everyone gets pulled into the act. With the timing and synchronization of a Ginger Rogers-Fred Astaire dance routine, the family waltzes around the compulsive worker's moods and actions. When Dad is home and not working, everyone is happy. When he is more often absent because of work, everyone is upset. Children learn to gauge their emotions and behaviors by the perfections of their high-achieving parents and they try to please them, an impossible task, as I will discuss later in this chapter.

The overdoer is obsessed with work, and the rest of the family becomes just as obsessed with trying to get him to cut back. The harder they try, the deeper the overdoer digs heels in and works longer and harder. Spouses are consumed with trying to get their partners to curb their compulsive behaviors and put some time into the relationship. Many overdoers give lip service to these pressures and go through the motions of being present. They may go to a cocktail party or a child's ballgame or recital, but they are present only in body. In their heads they're back at the office working. Many children, hungry for attention from their psychologically absent parent, complain about their parents' mental absenteeism.

Nancy Chase, 38 years old, was watching the 1991 World Series between the Atlanta Braves and the Minnesota Twins when she had a sudden insight. "It suddenly occurred to me that my father never would have taken me to a ballgame or something fun like that. He was too busy working. He wouldn't come home until the wee hours of morning. I'd be so excited and want him to play with me so badly, but he was always too tired."

The partners and children of overdoers often feel unloved and abandoned. Many families complain that even when overdoers are physically present they are emotionally unavailable — disconnected from the family. This is a sore spot for family members who are resentful and hurt because they always take second place to busy pursuits. I have observed identical patterns of attitudes, feelings and responses in all of the families with whom I have worked. This indicates that compulsive overdoing is not just an individual problem but is one that affects and requires treatment for the entire family.

Enabling

The irony of overdoing it is that the family's attempts to control the compulsive busyness only lead the overdoer further into it. Everyone in the family ends up unwittingly enabling the compulsive habits. Children like Nell, in order to have time with their parents and to get their approval, contribute unknowingly to parental work addiction. Judy, the spouse of a compulsive overdoer, tried to build family life around her husband's impossible schedule and made excuses to friends for not being able to attend social functions. Others join their spouse's compulsive overdoing, working alongside of them just to have time with their loved ones.

Joining in the compulsive overdoing is typical behavior for the spouse who initially struggles to keep the relationship intact. As they become involved in overdoing it, they too begin to show signs of stress that overdoers typically show, as Madge illustrates in this letter to me:

> I have to remove myself from him or I'm going to die. I've taken on my husband's work addiction and it's killing me. He heads a multimillion dollar business. Work is everything to him. He's always working, always on a "high." Work is his life. I feel totally alone with my two kids. People don't understand how bad the situation really is. To everybody else, he's perfect. I feel like I'm one of his employees. He denies there's anything wrong and gets hostile, aggressive and restless if I try to interrupt his excessive working.
>
> People want to know why I'm always complaining. We have two beautiful kids, he has a great job, he makes lots of money, and I don't have to work. So why do I complain? I have become the bitchy wife in the eyes of our friends. I tried to keep up with him for as long as I could, but then his obsession with work got the best of me. I couldn't keep up with him and I burned out trying.

Madge ended up in Duke Medical University to be treated for allergies, headaches, stomachaches and all the other stress-related symptoms that compulsive overdoers usually show.

I continue to be amazed that the majority of overdoers who see me for counseling try to have their initial appointments scheduled by their partners. I always request that the ones who are overdoing it call so that they can begin to take responsibility for their own recovery. Still, in the process of counseling, spouses seek ways to take responsibility for the compulsive overdoer's recovery.

Frances reminded Jon of his appointment with me three times in one week. On the day of the appointment, however, she forgot to give him a last-minute reminder. Jon forgot and, infuriated with his wife, blamed her for forgetting his counseling session when the truth was he was too busy working to remember. Frances responded with, "I'm sorry that I forgot to remind you." She fell into the trap of accepting the blame for something that was Jon's responsibility. This pattern is common and often permeates relationships in families with an overdoer.

Pointing Fingers At The Bad Guy

Frances and Jon are doing a dance as are all partners in relationships with a compulsive overdoer. Frances becomes the fall guy when she doesn't manage Jon's affairs so that he can practice his addiction. Madge was blamed for wanting more intimacy and closeness in her marriage. Sometimes there is a tendency to make the overdoers the bad guys and blame them for all the problems in the family. They, in turn, blame their spouse for nagging, which makes them more prone to compulsive overdoing. Sometimes kids act out the family distress and become scapegoats for the family's problems.

The more loved ones complain about the overdoing, the more overdoers seek out compulsive busyness to escape from what they interpret as nagging and put downs. Cheryl said, "The more my husband complained about my overworking, the more tenaciously I clung to it." When spouses try to dictate to overdoers how to set boundaries or reprimand them when they relapse, the more shamed and out of charge they feel with their lives. The only solution to these feelings, from their perspective, is to immerse themselves further into abusive work habits in an attempt to gain control.

To help clients understand the viewpoints of different family members, I created Healograms, or visual representations of their relationships, career, spiritual needs, self and play.

Look at the sample Healogram on the next page. Notice that Don, who came to counseling because of his compulsive overworking, saw himself very differently than his wife, Sue, did. She said he spent more time working than he acknowledged. She rated his spiritual and play needs as zero (below the line). Also notice that Sue had very different views and expectations about Don's recovery than he did. She wanted his spiritual needs to be much higher than Don set for himself and even prioritized it as number one. Her goals for Don's development in the areas of the self, play and their relationship were much higher than his. Her expectation of his job was slightly lower than what Don envisioned. Don sees his career as having priority over his relationship with Sue. This is the kind of conflict that can arise as overdoers get into recovery and begin to balance their lives. The viewpoints and expectations of family members are altogether different and much greater than what the compulsive overdoer can deliver and, when turned into disappointments and disapproval, can sabotage the recovery process altogether.

Don, The Compulsive Overdoer

Don's Vision Of Himself Now

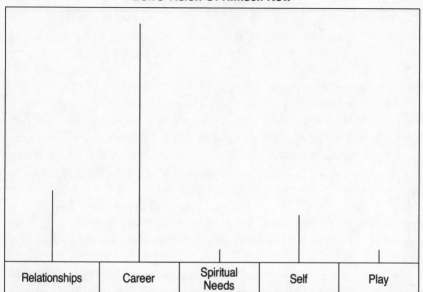

Don's Vision Of How He Would Like To Be

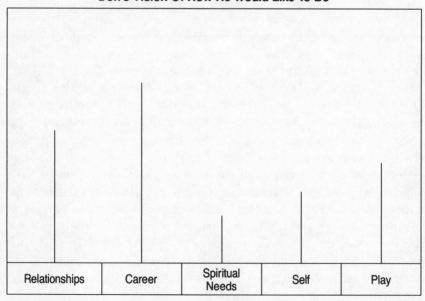

Sue, Spouse of Compulsive Overdoer

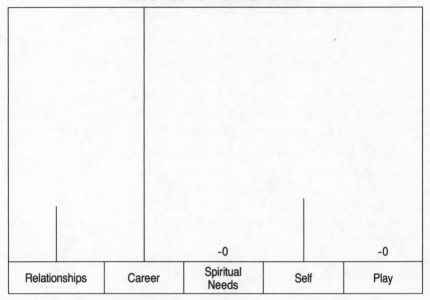

Sue's Vision Of How Don Is Now

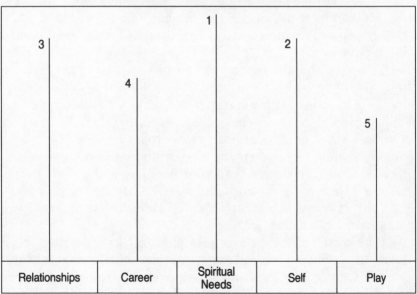

Sue's Vision Of How She Would Like Don To Be

Changing The Dance

As long as family members point to one person as the source of their problems, they all stay stuck in denial. The truth is nobody is to blame. There is no bad guy. Once each person stops pointing and takes responsibility for his or her own feelings and actions, relationships can be mended. It is important for everyone to identify and work on their own issues. Recovery is about changing the dance routine. As one person changes, the whole family system must shift to accommodate that change. Following are some things partners can do, who live in relationships with overdoers:

• *Get rid of the "elephant in the living room."* Refusing to acknowledge and discuss the problem causes tension to build. Dancing around this huge elephant often leads to angry outbursts over trivial events that have nothing to do with the real problem. It is important to talk about what's going on from your standpoint in a nonthreatening, nonjudgmental way. By identifying the problem and getting your feelings out in the open, you will reduce the tension and address the real source of the conflict.

• *Express your feelings in a positive way* without being combative, so that your partner will not tune you out. Let her know how you feel calmly, without ranting or raving, by talking about your feelings of abandonment, anger, resentment, hurt or sadness. Share your hopes and dreams and disappointments for the relationship. Stand your ground by letting her know you are concerned about health issues and about the relationship drifting apart. Tell her how it feels to be kept waiting or to be stood up. Let her know how it feels to live with a stranger and to have to assume responsibility for the other parts of your lives together. Keep in the context of a shared relationship and togetherness and let her know you miss her. After you have finished speaking, ask your partner if she can understand your position, and then it is your partner's turn to speak and your turn to listen. Try to address the conflict by working out a mutual compromise with suggestions from both sides.

• *Have constructive outlets for your feelings,* such as writing them down in a journal or talking them out with someone. Work through your feelings of abandonment or resentment with a support group or counselor, not the compulsive overdoer. Complaining and criticizing only make the overdoer cling more tightly to compulsive working because of feelings of guilt and failure and a need to escape what may be interpreted as put downs.

• *Understand the compulsion of overdoing it* and that your loved one cannot control this drive. Recognize that this compulsive busyness is a cover for low self-esteem, past hurt and fears that are difficult to face. Have compassion for the difficulty your partner has in controlling overdoing it, but don't make yourself a doormat.

• *Detach with love, not anger.* You didn't cause, cannot cure and cannot control your partner's abusive overdoing it. Focus on yourself and take care of yourself and the kids, if children are involved. Step aside and refuse to get caught up in the chaotic frenzy of your partner's pace. Avoid taking his "inventory" or telling him what he needs to do to refrain from overdoing it. Use this energy instead to take charge of your own life. Take the Healogram on page 193, apply it to your life, and develop your own self-care plan.

• *Go forward with your own life;* stop postponing it for your partner. Avoid building your life around the overdoer's busy schedule. This only sets you up for further hurt and disappointment. If you've planned a trip to the zoo with the kids and your partner cancels because of last-minute demands at the office, go without her. When she promises to be home in time for dinner and doesn't show, eat on time. Don't put dinner on the table at midnight; let her fix her own. Always include the overdoer in your plans, and let her know you missed being with her and how disappointed you were, but don't put your life on hold.

• *Avoid enabling your partner's overdoing it.* Refrain from joining in his compulsive work habits out of desperation to spend time with him or from bringing him work to do when he is in bed sick. Refuse to make alibis for his absenteeism or lateness at parties or family get-togethers, and let him be responsible for explaining. Refrain from assuming all of your partner's duties around the house, returning phone calls for him, fulfilling his family obligations or covering for him in a business meeting or social gathering unless you want to do it. Be careful not to put him in a double bind by complaining about his overdoing it in one breath and in another making unreasonable financial demands for luxury items.

• *Set flexible boundaries for yourself.* Don't get involved in helping her solve problems at work, but do listen with genuine interest to what she has to say. Negotiate boundaries around the amount of time you spend together discussing work. Don't allow work to dominate your conversations, but be open to discussing work frustrations and successes (yours included), as all healthy couples do.

• *Be willing to take an objective look at how you participate in the dance,* and be open to making healthy changes. You have built up certain behaviors over the years in response to your partner's compulsive overdoing it. For example, you may have gotten into the habit of nagging or being cynical about your partner's condition. You may have single-handedly raised the kids, when suddenly your spouse decides to take a more active role in parenting. This can arouse anger and hurtful feelings of "it's too late" and can lead to battles over turf. But if you expect the overdoer to change, you must be prepared to change too.

• *When overdoing it becomes life-threatening, intervene with your partner.* Forgetfulness, chronic fatigue, grouchiness, mood swings and physical ailments related to stress are signs indicating that the body is burning out. Lovingly share your concern for your partner's health, and encourage him to consult a physician. Ask your partner to go with you for counseling, and if he refuses, get help for yourself through a support group or individual counseling.

Passing On The Pain

Psychologically unavailable to their kids, overdoers generally do not take an active role in their children's development. When they do, it is often to make sure that their children are mastering their perfectionist standards. The household is run like a work camp, and family members are often treated like employees on work detail. Expectations are so out of reach that children are doomed to fail. And when they ultimately do fail, they internalize it as poor self-esteem. They carry the same legacy many of their parents have: They feel incompetent and unworthy and that something is wrong with them for being unable to meet adult expectations.

At age 47, Vanessa still remembers her mother as a perfectionist housewife, impossible to please:

We used to have this joke around my house, "There's three ways to do things: the right way, the wrong way and Mother's way," and now I think that about myself. "There's three ways to do it: the right way, the wrong way and Vanessa's way." I lived in a house where you'd throw Kleenex in a wastebasket, and my mother would empty it three or four times a day.

As a child, when she did something wrong, her dad would get over it right away. But her mom gave her the cold shoulder for a long time until she proved she could be the perfect little girl. Today that perfect little girl is addicted to co-dependent relationships. She continues to get herself involved with men who emotionally reject her. She relives her relationship with her mother many times over by making herself a doormat for the men she dates so that they will love and approve of her. She attends Co-dependents Anonymous to help her learn to break her cycle of addictive relationships.

It is difficult for youngsters to live with a compulsive overdoer because there is no visible cause for the confusion, discontent and frustration that they experience. If Dad drank excessively, the child could point to the bottle. If Mom was strung out on pills, that might explain her behavior. But the Puritan work ethic prevents us from seeing our parents' work addiction is at fault. So many children of perfectionist overdoers logically conclude that there is something wrong with them. Because they cannot measure up to their parent's standards of perfection, they are not good enough.

We all want the best for our children, and most parents do their best to see that their kids get what they need. But unless the cycle of overdoing it is broken, parental perceptions of "the best" are distorted by their own sense of failure that is unwittingly passed on to their children in the form of harsh criticism, high standards, and perfectionism.

Breaking The Cycle

Parents can do a number of things to avoid leaving their offspring with a legacy of dysfunctional behaviors. First and foremost is to get help for themselves so that they can see how their overdoing it is influencing their children's development. Individual counseling or such 12-Step programs as Workaholics Anonymous,

Co-dependents Anonymous or Adult Children of Alcoholics can be helpful. Aside from personal recovery, the following guidelines can be practiced daily with your children:

1. Limit the amount of work you bring home in the evening and on weekends, and save some time for your youngsters. Plan special times together as a family (without television). Be emotionally as well as physically present for kids. Participate with them in fun activities and listen to what they have to say.
2. Focus on children's positive actions rather than harping on the negative.
3. Give children opportunities to play, relax and have fun with other youngsters their age rather than spending their time with adults in adult activities.
4. Love children unconditionally. Set reasonable limits on their behavior, but never withhold love as a punishment for children's mistakes.
5. Encourage them and enjoy their successes with them, but let them know that it is acceptable for them to fail and that they do not have to be perfect in everything all the time.
6. Be there for children after a big failure, wrongdoing or letdown. Help them understand and accept that failing is part of being human. Allow children to make mistakes, and help them to see their mistakes as learning experiences. Teach them that no one is perfect and that they do not have to be super-responsible.
7. Avoid hurrying children. Let them grow and develop at their own pace, according to their unique developmental timetable.
8. Encourage children to face challenges that match their developmental abilities, but help them learn not to bite off more than they can chew. Avoid unusually high expectations and burdening them with adultlike responsibilities, even when they appear eager to accept them.
9. Encourage children to balance their lives with work and play. Make special efforts to provide them with opportunities for a lot of playing. Play is the work of young ones and is at the very root of everything they become.

10. Let children know that it is okay for them to relax and do nothing. Some of our fondest memories are of our childhood play experiences. Reassure them that they do not always have to be producing a product to please someone else, but that it is acceptable to please themselves — and that can also include doing nothing.

11. Affirm children for who they are, not just for what they do. Provide unconditional support for them as individuals — not support for what they produce or accomplish. Let them know that you accept them, regardless of whether they succeed or fail. Hold them in esteem by letting them know they are special even when they are not producing a concrete object.

12. Have reasonable expectations based on what children are capable of performing at their age. Take into account their individual interests and personalities.

13. Let children have some daily flexible schedule at home with free time built in for choosing activities that match their interests. Teach them to be open to spontaneous and spur-of-the-moment activities. The best way to teach this, of course, is by example.

14. Protect children from the harsh pressures of the adult world without overprotecting them, and give them time to play, learn and make-believe.

15. Provide children with a peaceful and pleasant home atmosphere, shielded from excessive marital disputes and don't involve them in parental conflict.

16. Try not to pass needless stress and worry on to children. Give them opportunities to talk about their own worries and stresses. Adults can save theirs for the therapist's couch.

17. Guide children toward wise decision making by allowing them choices limited to match their emotional maturity.

18. Reward children for their triumphs and successes, no matter how small. Let them know you love them and are proud of them for who they are, not for what you want them to be. In other words, let them know that they already are somebody.

19. Refrain from making snap judgments and criticizing children sharply.

20. Always start the day on a positive note with calm routines and pleasant words.
21. Refrain from burdening kids with adult responsibilities of raising a sibling or keeping house.
22. Provide children with guidance when they must make significant and difficult decisions that would benefit from your input.
23. Avoid modeling your family after "Ozzie and Harriet" or "Donna Reed." These fantasy stories create more problems for children because they don't show that all healthy families have problems and conflicts that can be resolved through communication.

Widow Of A Compulsive Overdoer

For years Carla Wills-Brandon told people she was the widow of a compulsive overdoer. Though her husband, Michael, was alive, he was the phantom in her life. During those few times when he was at home, he was usually involved in some grand, overwhelming project around the house. One time she came home from the office, dead on her feet and in need of a long hot bath, to find that Michael had taken apart the microwave oven. There were wires of all colors everywhere. He had made such a mess that, after much arguing, Carla had to call in a specialist to put the oven back together again. The repair man, says Carla, was a good old Texas boy who looked Michael straight in the eye and said, "Son, you came real close not only to blowing yourself up, but half the neighborhood!" Carla shared the trials and tribulations with me of being what she calls the "widow of a compulsive overdoer:"

Michael and I tell people we decided to get married because he needed another dissertation project to work on. My husband is a psychologist, and for years he enabled my disease of chemical dependency by treating me as a home-improvement project. Because he refused for so long to admit defeat, his enabling behavior almost killed me.

When I finally reached sobriety or "thawed out" from all the drugs and booze I had ingested over the years, I looked forward to living life with my husband as his lover and companion. Unfortunately there was a catch. I wasn't the only addict in the family, and I was shocked to see just how addicted Michael was DOING! DOING! DOING! For the first few years of my own recovery, I constantly felt guilt and shame for not being able to keep up with him. Also, he wasn't too happy about how self-reliant I was becoming and would continue to DO for me under the guise that he could still do it better.

Since both of us were therapists, we decided to open up an office together. While I was seeing only five patients per day, my husband would load himself down with 10 to 12 people in need of help. He couldn't understand why I refused to increase my caseload, and would tell me I was not pulling my weight in the office. When I felt sick or was ill, I would stay at home and cancel my patients. This would infuriate him. He went to the office when he was sick and on several occasions became so ill he would end up on the bed, unable to lift his head.

Michael would really come unglued when I would take a day off from the office, or what I call a mental health day. During this time, periodically, I needed to take care of my emotional well-being with my own therapy or with time to myself. When I would do this, all hell would break loose. I would usually have to do it without telling him, and if he did find out, I would have to fight for my right to take care of myself.

When I would do this, Michael would shame me about how I was abandoning my patients and being irresponsible. As he would sit at his desk, making phone call after phone call, wolfing down his lunch of Dr. Pepper and peanuts, he would tell *me* I had problems. At one point in our marriage, he would race home from the office at lunch-time to work on home chores. With sweat running down his face, he would return to his desk, which was always piled high with more projects, for his afternoon patients.

During this time I felt nuts! From all of our friends I would hear, "Carla, you are so lucky to have a man like Michael! You should be grateful that he stuck by you through your alcoholism." Well, this just made me want to throw up! On the outside Michael looked like the all-time high achiever, plus he was being paid very well for all that he was doing professionally. At one time he was consulting three hospitals along with seeing an overwhelming number of patients. Along with this, he spent hours involved in court custody cases.

The problem with all of this overdoing for others was that there was no time left for me and our relationship. Everybody else got a piece of Michael except me. At night he would come home from the office, usually late for dinner, only to collapse on the couch and fall fast asleep. With this, I would either rage with anger or grieve with loneliness. If I felt rage, I would take my wooden baseball bat and beat the bed with all of my might while screaming at the top of my lungs in anger at *him*.

Though my yelling could have awakened the dead, Michael rarely heard me because he would be so drained from all of his activities. If I was in grief, I would sob by myself and wonder what it was I was doing wrong to cause him to be so tired all the time.

I thought if I were prettier or sexier, he would spend more time with me. His mistress was his work so I didn't receive a whole lot of support from my friends. They would say, "You should be grateful that he doesn't drink, screw around or beat you." With statements like this, I would feel more shame and ask, "What is wrong with me?"

One day he came home and informed me that he was tired and no longer wanted to work. At first I was overjoyed! I thought maybe, just maybe now he will pay some attention to our dying relationship. Well, there wasn't more time for intimacy and what Michael did do was go 180 degrees in the opposite direction. His physical appearance went down the tubes, and he quickly put on ten pounds. Along with this he let everything go, the yard, his cars, his office practice and his finances.

I thought I was living with a manic depressive. I couldn't believe what I was seeing. Suddenly I .elt really frightened and fearful for our economic security. As a result of this I began writing in order to create another source of income to provide me with a sense of financial security. Because of this and my own continued recovery, I became successful professionally and my own sense of self-worth began to increase.

One day it hit me that I had been enabling his compulsive over-doing by:

1. Trying to keep up with his pace and work schedule.
2. Believing his need to always be busy was somehow connected with my being defective.
3. And buying into society's myth that says living with a "do-aholic" isn't as bad as living with an alcoholic.

I decided I could no longer live the way I was living. I knew Michael's compulsive overdoing covered up a whole lot of unresolved pain about a number of issues and that as long as I continued to put up with his behavior he would never heal. At one time Michael's enabling behavior almost destroyed me, and I began to realize the tables had turned and that my enabling could kill him.

One Saturday I spent the afternoon sitting on the couch watching
Michael run. Before this, I had always been running with him, trying
to keep up so as not to be accused of being lazy. It was amazing to me
to just sit and watch him go. He was moving so quickly it took him
a while to notice I wasn't doing anything. When Michael finally did
notice I wasn't involved in the usual load of Saturday chores, he asked
me, "What are you doing?" I replied with, "It's Saturday and I'm
resting." He looked at me as though I had lost my mind and continued
doing whatever it was he was doing at a 100-mile-an-hour pace.

For that week I didn't make the bed, do the dishes or cook meals.
I took a day off and went fishing and started having lunch more
often with my friends. I spent more time writing, as I had grown to
really love writing and I saw even fewer patients in the office. One
day I left town while he was at work and went to visit a woman
friend of mine for a week. While away, I called him and said, "Michael, I love you but your compulsive overdoing is as destructive as
my alcoholism was. If I am to continue living with you, you must
agree to seek out help."

To make a long story short, Michael did agree to get some help, and
today he is recovering. He recognized that he was addicted to the
adrenaline rush of doing and made a decision to do whatever it took
to recover. Because I finally gave up control and admitted I was powerless, I was able to get out of his way and let him suffer the consequences of his destructive behaviors. Once I started taking care of
myself and not enabling Michael, he was able to see how his compulsive overdoing was destroying his life and hurting those around him.

Periodically Michael slips back into his old compulsive busy habits,
and I find myself enabling, but thanks to our recovery, the barrier of
compulsive overdoing that kept both of us from experiencing true
intimacy for so long, has lost its power.

Part of our recovery has been to set aside more time for our
relationship. Not only do we have a once-a-week date night, but we
also go on vacation several times a year. The first time we took a
vacation together in recovery, Michael could only be away from the
office for three days. We were on the coast, and as I lay on the beach
enjoying the water and sun, Michael was up at the hotel helping the
housekeeping staff move furniture. Today if we go to the beach for
a vacation, Michael is beside me holding my hand.

Your Self-Care Plan

Family members often become so obsessed with controlling the overdoer's compulsive behavior that their own lives crumble. It is important for family members to keep the focus on *themselves* and to keep *their* lives balanced while they let the overdoer attend to his or her own life. The following Healogram exercise can be used by overdoers, their partners or children to assess and achieve healthy balance.

By completing the Healograms on the next page, you can see how balanced your life is and identify areas you want to focus on. Start with "My Healogram As I Am Now" and consider how you distribute time and energy in your relationships, career, spiritual needs, self and play.

First, in the area in which you spend *most* of your time and energy, draw a vertical line, which will be the highest in the graph. Next, in the area in which you spend the *least* amount of time and energy, draw a vertical line that will be the shortest in the graph. Then fill in the other lines, which correspond to the proportionate amount of time you spend in the remaining three areas. Using the same directions, draw vertical lines for "My Healogram As I Would Like To Be."

The differences between the two Healograms will guide you to balance your life. There are no right or wrong answers. The usefulness of the Healograms is in how *you* see it. After completing the Healograms, respond to the following questions:

1. What have you learned about yourself?
2. What do you like about what you see?
3. What do you dislike about what you see?
4. What could you change?
5. Do you want to change?
6. How would you do that?
7. Will you do it?
8. When will you begin?

My Healogram As I Am Now

Relationships	Career	Spiritual Needs	Self	Play

My Healogram As I Would Like To Be

Relationships	Career	Spiritual Needs	Self	Play

8

Overdoing It In The Workplace

*Often persons who come from
dysfunctional families find organizations
repeating the same patterns they learned
in their families. Even though these
patterns feel familiar, they do
not feel healthy.*

— Anne Wilson Schaef and Diane Fassel
The Addictive Organization

Ellen's abusive work habits as district sales manager for a major computer sales corporation have made it so unbearable for her sales representatives that they have devised their own coping strategies to survive. At 47, Ellen arrives at work by 7:30 A.M. and doesn't get home until eight or nine o'clock. She generally works at home for another couple of hours before she goes to bed. Frustrated at her work abuse, Ellen's husband took a job traveling because his interests and needs were not being met in their relationship. Her obsession and constant driving within her profession left no time for family life, and her social life included only people within the company.

According to Alec, age 27, who works under Ellen, she will not leave the sales reps alone to do their jobs. Instead she is burning herself out trying to keep her hands in everything they do. She spends most of her time working their accounts rather than managing them. She cannot delegate and wait until a task is accomplished. She has to be intimately involved while the task is completed.

Alec observes that work is everything to Ellen. There is nothing else in her life. Her business associates have never known her to take a day off without leaving one of them an electronic message. Most of her employees are frustrated. They are constantly beaten up by

197

her to get things done in a timely manner. Alec complains that she's always breathing down his neck by telephone and electronic messages. She wants things to go her way. She's a perfectionist, afraid that nobody can do the job as well as she can. So she keeps her hands in everything.

Alec says the morale of the sales reps is rock bottom, and their spirits are shattered. They are either not accomplishing enough in a time frame to satisfy Ellen or they cannot do their work because she keeps throwing other ideas at them that they consider to be insignificant.

According to Alec, the staff's frustration levels rise and fall in response to Ellen's unpredictable behaviors. He describes some of her erratic moods and the effects those moods have on the sales force:

We're ending our year right now, and we're talking about splitting my territory and putting a new rep in the southern part of the state. In a four-day period, over a weekend, she changed her mind six times by electronic messages. She kept calling and saying here's the way we're going to do it. Then she'd call back and change. The sixth message said, 'I think what we're going to do is have you turn the files over to this person. Well, no. We'll talk about it on Monday.' The way I overcome that unpredictability is to give her the answer she wants to hear and then push on and do things the way I think they should be done. I'll say, 'Oh yes! Sure, sure! Great idea!'

A lot of times my agreeing with whatever she says satisfies her desire to stay in touch with whatever I'm doing. If there's something of value in what she says, I'll accept it. If not, I ignore it. Once the task is accomplished, there's no question about how it got accomplished. So I avoid a lot of conflict and frustration on my part by lying and pacifying her. I overcompensate for what she does or I ignore her phone calls for a couple of days and try to sidetrack her.

Some of my fellow workers try to respond to everything she wants, and they're getting as crazy as she is, just constantly working. You can be buried in the middle of two or three things and she starts this routine. I've seen people come into the office with bloodshot eyes, completely drained. They look as if they haven't slept in three or four days. It's really rough.

We always know the reaction we're going to get out of her. She's going to give the immediate response that pops in her head. It's sometimes Jekyll and Hyde because it's tough to read which way she'll go immediately. She's constantly flying off the handle and jumping down people's throats, venting frustrations of her own. If you're under the pile (that is, you've got too much to do and you're really suffering), she helps you build up a frustration level and get buried in your pile of work. Then, she will pounce on you too. When she notices we're covered up with things to do, she starts harping on what we're doing and picking on a selected victim. Everybody always knows when they get on her list. She starts looking over our shoulders. She sees us as getting buried and not responding like she would, then she jumps us. Rather than helping take the load off, she puts more stress on us.

Addictive Work Settings

The editor of a major publishing company offered me big bucks to sign a book contract because she said, "I know you're a workaholic like me and that you'll live up to your commitments and get the job done right and on time." A few years ago, I would have been complimented by her comment. But as a recovering work addict, I was horrified that she viewed my abusive work habits as beneficial rather than disadvantageous to her company.

Although corporate America traditionally has valued and perpetuated abusive work habits, the types of dysfunctional environments that it creates are rapidly coming under fire from critics. Anne Schaef and Diane Fassel reveal in their book *The Addictive Organization* how business and industry encourage the denial of compulsive overdoing and actually promote it because it appears to be productive. The authors suggest that American work organizations function as addicts by denying, covering up and rewarding dysfunctional behaviors among its employees. They show how dysfunctional managers and executives negatively impact the organizational system and the employees of that system. My interviews support their view that many employers are re-creating their dysfunctional family patterns in their work environments.

The following list shows the problems generated by overdoing it in the work place:

- Low morale
- Disharmony
- Interpersonal conflict
- Lowered productivity
- Absenteeism
- Tardiness

- Job insecurity
- Mistrust
- Lack of team cooperation
- Loss of creativity
- Stress and burnout

The Company Workhorse

Overdoers usually become highly successful in their chosen careers. But they pay a huge price for their overdeveloped sense of responsibility and accomplishment. Obsessed with the need to control people and things around them, they put their own feelings and needs on hold. This creates problems with being intimate and developing healthy interpersonal relationships.

Many jobs that require creative problem solving operate on the premise that two heads are better than one. Generally overdoers are not team players. Their need to control makes it difficult for them to solve problems cooperatively and to participate in give-and-take situations. They believe their approach and style are best, and they cannot entertain less perfect solutions. Spontaneity is diminished and creativity stifled when the narrow view of one addicted worker prevails.

The label "workhorse" refers to those who push themselves beyond human limitations. Pushing themselves is routine for workers who grew up in homes where normal was undefined.

Janet Woititz sampled 100 adult children of alcoholics and found that 87 percent had chosen stressful occupations. She concluded that adult children are drawn to stressful jobs without the tools to manage stress. Overwork and added stress help overdoers dilute their attention to personal needs. Overdoing is a part of their general pattern of overcompensating for poor self-worth from early dysfunctional upbringing. Overdoers can be difficult to work with because they create high stress situations.

Abusive workers show the side effects of irritability and impatience with co-workers. Flared tempers and angry outbursts are the norm. Disharmony prevails and group morale nosedives. As overdoers try to squeeze more work into less time, burnout occurs for them and those under their supervision.

A super-overdoer who supervises staff for a national broadcasting company told me that since he took his supervisory position he has fast-forwarded the pace of work. He pushes his staff in order to get everything out of them that he can. And he constantly monitors them for burnout. When the signs of stress appear, he orders them to slow down, go on a break or take a short vacation.

People who overdo it on hazardous jobs often place themselves and others in danger. Rushing a job that requires manual dexterity with tools, machinery or heavy equipment can cause physical injury as well as damaged goods. Other occupations such as airline pilots and brain surgeons — where patience, precision and clear thinking are paramount — do not lend themselves to the overdoer's style of being mentally preoccupied with the next thing to be done. When fatigue and stress escalate, the likelihood of accidents and errors also increases. Thus many compulsive overdoers are less efficient than co-workers who put in fewer hours planning and working toward a job goal. As they continue to overinvest in their jobs, stress and burnout grow and efficiency declines.

The Compulsive Overdoer As "Boss"

Many compulsive workers are rewarded for their attempts to change and control other people by being promoted into management positions. Their over-responsibility, poor communication skills, inability to express feelings and insensitivity to employees, however, usually make them ineffective managers. Organizational consultant Joan Kofodimos sees the emphasis on overdoing it to the exclusion of the executive's underdeveloped personal side as an imbalance that brings serious problems to the workplace:

> An executive who is unaware of her own emotional life is likely to be insensitive to the needs and feelings of co-workers. Thus lacking in compassion and empathy, she is unlikely to receive their whole-hearted support and commitment. If she is uncomfortable expressing feelings, she might fail to provide positive feedback, praise or appreciation. If she denies her vulnerabilities, she might not seek needed help or advice. If she is reluctant to own up to weakness, she might resist critical feedback. If she needs to be perfect and control every issue in her unit, she might be unable to delegate responsibility. All of these are side effects of an overwhelming drive for mastery which can compromise success and accomplishment.*

An employee criticized her boss when he asked her what she thought about his management skills.

> I went to him with something very crucial. He didn't really have time, but he worked me into his schedule. The whole time he talked to me he signed vouchers, answered the phone and hung it up again. Then, he said, "Yeah, yeah, tell me more." I felt like I never had his attention. He didn't listen to anything I said. I don't do that to people. I come around from my desk and sit in front of them and really listen to what they have to say.

---

*Reprinted from "Regaining Balance." *Executive Excellence*, by Joan Kofodimos. August 1990. Used with permission of the author.

Supervisors and managers who overdo it push their employees into abusive work patterns, even when it goes against the grain of the subordinates' natural pace. Margaret, a nurse practitioner, shook her head in disbelief as she told of the unreasonable demands that her supervisor makes on the staff. The supervisor instructed Margaret to be prepared for an 11:30 P.M. phone call from another nurse who works the same job on the second shift. The late shift nurse did not know how to use a particular machine, so Margaret would have to teach her by phone and miss her regular 10:00 P.M. bedtime. Margaret pointed out that she had put in a stressful full day, was not being paid for the requested late-night work and had to report back on duty at seven the next morning. "Don't you think that's an unreasonable request?" Margaret asked her supervisor three different times.

"No, I don't," replied her supervisor, a compulsive overdoer. "I don't think it's unreasonable at all."

Cleveland, who works for a major corporation, told me about his manager's abusive work habits, which included unreasonable demands and the inability to delegate:

> We had an opportunity to do a presentation for a quarter million dollar bid at an engineering school. I found out about the deal and went to my manager and told him we need to go for this and showed him my outline. He got on the phone and started calling the potential clients and got everything hyped up and essentially took over my job.
>
> He came back to us and said we were behind the eight ball here and that the other vendors were six to eight weeks ahead of us. He started saying we got to get this much done, and we've got to get it done this week. He started throwing together a time line which was completely unrealistic if we were going to do a good presentation. In an attempt to slow him down I told him to leave it alone and let me take it, and he agreed to do that.
>
> But as we started to develop the presentation, we started getting more messages like, "Have you thought of this?" "How's this going?" "Are you bringing other parties within and outside the company into the presentation?" He even called some outside sources and invited them to take part in the presentation, after I had already booked their competitors. He had to run the show which made us lose the whole deal!

When hiring personnel, some bosses clone their employees in the perfectionist images of themselves, as the interviewing practices of one employer illustrate:

> I dot every "i" and cross every "t." I try to head problems off at the pass by finding people like me to hire. When I'm interviewing, I pick up on people and say, "Hey, you're my kind of person." Until recently, I have not made any mistakes in picking out that trait in my personnel. Staff who were laid back or couldn't buy into the loyalty and hard work eventually left. I look for enthusiasm, loyalty, a sense of commitment and a desire to do the job and do it well.

The work-addicted boss is overcritical, overdemanding and intolerant of mistakes. Employees get very little positive feedback for their efforts, which rarely are good enough to match the boss's expectations. No matter how hard they try to please, nothing is ever good enough to satisfy the abusive worker's perfectionist standards. The overdoer's mood can swing from high to low in a workday or workweek. It can be formidable working for a supervisor, manager or foreman who experiences the adrenaline highs and irritable and restless withdrawals. Employees are never sure what to say or do. They waste enormous amounts of energy trying to second-guess their employers. They suffer tension, poor self-esteem and loss of control.

Managers who compulsively overdo it on the job carry their family dysfunction into the workplace and re-create it in their relationships with employees, who become in effect their family. In that "family" the bosses function as "parents" and the subordinates as "children." The dynamics, then, in compulsive work families are similar to those that are created in true alcoholic households. Betrayal, deception, lies and mixed messages are some of the interactions that occur between overly-responsible employers and their employees.

As the moods of the boss swing from high to low, employees try to appease him or her by swinging back and forth as well. Overdoing managers are notorious for making and breaking promises because unrealistic time frames cannot be achieved. So a new plan is substituted. The climate is unpredictable and inconsistent, and morale is low, just like that in the alcoholic home.

Apprehension, fear and insecurity are normal reactions for employees in unpredictable job positions. Workers become frustrated and exhausted trying to keep up with their boss.

Having an overdoer for an employer for a prolonged period of time can lead to severe psychological damage. Emotionally battered and bruised, many workers limp through their careers. Poor self-esteem, lack of control over their careers, poor coping skills and problems in interpersonal relationships result when employees attempt to meet dysfunctional demands from the powers that be. Energy that workers ordinarily put into quality production instead goes to covering tracks, lying and engaging in deceptive practices. Ellen's case illustrates how this negative cycle works.

Dysfunctional Work Roles

The roles subordinates of tyrannical managers take to survive are identical to the ones children acquire in addicted families. The interworkings of the company department are dependent on each employee functioning as an interdependent part of the overall system. As the department works together to run smoothly, any change in one part will result in automatic changes in other parts. The department will always try to keep itself on an even keel. As the head of the department gets out of kilter with overdoing it, all other members are thrown off balance and shift their behaviors to survive and to accommodate the unbalance. As Ellen's managerial style became more dysfunctional, for example, Alec and his co-workers shifted from their ordinary way of response to such dysfunctional behaviors as deceptions and lies. Thus, many of the same interactive patterns of addicted families have been re-created in the workplace.

As overdoing patterns progress, the whole department becomes sicker too. Everything revolves around the overdoing boss, whose behavior dictates how subordinates interact inside and outside the work force. Each worker adapts to the boss's behavior by developing behaviors that cause the least amount of personal stress. Workers adapt roles of superiority (Company Hero), aggression (Company Rebel), withdrawal (Lost Worker) and wit (Company Clown). These roles parallel those that Sharon Wegscheider-Cruse identified among children in dysfunctional families, namely, the family hero, scapegoat, lost child and mascot.

The organization itself is the *chief enabler* because it stresses continued productivity at any cost. As the boss's work habits become progressively more abusive, the higher-ups toss accolades that encourage him or her to keep up the good work.

One worker in the department, usually with the most seniority, often emerges as the *company hero*. This role brings harmony and stability to the company. Heroes try to protect colleagues from the boss's abusive managerial style. They may jump in to help out a co-worker who is overloaded, organize a group to rebut unrealistic deadlines or even stand up against the boss to express the frustrations of the work family. Lech Walesa, organizer of Solidarity, is a work hero for millions of people in Poland. Cesar Chavez fills that role for the United Farm Workers of America.

Some employees adapt the role of *company rebel* to cope with the unreasonable job demands. Company rebels are disruptive. They never seem to do anything right. Rather than follow company policy, they take shortcuts, undermine the boss's authority or engage in bitter squabbles with employers and co-workers. Rebels internalize frustrations by getting into trouble on the job. They may take money from the business, telling themselves, "This company doesn't care about us anyway" or "They owe me a few extra dollars with all I've done for them and the low salary they pay me." Rebels may also act out their frustrations by physically assaulting or verbally abusing the boss or co-workers. They may even throw a fit and destroy company property.

A college professor aggressively tried to undermine the chair of his department in almost every academic policy that was put forward. The verbally abusive faculty member even went so far as to call a collegewide meeting of faculty to protest, point by point, the items on the chair's agenda. The professor's unruly and unprofessional behavior eventually estranged colleagues, who did not wish to be associated with his aggressive style. Of course, rebels do not last long. Typically they are fired or referred for counseling or both.

A few employees become *lost workers* and turn their feelings inward. They are neither troublemakers nor leaders. They adapt to the departmental dysfunction by following directions and accepting whatever comes their way, no matter how inconsistent or contradictory. They clam up and withdraw from co-workers, remain quietly in the background and try to behave as they are expected. They adjust because they do not make an emotional investment in their jobs. If they are not emotionally involved, then the chaos and job stress don't affect them as badly. At their first opportunity they abandon ship by finding employment elsewhere, perhaps never voicing their frustration and dissatisfaction.

The fourth role in the company is that of *company clown*. Company clowns divert their anguish and frustration with humor and fun. They are always full of wisecracks and jokes to entertain co-workers. They make light of the boss's demands and try to keep the tone upbeat, everybody happy and nothing too serious. Although they are the life of the party, underneath their jovial nature, clowns have difficulty handling stress. They are sad, afraid, insecure and alone. Their role as stand-up comic keeps them out of serious work commitments, and employers might wonder if they take their work seriously enough to make important decisions or to handle responsibilities.

The four roles of superiority (Company Hero), aggression (Company Rebel), withdrawal (Lost Worker) and wit (Company Clown) are workers' responses to a dysfunctional work system. Company heads who have internalized dysfunctional behaviors from their families, transfer them into the workplace and re-create them in a new and dysfunctional departmental system that filters down to everyone in the organization. Thus, the dysfunction is perpetuated and spreads throughout the entire business organization.

Overdoing It And Counterproductivity

Overdoing it is prized by corporate America despite the fact that, when converted to dollars and cents, it is clearly counterproductive. Big business promotes all-or-nothing thinking, which I discussed in Chapter 2, by suggesting that you give it all you got or you're out. There is no in-between. But such abusive work practices actually circumvent economic growth and prosperity. The greatest cost factors are absenteeism, tardiness and low morale because of stress and burnout. One overdoer put it this way:

Work reinforces our addictions. We are rewarded for killing ourselves. My boss has too much to do. He has more to do than it is possible for him to do. So do I. I work two jobs. They want your body and soul. When everybody is carrying that much of a burden, managementwise, you begin to hear people saying a lot of negatives. As that happens, it starts eroding at the base of the company of your middle management. Then, if middle management is negative, it filters on down to the work force, and you lose the whole thing.

Stress and burnout lead to health problems, which in turn lead to absenteeism, tardiness and reduced productivity. Ultimately businesses lose money because of abusive work habits. Overdoers have poor nutrition since they eat on the run and do not always get proper exercise because it interferes with work. Work productivity is also negatively affected when overdoers suffer from depression, which lowers motivation and increases work absences. High blood pressure, heart disease, abdominal problems and a host of other illnesses also cost businesses money. Heart disease alone, which is linked to job stress, is responsible for an annual loss of 135 million workdays.

Premature deaths from heart disease and suicides — often stemming from problems within the organization — contribute to a tragic loss of human potential. Overall estimates reveal that problems caused by stress and burnout cost the nation's employers $150 billion a year.

Removing Abusive Work Practices In The Workplace

In the past the corporate world believed that ranks of compulsive overworking employees would guarantee greater production. But in truth corporations achieve more creative results and higher revenues from a more balanced work force. Salespersons who have achieved balance in their lives, for example, are more apt to attract potential clients than obsessed, high-pressured reps who are more likely to turn clients off and drive them away.

How can corporate America eliminate the problems of overdoing it and benefit with increased dollars and cents? That question is being asked more and more today. Many businesses are refusing to hire known compulsive overworkers. Finding cost-effective ways to balance work and other responsibilities is now a major concern for employers in the United States. Employee assistance programs have assumed responsibility for helping with family-related problems that result from stress on the job. And more bosses are telling employees, directly or indirectly, to slow down.

Ellen's boss rejected a vacation card she had submitted because she had left him electronic messages that same day. He told her, "You were not on vacation because you sent me a message, so take another day of vacation. Get away from the office and forget about work for a while."

The following suggestions are designed to help corporate America eliminate abusive work practices and reap quality production and financial benefits:

Raise Employer Awareness

The first and most critical step in removing abusive work practices is raising executive awareness. As Joan Kofodimos suggests, employers often have a vested interest in keeping the issue off the organization's agenda: "Some organizations are unwilling to address the issue of work-family balance because decision makers are often themselves using work to escape failure in their personal lives."* Trained consultants can work closely with organizational personnel to brief them on the problems that workers transfer from home into their jobs. The dangers of dysfunctional work patterns and how to spot their symptoms in themselves and employees can also be addressed. A plan of action for interrupting these destructive patterns and improving the work climate can be adapted to the company's unique needs.

Conduct In-Service Workshops
For Employee Assistance Program Personnel

More assertive efforts by Employee Assistance Programs (EAP) to identify and discuss dysfunctional work patterns will give employees seeking help a bona fide support system. These programs can be instrumental in drawing attention to and promoting support for those who need it.

Executives Out of Balance: Integrating Successful Careers and Fulfilling Personal Lives (San Francisco, CA: Jossey-Bass, 1993).

Raise Employee Awareness

Establish addiction awareness days for employees with posters and special seminars featuring the many types of addictions that exist in families and in the work force. Present the information through outside speakers so that all workers learn about the effects of addictions and dysfunctional families in a nonthreatening way. Awareness days can serve as a springboard for establishing special groups for compulsive overdoers.

Encourage Support Group Meetings

Such 12-Step groups as Workaholics Anonymous can meet before or after work or during lunch in designated places at the work site. It is important that corporate America see the denial in recommendations from business consultants who eschew the need for a group founded on the principles of Alcoholics Anonymous. By meeting together and talking about their problems, compulsive overdoers are less isolated, less ashamed and have a rich support system to draw upon in the job setting. With minimum effort, healthier work environments can be provided for millions of workers.

Disseminate Information To Employees

Companies can, through avenues already available in the organization, offer aerobics classes, meditation workshops, stress-reduction classes and exercise programs. These can raise employee awareness of the signs of stress and burnout and how to combat them. Companies can present special seminars on overdoing it and balance, how to recognize warning signs and how to interrupt them before they take their toll. Community speakers can be brought in to talk about the usefulness of 12-Step programs and where they are located in the community. Company bulletin boards, newsletters and other publications are valuable for disseminating information on these topics.

Start A Lending Library

A corner of a waiting area, health station, lounge or other underused area can house a lending library. Stock it with pamphlets, books, newsletters and magazines dealing with overdoing it, healthy work patterns, work and personal balance, and stress and burnout. Materials can be catalogued and checked out on a regular basis, using an honor system. Reading these materials promotes knowledge, changes attitudes and reduces feelings of isolation.

Sponsor Company Celebrations

Work does not have to be serious all the time. The company that plays together stays together. Fun and light-heartedness relieve stress and make the work environment more enjoyable. Social times also unify employees and help them to function more cohesively. Company picnics, reunions, retirement parties, holiday office parties and special birthday parties for co-workers are just a few examples of how business can blend work with play. Downplay our society's emphasis on alcohol by serving nonalcoholic beverages.

Explore New Ways To Balance Work With Other Areas Of Life

Establish hiring practices that bring balanced employees on board who can build a work climate of security, satisfaction, creativity and productivity. Restructure the job responsibilities of employees so that they are encouraged to spend time in personal, home and social commitments. Some possibilities include:

1. *Paternity leave,* which gives fathers opportunities to participate in childbirth and child rearing.
2. *Flextime,* which allows workers to complete a fixed number of hours per week, geared to their personal lives.
3. *Job sharing,* which involves two people sharing one full-time job by arranging their work duties and schedules to meet employer needs.
4. *Flexplace,* which enables workers to perform their work duties at home and is likely to become increasingly popular as more computer links are made between office and home.

The Values-Behavior Discrepancy*

STEP ONE: Assign percentages according to the *importance* of each of the following areas in your life (they will total 100%):

Work	_____
Family	_____
Leisure	_____
Community	_____
Religion	_____
TOTAL	100%

STEP TWO: Assign percentages according to the amount of *time and energy* you devote to each of the following areas of your life (they will total 100%):

Work	_____
Family	_____
Leisure	_____
Community	_____
Religion	_____
TOTAL	100%

Based on these two sets of scores, do you see a discrepancy between what you said was important in your life and how you actually spend your time? Are your behaviors consistent with your values? Or does work get the lion's share of your time and energy? What goals can you set to bring your values and behaviors in line?

---

*Reprinted from *Executives Out of Balance: Integrating and Addressing the Work-Personal Life Imbalance.* Copyright 1993, by Joan A. Kofodimos. Used with permission.

The Living-In-The-Now Technique

The living-in-the-now technique can help you bring your personal side into balance within the impersonal workplace. It can show you another world that has always been open to you but that you normally do not recognize because of the organization's de-emphasis on personal development. It can help you become more sensitive to the needs and feelings of co-workers and be more supportive and positive in your working interactions.

The next time you go to your workplace (or its equivalent), pretend you have entered it for the first time. Look at the people and things around you as if you were seeing and appreciating them for the first time. Notice the entranceway, the architecture of the outside and inside of the building and the people at their workstations. What's in the hallways and hanging on the walls? Notice the textures and colors of the wall, ceiling and floor. Smell the flowers on someone's desk. Look at how your colleagues are dressed and the colors of their clothing. See who conforms and who marches to the beat of their own drum. Pay attention to the sounds you hear. Notice the smells in the air.

Be mindful of your co-workers' faces. Do they look happy or sad? Ready to brace the day or wishing they were back home in bed? Are they smiling or frowning? Who has wrinkles and worry lines, and whose face is stress free? Do people in this work environment touch or keep their distance? Do they affirm one another or put each other down with sarcasm and cutting remarks? Are they pulling together as a team or working against one another and coming apart at the seams? Pay close attention to as many sights, sounds, smells, tastes and textures as you can.

Look in people's eyes, behind their facial expressions and into their hearts, where their true humanity resides. What do you see? What do you feel? What unseen baggage are your colleagues carrying with them into the workplace? How can you set the excess baggage aside and experience the true human being that lies beneath the surface? As you experience your workplace, you discover that the little things that you haven't noticed before are actually the most important things of all.

After you have finished this process, write your thoughts and feelings in your journal.

9

Facing Yourself: Doing Less And Being More

*We're so engaged in doing
things to achieve purposes of outer
value but the inner value, the rapture
that is associated with being alive,
is what it's all about.*

— Joseph Campbell

Martha is a 38-year-old trainer for a major computer corporation:

I've grown up in the culture of my company. I've been there for six years and it's always been as any high-tech company. It starts quickly, the technology is there and it grows and grows. There are many high-energy people, and it's a young company in years and personnel. There are a lot of creative people, a lot of competition and many rewards from the corporation — nice recognition, bonuses and salaries.

One of the things we are told up front during the interview process is that this is not a 40-hour-week job and that more is expected. If you have that drive and desire, you'll succeed.

Five o'clock means nothing in my office. Everybody stays and keeps working. People know what the unwritten rules are. Everybody has so much to do because there are several projects going on at one time. We're spread very thin. You're not forced to stay there. It's just that to do the job you have to stay late. We do the jobs of many people and there are a lot of deadlines. If I have to teach a class the next day and I still have deadlines, I have to stay. Some people in similar positions say, "What the hell," and they go home. But they don't last long. The nature of the job requires that to do a good job you have to put in more hours than the usual nine to five. The whole industry is that way.

There is so much to keep up with that it's very frustrating. Sometimes I feel like I don't know enough to do my job because there's so much information that keeps me on my toes. I always fear that somebody else knows more than I do, and I feel depressed or guilty because I don't know as much as someone I work with or someone in one of my classes. As a trainer I have to be aware of changing trends in the market because it's a high-technology industry. Some software programs that are really hot at one point might just be a blank disc or have a newer version to replace it a year later.

I get in the office about nine and stay until six or seven. I rarely go out because it disturbs my day if I have to go out, even for lunch. When I do, it adds too much stress fighting lunch crowds and traffic. I usually eat at my desk and try and get some stuff done. I also do things while I'm on the telephone with business associates, like writing memos on the computer, filing something or reading.

My job has to do with patience because I'm a teacher and trainer, and I have to have that attitude when I'm doing my job in front of the classroom. But with peers or other people I work with, sometimes I'm not very patient. The area I'm most impatient with is travel-related services. Because I travel a lot, I'm easily irritated with bad service: restaurants, hotels and airports.

The fact that I get upset when I'm not in control goes back to not trusting other people to do things for me. I also don't like people to make decisions for me. I'm a real snob about my company and my position there. I know what I need to be concerned with and what I don't. If I'm in a situation where I feel out of control, such as substituting for someone on vacation, I have a hard time with my self-image. I feel very intimidated.

When I first started this job, I overcommitted myself because I wanted to make sure that I cooperated with the efforts of sales marketing and learned a lesson from that. Now I can commit to more because I can put things together faster. When

I overcommit, I end up working long hours and weekends to make sure it's the way I want it to be. I would be very meticulous about it.

Sometimes I get real high at work when I get recognition. It means a lot because I know I've done a good job. If I have done a class and it goes like clockwork, everything was perfect and the evaluations were great, I feel high from that — very content, very excited and very happy. When you're in front of the group, it's like acting or performing. You get an adrenaline charge and your heart pounds because you are entertaining or teaching, and you're the person everyone is focused on. It is a physiological experience.

It's essential for me to see the results of what I do in some way. It's hard to quantitatively prove, but if I see a light bulb go off in somebody's eyes, or if someone says that he really learned a lot from one of my classes, it gives me a sense that I've done my job well.

If I can influence people and change their minds, it makes me feel good. That's really what my job is: to sell my company, our products and our services. Money and recognition are the best ways to motivate people. I have received a lot of recognition on the job, which is important to me.

It's difficult for me to go out and put myself into positions to meet people. Work has always been an easy excuse. I met my current boyfriend at work. He's somebody who understands what I go through at work, and what the stresses and expectations are. His understanding makes our relationship easier because we both travel a lot. On the other hand, there's another aspect of work orientation; often we talk about work and end up squabbling about it.

In six years I've had five jobs with the company. Hiring is done within instead of from the outside. I've been in my current job for two years, and I'm starting to feel the pressure from others around me who are getting into new positions. People are probably thinking, "Why are you still doing this? Isn't it time for you to move on?"

It's very difficult for me to start projects. When I do get started, I'm okay. Although, I have a hard time making decisions about how to execute the job. If I'm under pressure, there's no time to think about it. That's the way it is at my company. Orders from corporate may say, "You have to do this task immediately," or "This procedure has been changed and you have to do it the new way."

I don't have any hobbies because I don't have much free time. I've gained 35 pounds since last year. Some of it has to do with personal stress in my life but mostly because of my work and travel schedule. When I travel, I overeat because I may be stressed out about training in a strange place. When the training session is over, I eat because it's a reward. I've done a good job, and I can relax now. In the six years I've worked for this company I have gained and lost close to 100 pounds. I must begin to plan time in my work calender to do healthy things.

Breaking Our Patterns Of Overdoing It

Tears streamed down my cheeks. Emotionally exhausted and slumped in my seat, all I could do when the flight attendant asked me if I wanted something to eat was wave her away with my hand. I had lost so much weight I looked like a refugee from Dachau. During the takeoff, I didn't care if the plane crashed. Nothing mattered. I was on my way for a sunny week in Jamaica to escape the pain of breaking up a 14-year relationship. My life was crumbling under my feet, and there was nothing I could do about it. I felt like half a person. I didn't care if I lived or died. That was the spring of 1983.

I didn't know it at the time, but I was living out the critical thinking patterns that I had learned growing up in my family. A few years later I would learn that these patterns had been in my family for three generations.

My grandmother was a compulsive overeater who died from a stroke attributed to her obesity. Her son, my father, was an alcoholic who died from cirrhosis of the liver. I swore I would never be like my "old man." I lived my first 30 years priding myself on the fact that I had "licked" the family disease because I had neither chemical nor food addictions. What I wouldn't discover until midlife was that my family's faulty thinking had been passed down to me and had burrowed itself into the very core of my soul. My general outlook on life was polluted, and my relationships eventually became contaminated. I saw myself as a victim of a bad life and a bad relationship.

"Why do all these horrible things keep happening to me?" I whimpered. "Maybe a trip to the Caribbean will ease the heartache."

All I could think about was how to get even with the third person who came between me and my beloved. I carried the hate and resentment as if they were excess luggage. I was so consumed with rage I lay awake until three or four in the morning, plotting and avenging my damaged emotions. Unknowingly all these negative obsessions hurt no one but myself.

My faulty thinking caused me to try everything to cope with my pain, except the things that could help me. I clung to my resentments, saw only misery and despair, blamed everybody else for my hardships and the breakup of my relationship and tried a change of scene to escape my pain. It never occurred to me that there was anything more I could do. My only option, as I saw it, was to react to life, rather than take action. In so doing I disempowered myself by playing the victim. I became cynical, negative and pessimistic — all of which ricocheted, slapped me in the face and multiplied my misery and despair.

Through meditation and affirmations, I was able to let go of my anger and resentment as I lay on the Jamaica beach. I started to notice changes in my life. The nightmares subsided. I felt an inner calm that I had never experienced before, and I slept like a baby for the first time in weeks. I realized that there was something I could do to change my life. I realized that no matter how dismal things appear to be I don't have to be a victim. I learned that I cannot control everything that happens around me, but I can always take charge of what I think, feel and do. This same awareness has helped me get in touch with my overdoing it, to slow down and to take better care of myself because I know I deserve it.

Everyone wants to live a happy life. But why are so many of us miserable so much of the time, constantly searching for serenity and calm with little success? Because we're looking in the wrong place.

An ancient tale about Nasrudin, who lost the key to his house on the way home one night, illustrates this point beautifully.

Nasrudin was down on all fours under the street lamp searching frantically for his key when a stranger came by and asked him what he was looking for. Nasrudin told him he had lost the key to his house. So the stranger, being a kind man, got down on his hands and knees and helped look for it. After hours of searching, the stranger asked, "Are you sure you dropped the key in this spot?" Nasrudin said, "Oh no! I dropped it way over there in that dark alley." Frustrated and angry, the stranger lost his temper, "Then why are you looking for it here?" Nasrudin replied, "Because the light's better here under the street lamp."

Those of us who overdo it are like Nasrudin. Our supercharged lives are stuck in fast forward and focused on the external world. We do not have an internal life. Overdoing it keeps us disconnected from ourselves, subtracts from our human value and prevents us from knowing who we are. We are so defined by what we do we don't know who we are on the inside. The only way out of this dilemma is to redefine ourselves from within.

If unhappiness and discontent are created on the inside, doesn't it make sense that to change our lives we must start there? As we learn to refrain from overdoing it we focus on an *inner* life, not an *outer* life. Wayne Dyer in his book *You'll See It When You Believe It* puts it this way:

> We live inside, we think inside, our humanity resides within, yet we spend time ceaselessly looking outside of ourselves for the answers because we fail to illuminate the inside with our thoughts. We resist the principle that thought is everything we are because it seems easier to look outside.

Once Nasrudin looks in the alley, he will illuminate his life and find his key. Once we look within ourselves, we achieve illumination and discover how to break our patterns of overdoing it.

Twenty-two-year-old Sheila worked for a computer company in New York City. She was bored and weary of the grind of morning rush hours, daily routines and afternoon traffic jams. She had few friends and was generally unhappy with her life. Finally, with her mother's encouragement, Sheila decided to go to California to "find herself." After a few months she decided that Los Angeles "was not what it is cracked up to be" so she moved to Seattle.

Unfortunately moving across the country won't help us find ourselves. We carry our old habits like luggage wherever we go. If we wake up feeling positive and optimistic in Detroit, we wake up feeling positive and optimistic in the Mediterranean. If we wake up anxious and pessimistic in Buffalo, we wake up anxious and pessimistic in the South Pacific.

Those of us who feel incomplete and unfinished often look outside to fill the void. We stuff our lives with projects, computer printouts, deadlines, unhealthy relationships and material possessions. We become addicted to acquiring power and get consumed with making it to the top. We aim for worldly achievements, approval and financial rewards. We become enslaved by greed, competition and material gain as we try to heal our past insecurities and feelings of inadequacy.

We look in the wrong place when we constantly *do* in order to *be*. We are often so busy "getting there," we forget we are already "there" and that there is nowhere else to go. All we really have is ourselves, and discovering the treasure of self is the key. All we need do is look within. It is this inner transformation that improves the quality of our lives.

Overdoing it keeps us stuck in the external world and in the cycle of never feeling good enough. Replacing constant busyness with a rich spiritual life can heal busy habits. Being puts us in touch with our inner world and takes us out of the future and puts us into the present. We discover how to *be* by living in the now and looking within and connecting with our own inner selves. Being allows us to accept and love ourselves unconditionally, *exactly* as we are. Once we face, accept and love ourselves, we no longer have to overdo to feel better about ourselves.

Healing from overdoing it comes from realizing that we cannot control anyone or anything but ourselves and that we can be responsible only for ourselves.

Only through interior change will you find what you have been looking for. It is not out there; it is inside of you. Everything comes from the way you think about yourself. If you want to change your life, change the way you think about yourself first. Everything else follows.

Inner healing occurs only through unconditional love. When you treat yourself as a worthy, loving and competent human being, others begin to treat you that way and the world begins to operate that way for you. Harmony in the world begins with harmony within yourself. You will allow yourself to be led from within once you realize you are your own best guru. That's why "guru" is spelled, "Gee-You-Are-You."

Self-Nurturance

When we put everyone's needs before our own, our needs get pushed to the back burner. Sometimes we resent not having time for ourselves. Self-nurturance is one of the most important qualities we can develop. It has helped me love myself unconditionally, to treat myself with kindness and caring as I would anyone I care about. It has allowed me to approach life with more calm, hope and optimism.

No one can give us free time but ourselves. During quiet, reflective moments we can gain clarity and receive answers to life's challenging problems. Self-nurturance can include listening to soft music, walking barefoot in a summer rainstorm, reading inspirational material, sitting by the ocean watching the waves, meditating in a quiet place or doing something we enjoy that we haven't done in a long time.

The answers within us always come when we put ourselves under the proper conditions. Meditation, prayer, contemplation and mental relaxation all help us receive the answers we need. These activities help us connect with our intuitive parts that guide us from the heart instead of the head — that show us how to *be* instead of *do*. Relying on this "inner knowing" is just as important as using common sense. It's okay to listen to our gut when it says stop, take care or slow down. As we eliminate overdoing it from our lives, we learn to listen with our hearts instead of our heads because this is how the intuitive self speaks to us and guides us.

When we reserve special time for self-nurturance, we send ourselves the message that we are important and worth our own care and attention. We create this time for ourselves by getting up 15 minutes earlier, going to bed 15 minutes later or taking 15 minutes at lunchtime. We can always find time for ourselves if we really want it.

The first rule of thumb is to provide ourselves with a mental sanctuary where thoughts and items of doing are not present. We can create this inner place of calm, harmony and contentment anywhere and anytime. There is a power within us that brings peace, emotional and physical healing and serenity. With the help of this power, we can create the best life that we can envision. This power governs the universe and makes trees grow and flowers bloom. With a power this strong we can create the best life possible. We can always go to this inner sanctuary to become refreshed, relaxed and recharged.

How do you get to this sanctuary? Find a quiet place to sit, cross-legged or in a chair for about 15 minutes. Close your eyes and focus on your breathing. Take a few deep breaths in through your nose and out through your mouth. Let your body relax. Let go of any thoughts that interfere with this process. Feel all the tension in your body slowly drift down your arms and out through your hands and fingertips. Feel all the tension move down your spine, down your legs and out through your feet and toes.

Let your mind rest and your heart be your guide. Your sanctuary can be anywhere and contain anything your heart desires to bring you peace and serenity. As you begin to feel relaxed, create in your mind this safe haven. It can be a void of warm darkness or one of your favorite places at the seashore or in the mountains. Or it can be a place of your own creation where you've never been before. See this place in detail in your mind and create item-by-item all the things around you that will make this *your* sanctuary. This is a place you can return to anytime you choose. After you have a clear vision of your sanctuary, spend some time there. Before opening your eyes, make a mental note of it so that you can return to it for as often and as long as you like.

The Value Of Meditation

The purpose of meditation is to quiet the mind so that we can hear what is already there. It helps us look within, understand ourselves and establish inner harmony and balance. Scientific research has shown that when we engage in visualizations and meditations, our heart rate and brain wave patterns slow down. Meditation has a positive effect on the immune system so that certain life-sustaining hormones are secreted. Scientists have discovered that adults who meditate each day actually live longer than adults who do not. In other words, the scientific world now appreciates the value of going within and connecting with the energy inside of ourselves.

The use of meditations and visualizations is a far more constructive way to achieve our goals than to worry about "what if," to try to control situations or to get upset and angry when things don't work out to suit us.

Guided visualizations give us a beginning structure for meditation. We receive step-by-step instruction on what to visualize. Guided visualizations are especially good for those who are still developing their ability to image. Practice is the key to successful visualization. The more you practice, the sharper and more powerful your visualization will become.

Some beginners are afraid to go within. They are afraid of their feelings and of facing emotions that are stored there. They are afraid that if they dredge up old feelings, they will open a floodgate of tears that, once started, they will not be able to stop.

A woman in one of my seminars in Texas sat in the front row during a guided visualization that I conducted. She wrote frantically, filling each page with words (she was overdoing it) the entire time that the other participants experienced an inner journey. Later she apologized and said that she was afraid of what would happen if she took part. Her note-taking was simply a way of blocking any emotions from surfacing. A therapeutic interpretation would say she was dissociating by compulsive doing to avoid facing her feelings.

Going within to face our hurt and pain is the only way we will ever heal. As long as we flee from our inner feelings, we can never resolve them. There is nothing within us that can harm us. In fact, the inner self is the part that protects and nurtures us from the outer world. It is the safest haven we can ever find. Once we confront our deepest fears and experience them fully, they lose their power to dominate our thoughts. We can only heal.

Inner Self Meditation

The following meditation can help you connect with your inner self, the seat of all the answers to your problems. Get comfortable in a relaxed position and in a quiet place where you can put yourself fully into this journey. You may want to tape this meditation, pausing where appropriate, with soft music, and play it back, or have a friend guide you through. I recommend Pachelbel's Canon (extended version) on the tape, "Timeless Motion" by Daniel Kobialka.

Focus on your breathing. Take a few deep breaths. Let it all go. Get connected with your breathing. Breathe in through the nose and out through the mouth, in through the nose and out through the mouth.

Feel the seat underneath you, feel the clothes on your body. Hear sounds around you. Let go of thoughts about what happened at work or at home today. Forget about what you have to do later today or tomorrow. This is a time for you.

As the thoughts race through your brain, don't resist them. Don't try to stop them. Just let them go. Let the thoughts pass through your mind. Just acknowledge them and let them pass on by. Continue to be aware of your breathing. Relax.

Now go deep within yourself. Imagine yourself floating through the air. You're going on an inner journey, and you can take someone with you, someone you are very close to: a child, a parent, a companion, friend or co-worker. It can be someone you see every day. Or it can be someone you haven't seen in a long, long time, perhaps someone you thought you'd never see again. You can take anyone you wish, but only one.

Now, imagine that you're floating with your companion through the air. You're floating in the clouds. You're as light as the clouds. Look around you. What do you see? Look below. What's there? Look beside you. Who's floating with you? Look at your companion. How does it feel to have this person with you? Now look above you. What do you see? What's in front of you? Imagine the wonder of it all in your mind's eye.

Pause for a while on a nearby cloud. Standing there, look in the eyes of the person with you. This person cannot go with you any farther. Say good-bye to your companion in any way you choose. You will make the rest of the journey on your own. Now say good-bye and let that person go.

Turn away and continue floating. Look back and see the companion you left waving in the distance as you float away. You see that person getting smaller and smaller. How does it feel to say good-bye to that person? How does it feel to be alone? Take one last look, and now that person becomes a dot and disappears as the clouds surround you. Continue floating.

Now let go of all your worldly thoughts and possessions and worries and relationships. This journey is for you alone. Let go of problems in your relationships, your latest work project, your most obsessive worry that you're trying to solve in your life. Let it all go. Feel yourself becoming lighter as you give up these burdens.

Your heavy load is gone, and you feel peace and serenity. Imagine that you feel so light as you leave the cloud that you're floating again. This time you're floating higher and lighter than before. Your worries are gone. You're at peace. Experience you without those extra burdens. Continue floating and feel free of the heavy load.

You've left the ones you love behind and you've left your problems behind and you're floating through the clouds. How does it feel? How does it feel to be alone without the ones you love and the things that keep you busy or that bog you down? Experience that feeling.

Now in the distance you see a huge altar, a beautiful altar adorned with your favorite colors and precious gems. As you near it, stop. This is your altar. Add anything you want to it. In the center of that altar is a huge life-sized mirror. This magical mirror will enable you to see your inner self. Not the physical you, but the inner you. That part of you that you've never seen before.

Stand in front of the mirror and see the real you for the first time. This is your inner self. Picture your inner self. What does it look like? Who are you really? Is it a small child? Is it a figure in a white robe? Is it a beam of light? Is it an exact replica of you? Or is it a shadowy figure? Really look hard and see it in your mind's eye. Does this self look ashamed, afraid, hurt? Does it have emotional wounds? Is it in pain, sad or angry? Does it have scars from years of mistreatment? Is it crouching in fear? Or is it standing proudly erect?

This is the part of yourself you have lost touch with because of the details of your outer life. This is the self that begged for attention and care when you had more important things to do. This is the self you've called worthless and inadequate time and time again, that you've told, "You can't do it," that you've called "stupid" or "dumb" or "unattractive." This is the self you have scolded for making mistakes, that you've punished with shame and guilt and kicked around all these years, the self you have showered with abuse by overdoing it, poor eating habits or lack of rest and exercise. This is the self who has been with you since the day you were born and will be with you until the day you die. This is your best friend, the one who stood by you even when you abandoned it, that has the potential to love you more than anyone on earth. It's time to attend to the wounds of your inner self.

This is the self that longs to be touched, the self that so desperately wants to be loved, accepted and appreciated, that hasn't received that love because of neglect. This love, acceptance and appreciation have to begin with you. This is the self who needs your love. It can start here and now.

Step into the mirror and embrace that inner self. *Feel yourself becoming whole. You already have within you everything you need to make yourself complete. You don't need your work to fill that hole. You don't need other people to make you complete. You don't need busy activities or anything outside of yourself to be fulfilled. All you need is to be in touch with this inner part of you. This self you're embracing is the self who you'll pay attention to from now on, the one you'll love, care for and affirm. This is the self you'll be there for, the one you'll pamper, the one you'll forgive and allow to make mistakes, the one you'll care for.*

Enjoy your own company and be your own best friend. The answers are not in the outside world, where we spend most of our time. They are right here within you. As you love yourself fully, all the other problems in your life will solve themselves. You never have to be alone again because you have this inner you, that deepest part of you that has always been there and always will be there.

Turn and walk away from the mirror and the altar, carrying your inner self inside of you. Imagine yourself floating again. You're as light as air. Soon you will be going back to the outside world again: The world of computers, rush hours, complex relationships, fast-track living, quick-fixing, stress and burnout. But this time you're not going back empty-handed. You're going back stronger to face the world. You're going back whole, confident and fulfilled. Because you have your inner self. See yourself floating through the clouds and slowly back into the room. Imagine yourself coming back into the chair underneath you. Feel the seat beneath you. Feel your feet on the floor. Hear the sounds around you. In any way you want, come back to the room. Open your eyes when you are ready.

Affirmations For Your Inner Self

Positive affirmations help us recognize and appreciate our inner beauty and worth. Sending ourselves balanced, positive messages helps reverse the inner negative voice that keeps faulting us as it plays over and over in our minds. Affirming ourselves helps us feel like the smart, capable and worthy human beings that we truly are. The following affirmations bring self-acceptance and tranquility:

My worth doesn't depend on everyone liking me. Things do not have to be perfect for me to be happy. Life is uncertain, and people, myself included, are not perfect. I forgive myself for my imperfections and accept myself as I am. I am coming to love and see the beauty within me. I am loving and affirming myself more and more each day.

My happiness comes from within, not without. I do not depend on the outside world to make me happy. I do not need anything or anyone beyond what I already have to make me happy. I have everything I need for happiness to fill my life. Wanting what I have makes me happy and leaves me fulfilled.

Today I no longer look for something or someone to make me feel complete. I am at peace within myself.

When I count my blessings, I see that I have much more to be thankful for than to fret about. Life is full of disappointments, but I choose to experience them as lessons that build inner fortitude and a stronger foundation for my future spiritual growth.

I look within myself for answers to my spiritual quest. I know that through the divine inspiration of my Higher Power spiritual fulfillment is mine.

I do not need another person, my job or material possessions to make me feel complete. I am whole just as I am. My relationship to my Higher Self helps me to feel this wholeness more and more with each new day.

My value as a human being begins with me today through self-acceptance and self-love. Today, I will build time for me into my daily life. I feel renewed as I quietly sit, reflect and pay attention to my inner self.

There are many ways to use these affirmations. You can write them down and read them to yourself over and over again. You can record them on tape and play them back or put them up in strategic places around your house. The bathroom mirror is a good location where you'll see the affirmation first thing in the morning.

One of my favorites for the bathroom mirror says,

I am looking at the only person in the world who can determine my happiness.

Keep a bulletin board with all the affirming notes, gifts and sayings that people send you. Look at them often to remind yourself that others see you as a wonderful human being. When you are facing a particular problem, make up special affirmations to give yourself confidence. Keep a notebook or journal of affirmations you've created or found in other places. If you have a telephone answering machine, call yourself from work and leave an affirming message. It's a wonderful experience to come home from a hard day and hear a loving and affirming message from yourself just as if it were from someone else who cares about you.

Each breath we take is exclusively ours. What splendid creatures we are! How lucky we are to have this once-in-a-lifetime chance to live our lives in our own unique way!

I challenge you to affirm and love yourself. Be yourself. Pamper yourself. Forgive and care for yourself. Enjoy your own company and be your own best friend. Do the things for you that you would do for the ones you love the most and as you do so will you be.

Facing Yourself

A final meditation will allow you to face yourself. This meditation helps you get in touch with your inner child . . . that part of you that you may think is gone, but is still there, only a breath away. Connecting with this inner part of yourself helps you learn more about who you are and how you can care for yourself. Record the meditation on a tape recorder with soft music, pausing where appropriate. Play it back later to guide yourself through.

Get comfortable, uncross your legs, close your eyes.

Now focus on your breathing. Take a few deep breaths. Let it all go. Connect with your breathing. Breathe in through the nose and out through the mouth. In through the nose. Out through the mouth.

Feel the seat beneath you. Feel the clothes on your body. Hear the sounds around you. Let go of your thoughts about what happened today or yesterday. Don't try to force or resist whatever comes up, just be aware of your thoughts, letting them pass by. Forget about what

*you have to do after this meditation. This is a time for you. Feel the
tension drift down your arms and out through your hands and fingertips. Feel the tension slowly moving down your legs and out through
your feet and toes.*

*You're going to go back in time, through a review of your life to see
how you got to where you are.*

*Imagine the day you were born. The beginning of you. Imagine
what the room must have looked like. Experience the feelings that come
up. Let your thoughts go and try to feel what it must have been like.
Feel the connection with your mother. What sensations do you have as
you move through the birth canal? As you emerge into this world see
your first fleck of light, sounds of voices, hands on your body, being
cuddled in soft, warm arms. Notice that your mouth receives a nipple,
either a breast or a bottle.*

*Who's loving you now? How does it feel? Is anything missing? How
do you feel about yourself as a newborn?*

*Time passes and you're an older infant — still in the first year but
a few months older now and a little wiser about how this world and
the people in it work.*

*Try to remember back to anytime during your first year. What did
you look like? What did you wear?*

*You're still dependent on those around you for all of your needs.
Who is there for you? Who is loving you?*

*This is a time of building trust or mistrust. Who do you trust to take
care of you? Is there anyone you've learned to mistrust? What messages
are given to you? How do you feel about yourself at this stage?*

*Time passes and you continue to grow and develop. You enter the
toddler years — somewhere between one and three. This is a time of
independence. Your world widens, and you learn to talk and to move
around on your own. You can pull up, stand and walk. You can climb
to get things you want, even some things you're not supposed to have.
You're curious about this fascinating world and you want to explore it.*

*What is this experience like for you as you explore your house and
yard and the people around you? Who's watching over you and
setting boundaries when you go too far? What happens when you
overstep your bounds? Are you criticized and shamed or protected
and nurtured?*

*Who's there for you? Who's showing you right from wrong? Who's
bouncing you on their knee and playing with you? Who's loving that*

little toddler in you? Do you feel affirmed and nurtured or criticized to death? Is anything missing at this stage?

Time marches on and you continue to grow and develop into a preschool child, between the ages of three and five. This is a magical time when you fantasize and develop a wonderful imagination. You believe in the tooth fairy and you believe that Mickey Mouse is real. Sometimes your imagination runs wild and you're afraid of the dark. You even believe that the teddy bear that lays on your bed all day can carry you off into the middle of the night.

Who's there for you in this period of wonder and magic? To protect you and reassure you when you have a bad dream? To tell you that they will always be there for you? To comfort you in their arms when you fall down and skin your knee?

What does your house look like? See a mealtime and remember who sits in each spot at the dinner table. What are your favorite games and toys? Who are your playmates? Do you have a preschool teacher?

What messages are given to you at this age? How do you feel about yourself? Who tells you that you are loved? Is anything missing?

The world is widening as you move into school and your neighborhood. The magic of childhood starts to evaporate. You're a school-age child between ages six and 12. You don't believe in Santa Claus or the tooth fairy anymore. You don't want to give it up, but you know you have to move on. You understand rules now, and you know when you break them. You take on the worries of the real world: fear of earthquakes and tornadoes, a parent's job loss, fitting in with your friends.

You'll do just about anything to be accepted. Who is your very best friend in the whole world? The one person you can tell anything to and trust? When you choose teams on the playground, are you chosen first or last? How does that feel? How do you feel about yourself at this stage? Do you feel competent or inferior? What do the adults in your life tell you about yourself? Who tells you that you are loved? Is anything missing in the school-age years?

Time passes and you step onto the bridge between childhood and adulthood, the teenage years. You're starting to become a grown-up. You're not a child anymore but still not an adult either. You're trying to cut through the confusion and figure out who you are.

What is it like as your body starts to change. When you look in the mirror, what do you see? How are you treated by those around you?

Your parents? Peers? What messages are given to you by these people? Do you feel accepted and affirmed? Or rejected? Who's there for you when you need them? Who helps you sort yourself out and figure out what you'll do with your life? Who would you like to have been there but wasn't? How do you feel about yourself as a teenager?

You're walking across the bridge from the teen years and you're on the other side. You're a full-fledged adult now. Do you feel like one inside? Where did all those children go? Are they still there? Can you still feel that helpless infant sometimes or the rebellious toddler? What about the magical preschooler who gets excited about life? Or the school-age child who wants to fit in and be accepted? Or the confused teenager who struggles with who he or she is?

Yes, all of these parts are still within you, and they always will be with you.

Who's there for you today? Who can you depend on? Who loves you unconditionally and with all their heart and lets you know that you're okay just the way you are? How do you feel about yourself today?

Now go back to the one stage where you had trouble feeling good about yourself. See the people in your life at the time. What stage are you in? How old are you? Who's with you and what's going on?

Now tell whoever is there that you're taking this child away from this situation and that you're not going to let this child part of you be hurt again. Because from now on you'll take care of this part of you. Pick yourself up and hold that child in your arms and say and do for it whatever it needed back then and didn't get. Say and do those things for yourself now. Give yourself the love you didn't get.

Know that you are okay just as you are and that you're lovable. Know that you will always love this small child inside of you.

Now turn and walk away carrying that child part within you. Feeling the love inside yourself, start to come back into the room. Feel the seat underneath you. Feel your feet on the floor. Hear the sounds around you. Take a deep breath, and in any way you want and in your own time, come back to the room. Open your eyes when you are ready.

Process

Sit for a while and reflect on the experience. Feel your
feelings, whatever they are. After you have felt your feelings, reassure yourself that the adult part of you can take
care of the child within you. Then process the following
questions silently or in your journal.

1. What were the messages?
2. What feelings came up? In response to what?
3. Which stage did you go back to?
4. What was it like when you took yourself out of the
   childhood situation?
5. Was anything missing in your life? What did you give
   yourself? Who wasn't there that you wish had been?
6. What did you remember from your childhood that you
   thought you'd forgotten?

Facing Themselves:*
Two People Who Do Less and Live More

Charles Steinberg, M.D.,
Part-time Doctor

The work of a physician is geared generally to the Type-A personality, the person who wants to achieve endlessly, to do more and more. We're trained to be that way. Amid all of our medical education no one teaches us how to say no, how to look at a day's schedule full of appointments and tell a sick person that, no, we cannot fit in one more.

During my residency, I remember, the chief of our every-other-night on-call duties would tell us that the only problem with our schedule was that we were still missing half of the action. I was working with seriously ill newborns, and it was nonstop and stressful. I decided back then that though I may have had to work that way to get my credentials, it wasn't how I wanted to live.

I've been a physician for 15 years now, the last six working primarily with people with AIDS and HIV infection. When I first opened my practice, I set up a schedule totaling about three-quarters full time, leaving myself plenty of time for breaks and allotting significant time for each patient appointment. That was a fine arrangement for a while. But then the AIDS epidemic began to outpace my schedule.

It's not just the great numbers of people who have been afflicted; it's also what working with AIDS entails. Along with the medical work there's also a large degree of personal, emotional, psychological, even spiritual involvement with people, some of whom will die while under my care. As important and rewarding as this work is, I've also found it rather devastating.

So I've cut back even further on my schedule. I'm now scheduled to see patients about 18 hours a week, or a little less than half time. The way I've set it up, it amounts to five half-days a week. By choosing the schedule that I have, I actually have

*"Slowing Down" by Charles Steinberg and Autumn Preble. Copyright 1991 by *New Age Journal*. Reprinted with permission of *New Age Journal*, Brighton, MA.

chosen to earn about a third of what the average doctor makes. I'm fortunate enough that that's still plenty. It's a trade of time for money, and that's fine with me.

What's been nice about cutting back on my schedule is that I now have a built-in flexibility. At least once or twice a week my free time gets filled by something unexpected — maybe a patient takes ill and I have to meet him at the hospital. That's a frequent occurrence in AIDS work. But now it means that I miss an afternoon hike or some fishing. It used to mean that I'd have to push other appointments back into the evening, really cutting into my family life.

My family life has benefited greatly from my down-sized schedule. I've had more time to see my seven-year-old son grow up and to go on camping trips with my 19-year-old daughter or 23-year-old son. Last year my wife accompanied me to the International AIDS Conference in Florence, and when it was over, we spent three weeks traveling around Italy. Travel has been important; we go away at least ten weeks a year. But even week to week, when I'm free for an afternoon in Boulder, I'm able to do things I never could do with a full-time job. For one thing, I've been able to develop my photography to the point where I'm starting to sell some pictures; it's evolved from a hobby into a second profession.

To be away from my office so much, I've needed the support of physicians willing to at least monitor my patients while I'm gone. My patients also have been great about this. They may have an anxiety attack when they know that I'll be out of town for an extended period, but they've supported me for taking care of myself. And they've also taught me a great lesson: With death staring them in the face, they've taken the attitude that now is the time to live the way they want to. That's been a deep teaching for me, the son of a physician who died six months after his retirement. My father never had the opportunity to live because he put it off. I'm 44 now, and I can pedal a bicycle, paddle a canoe or hike a mountain all day. When I'm 74, I'll still be doing some of those things, just not as much. But I'll probably also still be working at that age. With my schedule, I see no reason to retire.

I think my schedule has made me a better doctor as well. In medicine when it gets busy, it's easy to click on automatic mode, go from chore to chore and check them off the list, and really not infuse each patient appointment with that spark of humanism that makes it a healing encounter. I do a meditation at the start of each day to remind myself that that's why I'm here — not just to write prescriptions. And if I'm getting the rest, the support, the physical exercise, and the time to play that I need, then I think I am much more able to deliver what my patients value the most: my humanness as well as my professional skills.

Autumn Preble,
Full-Time Mother

When I got pregnant nearly seven years ago, my husband and I were living in Oxford, England, as co-directors of an American university's semester-abroad program. I was working seemingly endless days and was very much identified with my job. My expectation was that I would take some time off to have the baby and then return to work. I couldn't imagine *not* working. I had the image of myself sitting at a desk with my child beside me in a baby bouncer, bouncing happily away.

Then I had the baby, and something shifted in me. I think it was my priorities. The first year of child rearing took every bit of strength that I had — physically and otherwise — to meet my new demands. I found that I no longer was even thinking about going back to work. One day I looked at my engagement calendar and realized that, whereas I used to be able to jam my day full of appointments, I now could schedule only a few things. And I remember thinking that that was okay. Maybe it's partially the influence of the Zen study I've done, but for all of my adult life it has been a value of mine to put space around things, to pay attention to what I'm doing. And in this case that meant being able to relax and watch my child's small steps — literally and figuratively. I wanted to be a parent who has some awake, daytime energy to offer my child.

I had heard so much about women getting pregnant, leaving the work force and getting a dull mind. But that hasn't been true at all for me. One reason is that I simply find being with a child and thinking about child-raising issues to be incredibly stimulating. And I think it actually *sharpens* your mind to be interrupted ten times during a conversation — as so often happens while caring for a child — because you learn to pick up threads and carry on.

Also I happen to be surrounded in my community by other older mothers who themselves are choosing to spend priority time raising children. When we get together, we talk on a deep level about our children: their spirituality, their personal growth. We also talk about *our* personal growth through parenthood. There's a great deal of strong thinking going on.

Sometimes that is not enough, though. At times I'm bothered by the fact that there's no paycheck to tell me, in dollars and cents, what I am contributing. I grew up in the '60s, went to a good university, and spent years out in the world building a career. So sometimes I question what I'm doing now. I'm 40, and I hear inner voices that are not terribly supportive, asking what I have to show for myself.

Fortunately our family has done all right financially since I've left the work force. We'd have more money if I were out working, of course, but we're doing just fine as it is. And, as I sometimes have to remind myself, I *am* working. If I had a job, I'd have to come home and care for Brendan in my "off" time; now caring for him is my "on" time.

Balancing a job and motherhood also would leave me little time or energy for other activities. As Brendan has grown, I've been able to find time for two artistic passions of mine: dancing and sculpting. Sometimes I have to grab whatever time becomes available, but I'm comfortable with that. It's just nice to *have* time available; otherwise my life would be very stressful. I have a great deal of respect for women who juggle mothering small children and a job, but I can no longer imagine myself doing that.

I still struggle with my decision from time to time. But when I'm searching for validation, I like to remind myself that, in a quiet way, I am making my mark on the world simply by living intentionally. Of course, the best validation may be in the shining, brown eyes of a child I know is happy.

From Doing To Being

There once was a starfish who lived in the ocean. "Pardon me," he said to the whale. "Could you tell me where I can find the sea?"

"You already are in the sea," replied the whale. "It is all around you."

"This?" replied the starfish. "This is just the ocean. I'm looking for the sea."

The frustrated starfish swam away to continue searching for the sea.

"Look no further," yelled the wise old whale after him, "*Seaing* is a matter of *seeing!*"

As you make the shift in how you see your life you remain the same person on the outside. You may keep the same job and the same relationships. You may still get angry and impatient sometimes, and there will be occasions when you will feel sad or disappointed. Your transformation happens on the inside. You look at your life in a different way and see things with new insight and greater clarity.

Teilhard de Chardin described this change as "ever more perfect eyes in a world in which there is always more to see." You don't swim around the answers like the starfish, looking and wishing for something that is already his. Instead, you see what is yours and are grateful for it because you have made the shift from doing to being.

10
My Story

*Something we were
withholding made us weak,
until we found it was
ourselves.*

— Robert Frost

Flames engulfed our tiny wood-frame house. I was five years old. I remember standing, paralyzed by fear, as the fire roared and swelled. My older sister and I huddled together in terror as neighbors worked frantically to retrieve household goods. A gas stove had exploded, I heard someone say. Minutes before I had witnessed flames leaping up the kitchen wall and my mother's sharp demands for me to hurry for sand as she desperately tried to douse them. And I vaguely remember my mother's moans of horror after head-counting her three children and realizing that her 18-month-old daughter was still inside the burning house.

A legend grew from that incident and was told and retold by friends and neighbors for the rest of my childhood. A brave neighbor, so the story goes, rescued the toddler by rushing through the blaze, picking her up from a circle of dancing flames and tossing her like a football over the heads of curious onlookers into the arms of another neighbor. My older sister insists that the truth is less intriguing. She had picked up baby sister and carried her to safety before the fire started burning out of control; she had never been in danger. In the confusion no one agrees about what really happened that day, but my younger sister suddenly appeared safe in my mother's arms.

The fire continued to rage until our house burned to the ground. We were left with nothing, except for a few pieces of

furniture and the clothes on our backs. No one had notified my
father of the disaster. He came home as usual that afternoon to
find his house in smouldering ruins. He didn't know what had
caused the fire or if his family was safe. Standing beside him in
silence, I didn't know what was going through his mind. But like
all five-year-olds, I figured he was thinking the same thing I was.
Looking up at his sad and defeated face, I felt inside the way he
looked on the outside. Pondering the charred remains, we wondered and worried about what we would do now.

In many ways that fire symbolized my entire childhood. The
volatility, rage and chaos of the burning house embodied the
spirit of its inhabitants. When I recall my early family life, I think
of it as unpredictable and raging out of control. You might even
say it was hell. I always thought that mine was an unusual childhood — unique enough that it would make a best-seller. But after
years of studying chemical dependency and family systems, working with children of alcoholic parents and hearing other childhood
stories, I realized mine was not so different from all the rest. In
fact by comparison with most my upbringing was bland.

A Sea Of Denial

I grew up on the edge of a large city in the rural South. The
term "alcoholic" was not part of the language of that region. I
never even heard the word until I was grown. We had one local
drunk, Ed Quick, and even he was never called an alcoholic. The
only reason he was called a drunk was because he slept wherever
he fell each night — in a ditch, in the woods or on someone's
doorstep. He was the butt of jokes as well as the scapegoat for
other heavy drinkers who needed proof that, because they didn't
fall down in the street, they didn't have a drinking problem.

If you drank behind closed doors, your reputation could not be
impugned no matter how much you drank, how it affected you or
where you fell drunk in your own home. Drinking was part of
life. It was all around me as I grew up. Nobody thought twice
about it, and if somebody's drinking got out of hand, you'd simply
hear, "He tied one on last night" or "He had one too many." There
was community as well as family denial about alcoholism. To this
day my mother denies that my father was an alcoholic. "He was

a drunkard," she contends, despite the fact that he died of cirrhosis of the liver.

After I grew up, I learned that the county in which I lived has the highest rate of alcoholism in my home state, which, in turn, has a larger rate of alcoholism than is found among the general population. I was surrounded by alcohol from the day I was born. No wonder drinking and seeing neighbors drunk were so normal to my eyes. No wonder the denial in the family and community was so strong. We couldn't see the forest for the trees.

It wasn't the drinking per se that caused the turbulence in my childhood; in fact I have few memories of my father actually consuming alcohol. But it was the bizarre behavior that the drinking wrought, the breakdown of healthy communication and the development of childhood survival techniques that, while appearing to work at the time, would ultimately cause me great difficulty in adult life. I hold no memories of the old house that burned — only of those in the rebuilt house after I was five. Little did I know that the next five years of my life would be the worst.

New House, Old Habits

Within two years my hard-working and resourceful father had managed to finance the rebuilding of that house on the same plot of land. Ironically we had a new house, but our home — our family — continued to decay.

It was 1950 and my father worked as a machinist in a plant that manufactured guided missiles. He worked long and hard. My mother stayed home and managed the house. I have no memories of my parents smiling at each other, having fun or embracing. Through my childhood eyes, the only time they spoke was to complain or disagree, and the only time they touched was to hit or slap. My father drank in the open at home until my mother bitterly complained that he should not drink in front of the kids. Perhaps that's why I have few memories of his actually putting a bottle to his lips, but many of his drunken episodes.

Weekends Were The Worst

Friday nights were usually movie nights. When I was eight, Daddy, as I called him true to southern tradition, would take my younger sister and me to the movie theater about three miles from home and leave us there. He promised to be back by a certain time, but rarely was. More often than not, it became routine for us to walk out with the manager after seeing the same movie two or three times. Many nights we stood outside the theater as the marquee darkened and the street traffic hushed in the still night. We never knew whether or not he would remember to come back for us. Underneath the big-screen excitement of James Dean and Marilyn Monroe was a little boy's constant worry that his father had abandoned him.

Sometimes we got rides home with parents of our friends. I always rejected the manager's offers to take us home saying, "Oh, he'll be here after a while. He just got busy." Naturally I wanted to believe that, and above all I didn't want the manager to know the truth: that this man was so busy drinking he'd forgotten his children. Sometimes my sister would cry, and although I wanted to cry also, I had to make her think I was in charge of the situation. I was scared and mad because of the cold and the dark. How could our father be so thoughtless if he truly loved us? My feelings of abandonment were expressed through anger that camouflaged deeper emotions of hurt and rejection.

Sometimes Daddy would pull up at 12 or one in the morning. Other times strange men (who must have been more sober "drinking buddies") would come for us and say our father had sent them. We were always frightened of these strangers because we didn't know if they were telling the truth or if they would hurt us.

One Friday night Daddy dropped us off and told us that he would be back at a certain hour and that we should be standing in a specific spot at that time. As kids we became fastidious about times and locations because we had to make sure that any mixups were not our fault. We waited in the designated spot for hours, but he never came. It was late and dark. Finally, a taxi driver pulled up and said that our father had sent him to pick us up. Emotionally and physically exhausted, we reluctantly went with the stranger.

When Daddy never showed, the police would take us home. Riding in the police car embarrassed and scared me because I felt as if I had done something wrong, and I didn't want neighbors and friends to see the officers pull up in front of my house. After one or two rides in a squad car, I insisted, over the protests of my tired five-year-old sister, that we walk the three miles home. I learned quickly that the exertion and fear of a three-mile hike in the dark were less painful than the humiliation of standing in front of the theater or of riding in a police car like a criminal.

Saturdays would be different, we convinced ourselves, because that was the day we went into town to buy things. Daddy was a generous man and bought us practically anything we wanted within reason. He usually kept a bottle in the glove compartment of his Chevrolet. After parking the car he'd reach for the bottle and take a big gulp before going to the bank or to the five and dime. One day as he put the bottle to his lips, two of my schoolmates passed by. They looked at me and waved and then looked at my dad, and a strange look came over their faces. I was so ashamed that, after that day, I pretended I didn't see my friends when my folks took me to town.

Daddy would end up spending hundreds of dollars on clothes for us. But by the time we would get inside the department stores to try on outfits, he'd be stumbling and slurring his words. The stares from clerks and other shoppers would embarrass me so badly that I wanted to disappear. The expensive clothes were not important anymore, and I just wanted to leave.

To avoid the shame of being seen with my father, I eventually convinced him to set up an expense account for me and my sisters at the best shop in town. From then on I walked downtown after school and did my own shopping without the burden of Saturday morning humiliations. At ten years of age this experience made me more independent, and I learned to purchase and coordinate my own outfits when most kids' parents still did that for them.

Sundays in the South were big days for visiting relatives and eating large home-cooked meals. Our favorite place for Sunday lunch was my father's sister's house. She'd make huge platters of fried chicken, heaping bowls of rice and gravy, and mounds of home-made biscuits. As kids we loved to pop in unannounced and sit down at the table with her, my uncle and our cousins. We always felt welcomed and enjoyed the conversations and the delicious food. After eating, the children had a good time playing while the adults lounged under the shade trees.

Those wonderful, lazy Sundays were the best days of the weekend and usually the quietest because we were with other people who loved us and enjoyed our company. Or so we thought. Once grown, however, our cousins confided in us that they always resented it when we drove up right at lunchtime and interrupted their family meals. We learned that they were nice to us because they felt sorry for us and had been instructed to be kind by their mother. It was the least a dutiful sister could do for her alcoholic brother. The truth was we had been in the way: our best days had been enjoyed at others' expense.

Stuffing My Feelings

I was embarrassed by the way my father behaved and was afraid people wouldn't like me because of it. He seemed to care more for his bottle than he did for us. My sense of self-worth nosedived. If my father couldn't remember to pick me up at the movies, I figured I wasn't very important. My way to cope with these feelings at a very young age was to disconnect myself from my family. I became very shy and withdrawn. I felt alone. I thought others were better than me and that I was no good at all. For years I kept all my feelings bottled up inside.

Little did I know that my heart showed through my sad eyes and face. To my teachers at school, I was an average and shy little boy from an ordinary family who never made trouble and always wanted to do well to please others.

My third-grade teacher once asked me in front of the class, "Bryan, why don't you ever smile?" Although she was a kind person and probably had only the best of intentions, I was devastated. I realized she had detected my hidden secret and that I should smile more often to conceal my feelings. From then on and even into adulthood, my smile became my mask. Sometimes I found myself smiling for no apparent reason — not because I was happy but because I wanted to hide the fact that I was sad.

Taking Control Of The Situation

During the next few years, things got worse. To avoid confrontations with my mother, Daddy started hiding beer and liquor bottles. I was always discovering them in closets, cabinets and dresser drawers. One day I found a hidden bottle of whiskey in a kitchen cabinet. As a weak attempt to control his drinking, I poured out the alcohol and filled the bottle with apple vinegar, which resembled the color of the whiskey. "That would stop him once and for all" my ten-year-old mind reasoned. When he took a swig of the vinegar, he grimaced, became enraged and beat me unmercifully. I never tampered with his bottles again.

My father started "working longer hours" until eight or nine o'clock at night. Eventually he stopped coming home at all. He would stay out all night and sometimes he would stay away the entire weekend. That's when the violence erupted, and that's when my memories are sharpest, for that's when I had to take center stage.

My stomach flip-flopped. It always did that when Daddy finally made it home and staggered up the porch steps at a late hour. I quaked in my bed as I heard him fumbling around for his keys because I knew another sleepless night was about to begin. The lights would come on all over the house. My mother was up, determined to find out what woman he'd been with until three in the morning. My sisters would scurry around too, and true to tradition, the whole house would be in an uproar.

When Daddy was drunk, which had become frequent by now, I'd jump out of bed to manage the situation. My parents' words became sharper and louder, and more violent. A vicious cycle developed between them. The more Daddy drank, the more Mother complained, and the more she complained, the more he drank. She accused him of seeing other women. He accused her of making his life so miserable he had no place to come home to. They were so consumed with their own feelings and preoccupations they didn't stop to consider the children. We were left to survive on our own as best we could in a house that had become a battleground.

A new lamp had a maximum life of 48 hours. Kitchen knives, dishes, frying pans, knick-knacks, mirrors, pictures off the wall, hairbrushes, even furniture were all heaved, thrown, slung and slammed during angry outbursts between my parents. My house was always in disarray. I hid things so that they wouldn't get broken. Sweeping up shattered glass, plastic or debris became a weekly ritual.

My 17-year-old sister had married and left home, and I had become ringmaster of our family circus by the age of 12. To avoid violence, I tried to clarify verbal assaults, "Mother didn't really mean it that way." I ended up refereeing verbal bouts that sometimes lasted for hours. "Okay, that's enough, now stop it! Be quiet!" Sometimes my interventions developed into pleading as a last resort, "Please don't call her that." I would beg them to stop and settle their differences quietly. But ultimately, as quarrels turned into threats, I placed myself between my father's fist, defiant stare and bloodshot eyes and my mother's raised arm. It was like trying to separate two fighting dogs and getting bitten in the scuffle.

When I interfered, they would strike wildly at me or push me away so they could resume their battle. It was an impossible job, and I had to sidestep their swats at me. Realizing I couldn't prevent the inevitable, I busied myself jerking windows and curtains closed to insulate the domestic war from the eyes of curious neighbors and hiding wall hangings and fragile figurines from the coffee table, most of which were already dented or chipped from previous abuse.

I had become the one who ran the show: the protector, the peacemaker, the referee, the judge, the hero, the general. The seeds of overdoing it were being planted. Although I couldn't stop the violence, I could make sure the neighbors couldn't see, the house wasn't destroyed and no one was killed or sent to the hospital or prison. It was not a role I chose; it was one that I took out of a will to survive.

Eventually I discovered that my best recourse was to withdraw from my family altogether. From the time I could hold a pencil, I spent hours alone in my room writing mystery stories. I loved it because the characters I created would do anything I wanted them to do. I had full rein over them. Writing not only gave me a sense of control over my unwieldy life but also provided a sanctuary from all the inexplicable events that surrounded and threatened to engulf me. My pretend stories became plays that I'd make my neighborhood friends act out. I was not only the writer but also the director. We'd hang up old bedspreads for curtains and my front porch would be the stage.

In high school I wrote and directed the annual church Christmas play, designed the sets, and even played the lead character. I didn't know it at the time, but writing plays and directing others gave me a sense of immense power and stability that served as an antidote to the chaos of my home life. Paradoxically these activities were also the origins of an addiction to work that would stalk me into adulthood.

After years of seeing my parents out of control, I began to deplore any situation in which people could not control themselves. I learned very early to *always* be in control. When violence erupted between my parents, I learned to stay poised to keep them apart, to hide breakable items and generally to keep them from killing each other, one of us, or from destroying the house entirely.

Then, after calm descended upon us, as it always did in the wee hours of morning, I cleaned up the mess and made everything look as if nothing had happened. A scrupulous eye, however could see chipped glass figurines, dented furniture and holes in the wall.

There were many trips to the hospital and the police station, and the police visited us many times, sometimes at a concerned neighbor's request. I always hated it when the secret slipped out. In fact, I would rather contend with the violent nights than have anyone find out. Daybreak was always welcome. As quiet descended over the house, I could breathe a sigh of relief because I knew my family had made it through another night.

From the time I was 13 on I remember my father drunk. I honed my skills carefully and became an expert at assessing his sobriety by the time his feet left the 1958 Chevy and touched ground. It was a look he had about him, his vacant stare and downturned lips. I immediately began preparing the house for what had become the only predictable thing in my young life — turmoil. For the next 15 minutes, I would remove breakable objects, close the windows and curtains, hide anything that could cause harm and try to smooth tense conversations.

We walked on eggshells and were careful about what we said and how we said it so that my father wouldn't think we were laughing at him or making fun of him. Any subtle movement of the hand or head took on exaggerated meaning in my father's mind. Ultimately it did not matter what we said or did because he expressed his helplessness and frustration through violence.

One night in particular he had been drinking heavily. I was 15 and was sleeping with and caring for my 12-year-old sister, who'd just had a tonsillectomy and was still sick in bed. A roaring fire in our living room fireplace warded off the bitter cold. From the bedroom where I slept with my ailing sister, I heard the sounds of angry, muted voices. I put my arm around her to assure her everything would be okay. Suddenly the door was flung open and the lights came on. Deafening sounds of a drunken rampage broke the silence of the room. Daddy picked up an old lantern I had found in an abandoned house and slung it at us. It hit my sister in the head. As she began to cry he jerked the telephone cord out of the wall, marched into the living room and flung it into the fire. My mother yelled at him, and they pushed each other.

My attention was riveted on the melting telephone. That sight terrified me. I felt my lifeline to a world I longed to become a part of had been severed.

As my parents continued screaming and hitting each other, I bundled my sister up and drove illegally (I was only 15 years old) five miles to my older sister's house. In anticipation of my sixteenth birthday and getting my driver's license, I had been given an old 1950 Dodge with no heater. Although we could see our breath in the cold, our emotions numbed us to the weather. We drove in silence, frequently broken by my sister's whimpers. We must have looked like two waifs suddenly appearing in the cold on our sister's doorstep in the middle of her dinner party. Through tears of fear, anger and exasperation, I told her what happened. I'll never forget feeling her arms around me, the warmth and security of her house, the calm that suddenly embraced us.

Dr. Jekyll And Mr. Hyde

The morning after any of the drunken skirmishes, Daddy always acted as if nothing had happened. He was like a different person. But the rest of us had an emotional hangover. I was perplexed by his Dr. Jekyll and Mr. Hyde personality and wondered how he could forget or pretend to forget the terrible things he had done. I didn't realize at the time that his blackouts prevented him from remembering the events of the night before.

While my family still carried around their anger, my father had transformed into a sweet, gentle and caring man. It was a kind and considerate father who dropped us off at the seven o'clock movie and promised through genuine smiles to be back by nine. It was the snarling monster who returned at 12 o'clock or who never returned at all. Still, his gentle side appeared just often enough to keep my trust in him alive — trust that he would keep his promises and that he would eventually stop drinking.

His gentle nature would bait the family in going out to eat at a restaurant. As if we had total amnesia of past experiences, we always looked forward to the good time we would have. I wanted to believe that this time things would be different. But by the time we were seated, he would be drunk, bold, defiant and hostile. He would embarrass us with his coarse words and gruff manner. He insulted our waiters, and his loud voice and animated gestures were obtrusive on the mealtime conversations of those around us. He would knock over a glass of water or brush his sleeve through his food. His programmed response to our pleas for him to be quiet was "I don't give a damn! I can buy this place!"

I would be so embarrassed and humiliated I usually could not eat. It was not until I was 21 years of age that I realized he might not ever change. I remember looking across the table as he made a spectacle of himself, wondering where was that bright, capable man I admired, the man whose mind spun out inventions and dreamed new ideas? I loved that man, but I hated the monster that sat at the head of our table, boldly claiming he could buy the restaurant and everyone in it. Without saying a word, I left the restaurant before we were served and vowed to never eat publicly with him again until he was sober. That was the last public meal I ever had with him.

Despite all the bad times, though, my father was by nature a good man, loving and kind. I have many fond memories of being snuggled in his arms listening to bedtime stories on cold nights. His train stories were the best, and I loved how he mimicked the chug-a-lug of the locomotive whistle that lulled me to sleep.

He worked hard and always insisted on two things: that we brush our teeth before going to bed and that we do well in school and strive for a good education. He was a good provider for his family. We never lacked for any material comforts, although we were not rich. Daddy frittered away most of his money on gambling and drinking and our small, simple house always showed signs of neglect. Still, we had the finest clothes and the newest cars, and he paid every penny of our college tuition for as long as we wanted to go.

A brilliant and resourceful man, Daddy was an inventor in his spare time. From my earliest memory he sat in front of some contraption, contemplating the cosmos and staring into space. He only did this when he was sober and lucid. That's when I loved him the most. I could almost see his mind working, and I knew he was doing positive things.

He had mediocre success with a brand of curtain rods, trash can holders and a window-washing chemical that we bottled in a makeshift assembly line in our kitchen. One of us filled glass jugs with a powder, another filled it with water from the tap, while a third slapped on the label, which read "Red-Head Enterprises" — Daddy's affectionate way of acknowledging our behind-the-scenes help and his genetic gift to us of red hair.

Those days were the best because we were doing something productive, good and useful. There was a sense of close-knitness as we worked together as a family.

Daddy's biggest success came with the invention of a console-style beer can opener that was faster than the conventional hand-held type. It sold like wildfire, and he made lots of money. He signed a contract with a major corporation in Chicago, which distributed his invention in bars throughout the United States and the world. His claim to fame came one night in a comedy skit on the "Dick Van Dyke Show." We all gathered around our black-and-white television set and watched Rob Petrie carry my father's invention around his office, trying to figure out what it was. Although it would later become obsolete with the advent of the pop-top can, revenues from sales became our sole source of income for years.

Looking back, I find it ironic that I spent my early teenage years working part time in his small factory manufacturing beer can openers. Little did I know that I was aiding and abetting on a large scale the very disease that strangled my family. Revenues from these sales not only paid my tuition through college but also supported my father's drinking habit.

Childhood Trappings In An Adult World

I continued to overdo it well into adulthood, although I no longer lived in a chaotic family. On my own the need to control everything and everyone became an obsession. Things had to be done my way or not at all. But the old survival skills that saved me as a child caused me many problems in my interpersonal relationships at work, at home and at play.

As a grown-up I had great difficulty with weekends and holidays when there was too much free time. Waking up on a Saturday morning with nothing to do made me panic-stricken. I felt out of control, as if something terrible could happen at any moment during those idle hours. I didn't know how to be flexible and live by the moment. I was afraid of the unknown.

Eventually I discovered that weekends were difficult for me because, as a child, I never knew when a crisis with my father would erupt. Anytime there was quiet it was the calm before the storm. If I let my guard down, the rapid-fire of Daddy's inebriated outbursts would hit me. So I learned to live with this uncertainty by always expecting the worst and staying poised for it, even when everything appeared calm. In adulthood I got into the habit of packing my weekends full so that I knew exactly what would happen next and how to prepare for it. There could be no surprise; I made sure of that. Although staying busy seemed to alleviate a lot of stress, it left no time for spontaneous, relaxing moments, no time for play and no time for living in the now.

I excelled in school and discovered that I could be academically successful and unconsciously hold on to my old survival skills. School helped me feel good about myself, so I spent a lot of time studying.

Three degrees and a doctorate later, I learned that the work-world gave me the same sense of what I thought was fulfillment. I received my self-worth from work, and it became my life. I transformed my long hours of study into long hours of work: weeknights, weekends and holidays. I was hooked. I had become hopelessly addicted. I worked for the sake of work and the superficial and fleeting feelings of esteem and accomplishment it gave me. It also provided an escape so that I didn't have to deal with many feelings buried since childhood. It kept me disconnected from people and intimate relationships. Work was something over which I thought I had total control even though it actually had control over me. In work I had found my salvation, my nirvana — or so I thought.

My behavior was highly rewarded in my job, and I quickly made it through the professorial ranks. But the other three-quarters of my life — social relationships, hobbies and recreation, and personal relationships — suffered from neglect. I became obsessed with my career. I lived to work rather than worked to live. Like many children of alcoholics, work had become my bottle. I was driven. Like an alcoholic, I felt restless and became irritable when I went more than a few days away from my desk. Even when lounging on a tropical beach, all my thoughts centered around my next project.

Hardly a vacation passed that a stuffed briefcase of work didn't accompany me as part of my luggage. While others swam and played in the surf, I toiled over my word processor back in the cottage. My family and close friends became concerned, and after many stormy protests, work was no longer allowed on vacations. My response was what any normal work addict would do: sneak it into my suitcase. I hid my work as my father had hidden his bottle. When others strolled the beach, I feigned tiredness so that I could have a few moments of bliss alone with my addiction. It sounds strange now, but at the time these behaviors seemed perfectly normal to me. Anyone who tried to interfere with my plans was immediately subjected to my harsh retaliation.

Father Knows Best

Many politicians, writers, comedians and entertainers (for example, Ronald Reagan, Carol Burnett, Jonathan Winters, Chuck Norris and Suzanne Somers) are adult children of alcoholics; the shorthand term is ACoAs. Many ACoAs discover that they are reliving the same destructive patterns of their families of origin. Anywhere from 40 to 50 percent become alcoholics themselves; others become work addicts. One reason for this is that ACoAs do not know what a healthy family is supposed to be like. Because of their early wretched family life, they develop unrealistic expectations of the ways families function. Many times they develop a fairy-tale image, and when the dream doesn't come true, they feel as if they have failed.

As a child my vision of what a family should be came from the television shows I watched, "Leave It To Beaver" and "Father Knows Best." I dreamed of living in a beautiful house on a quiet and shady tree-lined street like the Cleavers or the Andersons. There would be peace and tranquility, and everyone would smile and talk instead of frowning and yelling. I would live happily ever after.

Needless to say, these unrealistic expectations were the source of trouble when I was forced to learn in adulthood that my family experience and my fantasy were two extremes on a continuum and that most families fell somewhere in between. It was a hard lesson to understand that it was okay — and even healthy — for family members to disagree. And that on occasion it was okay for members to become angry or hurt and to communicate these feelings to one another. But the main thing I learned was to keep communciation lines open in a rational way.

Through years of hard self-inventory and the help of Al-Anon, Workaholics Anonymous and Adult Children of Alcoholic groups, I came to see that my inner feelings and perceptions of myself had caused my life to continue on the same self-destructive course that began the day I was born. For a long time I had seen myself as a victim of an unstable childhood that had left me shy, insecure and unhappy. Viewing myself as helpless and bent and swayed by whatever life sent my way had become self-fulfilling.

By age 40, the cycle of misery continued just as if my alcoholic father (who had died five years before) was still in control of my fate. The most important thing I learned in therapy and Al-Anon and my own personal search is not to disempower myself. My approach to my upbringing became metaphysical. I no longer saw myself as a disempowered victim of an unfortunate set of circumstances. Once I learned to give up those feelings of victimization and to see myself as a person of worth and power, my whole life began to change. Using my childhood as a transformational experience from which to learn, I began to reinterpret my life in a much more positive and constructive way.

Everything that had happened to me as a child had happened for a reason, both good and bad. I was a kid who grew up in an alcoholic home, and it's a good thing I did because everything —

and I mean everything — in my life has led me to where I am right now. And I wouldn't trade my life for anything. I learned to separate abusive work habits from work effectiveness, and I became aware of the hidden motives for my work dependency. Now work no longer controls me.

Saying Good-bye

My father became very sick with cirrhosis of the liver and leukemia. He died after five years of suffering and struggling with failing health. It was not until the day of his funeral that I put all the complex pieces of the puzzle together and was able to resolve my conflicting feelings about him.

I sat alone by his coffin and looked at the tired face of a defeated man. For the first time ever, I saw him, not as my father, but as a fellow human being. I thought back over all the terrible times we shared, and feelings of sympathy and compassion swept over me. Here was a man, born into poverty, who had a hard life — much harder than mine — whose own father had died of tuberculosis before he was born. His life had been a perpetual struggle, but it had its peaks too. He had been a star basketball player in high school and had won several trophies. As an inventor he had great talent that never totally manifested itself. Somewhere along the way, consuming alcohol became his crutch to get him through the tough times. But, as is often the case, the tables turned on him, and it was he who was consumed by the alcohol.

I wept for the tragedy of a human life never fully lived, and I mourned for the relationship between father and son that never was. I did not shed a tear for the man I knew as my father. I yearned for the man I had glimpsed underneath.

Writing this book has become a communion between my personal and professional lives. Like everyone else, I have problems and concerns. But as a recovering work addict and adult child of an alcoholic, I have found, through extensive personal inventory, hard work and a spiritual connection within myself, that life can be, not only satisfying, but joyous!

Appendix:

Resources To Cope With Overdoing It

If you want to
kill time, why not try
working it to death.

— O.A. Battista

Audio-Visual

Overdoing It: When Work Becomes Your Life. A 30-minute documentary in which seven people give heartwarming stories that portray the consequences of work addiction — inner misery, family neglect, broken marriages and relationships, physical problems and, in some cases, death. Hosted by Dr. Bryan Robinson, this film shows why people become work-addicted, how the addiction has affected their lives and where they sought help. Available on VHS only. To order call 1-800-582-9522, or write WTVI Video, 3242 Commonwealth Avenue, Charlotte, NC 28205.

Further Readings

Becker, Robert. (1989). **Addicted to Misery: The Other Side Of Co-dependency.** Deerfield Beach, FL: Health Communications.

Berry, Carmen Renee. (1988). **When Helping You Is Hurting Me.** New York: HarperCollins.

Elkind, David. (1981). **The Hurried Child.** Reading, MA: Addison-Wesley.

Friedman, Meyer and Rosenman, Ray. (1974). **Type A Behavior and Your Heart.** New York: Knopf.

Kofodimos, Joan. (1993). **Executives Out of Balance: Integrating Successful Careers and Fulfilling Personal Lives.** San Francisco, CA: Jossey-Bass.

Miller, Joy. (1991). **My Holding You Up Is Holding Me Back.** Deerfield Beach, FL: Health Communications.

Robinson, Bryan. (1989). **Work Addiction: Hidden Legacies of Adult Children.** Deerfield Beach, FL: Health Communications.

Robinson, Bryan. (1990). **Soothing Moments: Daily Meditations for Fast-Track Living.** Deerfield Beach, FL: Health Communications.

Robinson, Bryan. (1991). **Heal Your Self-Esteem: Recovery From Addictive Thinking.** Deerfield Beach, FL: Health Communications.

Schaef, Anne and Fassel, Diane. (1988). **The Addictive Organization.** San Francisco, CA: Harper & Row.

Steinem, Gloria. (1992). **Revolution From Within: A Book Of Self-Esteem.** New York: Little, Brown.

Wills-Brandon, Carla. (1990). **Learning To Say No: Establishing Healthy Boundaries.** Deerfield Beach, FL: Health Communications.

Woititz, Janet. (1987). **Home Away From Home: The Art of Self-Sabotage.** Pompano Beach, FL: Health Communications.

Self-Help Organizations

Many support groups are available to facilitate spiritual growth in recovery from overdoing it. I recommend one of the groups founded on the 12 Steps and Traditions of Alcoholics Anonymous (AA). Co-dependents Anonymous (CoDA), Adult Children of Alcoholics (ACoAs) and Workaholics Anonymous follow the 12 Steps.

Co-dependents Anonymous, National Service Office, P.O. Box 5508, Glendale, AZ 85312. Co-dependents Anonymous is a fellowship of men and women whose common problem is the inability to maintain functional relationships. Its meetings are open to those who feel they are in a co-dependent relationship and feel overly responsible for others' feelings and behaviors.

Adult Children of Alcoholics, Central Service Board, P.O. Box 3216, 2522 West Sepulveda Blvd., Suite 200, Torrance, CA. A 12-Step program for recovery/discovery for adults who were raised in alcoholic homes. The office serves as a clearinghouse for information to, from and about the growing fellowship of adult children of alcoholics around the world.

Workaholics Anonymous, World Service Organization, P.O. Box 661501, Los Angeles, CA 90066. A 12-Step support group that has chapters nationwide. The purpose of WA is to help people to stop working compulsively. Start-up packets for beginning new chapters of Workaholics Anonymous can be obtained by writing to the above address.

Workshop Information

For information about Dr. Bryan Robinson's Workshops, write to him at the Department of Human Services, UNC-Charlotte, NC 28223 or call (704) 374-1418.

The Twelve Steps of Alcoholics Anonymous

1. We admitted we were powerless over alcohol — that our lives had become unmanageable. 2. Came to believe that a Power greater than ourselves could restore us to sanity. 3. Made a decision to turn our will and our lives over to the care of God *as we understood Him*. 4. Made a searching and fearless moral inventory of ourselves. 5. Admitted to God, to ourselves and to another human being the exact nature of our wrongs. 6. Were entirely ready to have God remove all these defects of character. 7. Humbly asked Him to remove our shortcomings. 8. Made a list of all persons we had harmed, and became willing to make amends to them all. 9. Made direct amends to such people wherever possible, except when to do so would injure them or others. 10. Continued to take personal inventory and when we were wrong promptly addmitted it. 11. Sought through prayer and meditation to improve our conscious contact with God, *as we understood Him*, praying only for knowledge of His will for us and the power to carry that out. 12. Having had a spiritual awakening as the result of these steps, we tried to carry this message to alcoholics, and to practice these principles in all our affairs.

In human affairs of danger
and delicacy successful conclusion
is sharply limited by hurry.
So often men trip by being in a rush.
If one were properly to perform
a difficult and subtle act,
he should first inspect the end
to be achieved and then once he had
accepted the end as desirable,
he should forget it completely and
concentrate solely on the means.
By this method he would not
be moved to false action
by anxiety or hurry or fear.
Very few people learn this.

— John Steinbeck,
East of Eden

Other Books By . . .
Health Communications

ADULT CHILDREN OF ALCOHOLICS (Expanded)
Janet Woititz

Over a year on *The New York Times* Best-Seller list, this book is the primer on Adult Children of Alcoholics.

ISBN 1-55874-112-7   **$8.95**

STRUGGLE FOR INTIMACY
Janet Woititz

Another best-seller, this book gives insightful advice on learning to love more fully.

ISBN 0-932194-25-7   **$6.95**

BRADSHAW ON: THE FAMILY: A Revolutionary Way of Self-Discovery
John Bradshaw

The host of the nationally televised series of the same name shows us how families can be healed and individuals can realize full potential.

ISBN 0-932194-54-0   **$9.95**

HEALING THE SHAME THAT BINDS YOU
John Bradshaw

This important book shows how toxic shame is the core problem in our compulsions and offers new techniques of recovery vital to all of us.

ISBN 0-932194-86-9   **$9.95**

HEALING THE CHILD WITHIN: Discovery and Recovery for
Adult Children of Dysfunctional Families — Charles Whitfield, M.D.

Dr. Whitfield defines, describes and discovers how we can reach our Child Within to heal and nurture our woundedness.

ISBN 0-932194-40-0   **$8.95**

A GIFT TO MYSELF: A Personal Guide To Healing My Child Within
Charles L. Whitfield, M.D.

Dr. Whitfield provides practical guidelines and methods to work through the pain and confusion of being an Adult Child of a dysfunctional family.

ISBN 1-55874-042-2   **$11.95**

HEALING TOGETHER: A Guide To Intimacy And Recovery For
Co-dependent Couples — Wayne Kritsberg, M.A.

This is a practical book that tells the reader why he or she gets into dysfunctional and painful relationships, and then gives a concrete course of action on how to move the relationship toward health.

ISBN 1-55784-053-8   **$8.95**

3201 S.W. 15th Street,
Deerfield Beach, FL 33442-8190
1-800-441-5569

Health
Communications, Inc.®

New Books . . .
from Health Communications

HEAL YOUR SELF-ESTEEM: Recovery From Addictive Thinking
Bryan Robinson, Ph.D.

Do you have low self-esteem? Do you blame others for your own unhappiness? If so, you may be an addictive thinker. The 10 Principles For Healing, an innovative, positive approach to recovery, are integrated into this book to provide a new attitude with simple techniques for recovery.

ISBN 1-55874-119-4   **$9.95**

HEALING ENERGY: The Power Of Recovery
Ruth Fishel, M.Ed., C.A.C.

Linking the newest medical discoveries in mind/body/spirit connections with the field of recovery, this book illustrates how to balance ourselves mentally, physically and spiritually to overcome our addictive behavior.

ISBN 1-55874-128-3   **$9.95**

CREDIT, CASH AND CO-DEPENDENCY: The Money Connection
Yvonne Kaye, Ph.D.

Co-dependents and Adult Children seem to experience more problems than most as money can be used as an anesthetic or fantasy. Yvonne Kaye writes of the particular problems the co-dependent has with money, sharing her own experiences.

ISBN 1-55874-133-X   **$9.95**

THE LAUNDRY LIST: The ACoA Experience
Tony A. and Dan F.

Potentially The Big Book of ACoA, *The Laundry List* includes stories, history and helpful information for the Adult Child of an alcoholic. Tony A. discusses what it means to be an ACoA and what the self-help group can do for its members.

ISBN 1-55874-105-4   **$9.95**

LEARNING TO SAY NO: Establishing Healthy Boundaries
Carla Wills-Brandon, M.A.

If you grew up in a dysfunctional family, establishing boundaries is a difficult and risky decision. Where do you draw the line? Learn to recognize yourself as an individual who has the power to say no.

ISBN 1-55874-087-2   **$8.95**

3201 S.W. 15th Street,
Deerfield Beach, FL 33442-8190
1-800-441-5569

Health
Communications, Inc.®